# DISCOVER
# SOUTH-EAST ASIA
# AND
# INDONESIA

PUBLISHED BY THE READER'S DIGEST ASSOCIATION LIMITED

LONDON   NEW YORK   SYDNEY   MONTREAL

DISCOVER SOUTH-EAST ASIA AND INDONESIA

Translated and edited by Toucan Books Limited, London
for Reader's Digest, London

Translated and adapted from the French
by Robin Hosie

**For Reader's Digest**
Series Editor: Christine Noble
Editorial Assistant: Lucy Murray
Prepress Accounts Manager: Penny Grose

**Reader's Digest General Books**
Editorial Director: Cortina Butler
Art Director: Nick Clark

First English language edition Copyright © 2002
The Reader's Digest Association Limited
11 Westferry Circus, Canary Wharf, London E14 4HE
www.readersdigest.co.uk

Reprinted 2004

We are committed to both the quality of our products and
the service we provide to our customers. We value your
comments, so please feel free to contact us on 08705 113366,
or via our web site www.readersdigest.co.uk
If you have any comments about the content of our books,
you can email us at gbeditorial@readersdigest.co.uk

ISBN 0 276 42521 9

*Discover the World:* SOUTH-EAST ASIA AND INDONESIA
was created and produced by
HUBERT DEVAUX & CO, Paris for
Selection Reader's Digest S.A., Paris, and first published
in 2001 as *Regards sur le Monde: L'ASIE DU SUD-EST ET L'INDONESIE*

©2001 Selection Reader's Digest, S.A.
212 boulevard Saint-Germain, 75007, Paris

# CONTENTS

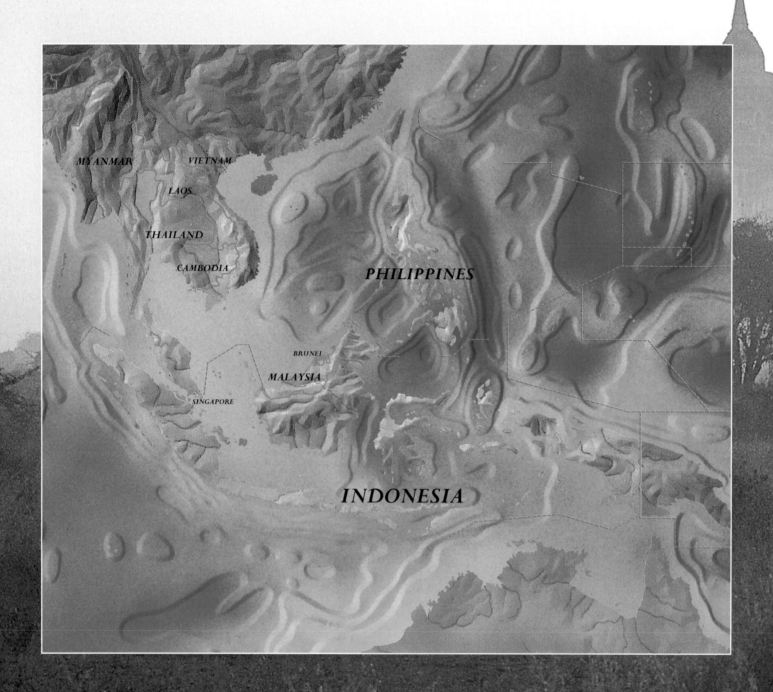

# INTRODUCING
# SOUTH-EAST ASIA AND INDONESIA

South-east Asia is a scattered jigsaw of islands, peninsulas, deltas and straits, strewn between the Indian Ocean and the Pacific. While the island nations have grown mainly through trade and sea power, the mainland nations and civilisations were cradled in the fertile river valleys and deltas. This volatile corner of the world's largest continent is a geographical and cultural extension of India and China. The rites and beliefs of Hinduism and Buddhism, Confucianism and Taoism have all left their mark – so, too, have those of Christianity and Islam, and the modern 'faiths' of colonialism, capitalism and communism.

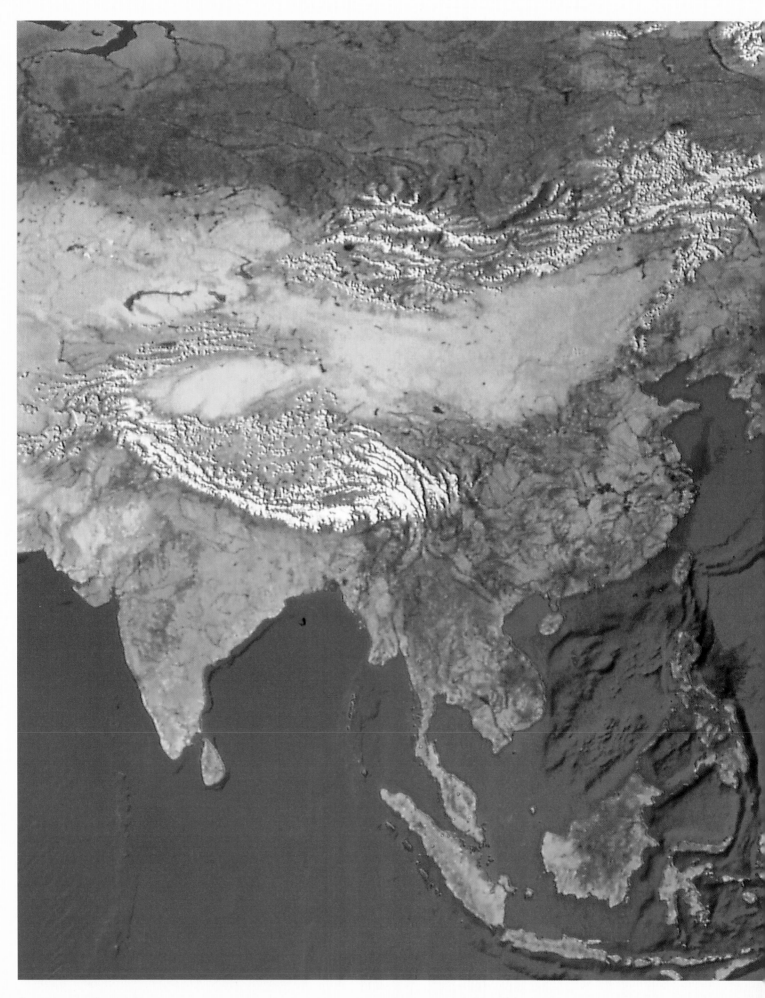

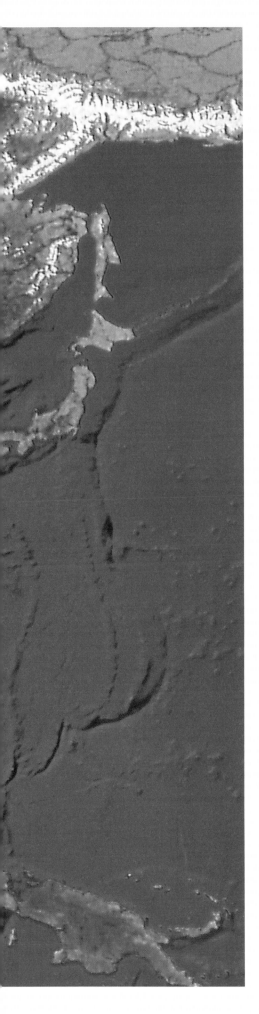

# Between two oceans

South-east Asia was intended by nature to be a Garden of Eden. The region, with heat and moisture in abundance, is a gigantic, steamy hothouse, where plants can produce fruit all the year round. Enormous butterflies, dragonflies and other less attractive insects thrive, alongside outsized frogs, spiders, snakes and lizards. The tropical forests are the home of noisy parrots and chattering monkeys; of the Asian elephant, the awesome tiger and the human-like orang-utan, whose name, in Malay, means 'man of the woods'. When man's ancestors entered this paradise, half a million years or more ago, all that they needed for survival was at hand: fruit, nuts, roots, succulent grubs and occasional large prey for food; trees for shelter and for the wood needed to fashion tools and weapons, and to make fire.

In temperate regions of the world, the rhythm of the year is seasonal, but South-east Asia does not have seasons in the sense of spring, summer, autumn and winter. Instead, it has the monsoon, when oppressive humidity is released in torrents of rain. This is an ideal climate for rice-growing, and throughout most of the region, agriculture long ago replaced hunter-gathering as the dominant way of life. At first, the work of digging and maintaining irrigation channels, flooding the paddy fields, and planting and harvesting the crop was organised at village level. But as the efforts of thousands of workers produced grain surpluses, what had been subsistence societies became more complex. Rice-growing is labour-intensive, and requires irrigation. Civilisations based on the management of water – the so-called 'hydraulic' civilisations

*Between two oceans  With a total population approaching 460 million, South-east Asia is made up of mainland states and far-flung island nations. Indonesia alone consists of more than 13 000 islands, scattered in a 3000 mile (5000 km) arc between the Indian and Pacific Oceans.*

– tend to be authoritarian, even despotic, because the work is hard, from digging canals to stooping, knee-deep in water to plant the rice. South-east Asia has had its full share of tyrants and empire-builders.

Outside influences have played a major role in shaping the region's religious, social and political systems. Hinduism and Buddhism spread from India into Burma, Cambodia and Laos. Northern Vietnam, once a province of China, fell under the spell of Taoist and Confucian ways of thinking. Arab traders brought Islam to Indonesia, and Spanish missionaries converted the Philippines to Christianity. Another import from Europe was colonialism. With the exception of Thailand, every country in South-east Asia has at some time been ruled or controlled by a Western power. The natural reaction to white domination was the rise of nationalist movements, which went on to triumph after the end of the Second World War. A string of Japanese victories in that war had demonstrated that white invincibility was a myth, and indigenous guerrilla movements had been supplied with arms to fight the Japanese.

Communists were often in the forefront of resistance movements. Vietnam had its Vietminh, Cambodia its Khmer Rouge, Laos its Pathet Lao, the Philippines its Hukbalahaps. But old rivalries ran deep. In Indonesia, where most communists were ethnic Chinese, the army turned on them in 1965. In Malaya, a Chinese communist insurrection was crushed by an alliance between Malayan nationalists and the old colonial power, Britain.

Today, the region is marked by contrasts, conflicts and internal tensions. Singapore and Brunei are among the richest countries in the world, whereas Cambodia and Myanmar (Burma) rank among the poorest in Asia. Democracy in Singapore, muscular though it may be in its style, contrasts with the harsh military dictatorship of Burma. The mineral wealth of the region and its strategic position astride the Indian and Pacific Oceans means that its future is of prime concern to nations outside its boundaries.

**Paradise disturbed**  *A canoe fitted with an outboard motor ruffles the calm of Lake Inle, Burma. The traditional way of propelling a craft on the lake is by 'leg rowing' – standing with a paddle strapped to one leg. The lakeside dwellers build houses on wooden piles and grow crops on floating islands made of thick carpets of reeds, entangled with flowers.*

**Where a dragon fought**  *Vietnam's Halong Bay (above) presents a seascape of haunting strangeness. A 17th-century Chinese traveller claimed that there was no other place like it on earth, and wrote that it was easy to lose one's way among the 2000 rocky islands that dot the surface of the bay. According to legend, the islands were created when a dragon god jumped into the bay to calm its raging waters. The struggle was so ferocious that the dragon's tail knocked great lumps off a nearby mountain, and they fell into the sea.*

**River of 4000 islands**  *The River Mekong thunders over rapids in the extreme south of Laos at Si Phan Don – 'Four thousand islands'. This stretch of the river lives up to its name in the dry season, when its flow diminishes and the islands emerge.*

9

**Land of warriors**  The spectacular limestone hills of Vang Vieng, in Laos, are home to a warrior tribe, the Hmong, who make a living these days by cultivating the opium poppy. During the final years of French rule in Indochina, they were recruited by the colonial power to fight Vietminh communist guerrillas. The hills are honeycombed with caves, many of which are held sacred by the Hmong.

**A god who demands sacrifice**  Rising above a sea of mist, the volcano of Bromo, in Java, may look serene, but people nearby live in dread. To appease the volcano god's anger they throw flowers and fruit into the crater – and sometimes chickens or a live buffalo.

**Small but deadly**  Taal, in the Philippines, is one of the smallest volcanoes in the world. But more than 5000 people were killed when it erupted in 1911, and another 200 died in a 1965 eruption. The volcano rises from a lake on an island, and its crater is a lake that in turn holds a tiny island.

**Taming the jungle**  The interior of the holiday island of Krabi, in Thailand, is covered with a dense tangle of tropical forest, which in places has been cleared for the cultivation of palm trees (left) and for rubber plantations.

**Where danger lurks**  The national park of Thaleh Ban, in Thailand (right), is the home not only of tigers, leopards, bears, wild pigs, gibbons and giant lizards, but also of a tribe who hunt their prey with blowpipes and poison darts. They travel through the jungle in small groups, seeking safety at night by sleeping in the trees.

**Man-made landscape**  *Around Sapa, in the north of Vietnam, terraces cut out of the hillsides for the cultivation of rice have added an extra dimension to the landscape. Sapa lies 5500 ft (1650 m) above sea level, and in French colonial days was a hill station where cool villas offered an escape from the stifling heat of the plains.*

**007's island**  *The island of Phuket became Thailand's most popular luxury holiday resort after Phangnga Bay, in which it lies, was used as the setting for a James Bond movie, The Man With the Golden Gun. Virgin forest is protected in the national park of Khao Phra Thaeo (left).*

# A brief history

Half a million years ago, sea levels were lower than they are today, because so much of the planet's water was locked up in polar ice caps. At that time a man-like creature reached Java across the land bridge that connected it to the Asian mainland. Java man walked upright, and for this reason has been given the scientific name *Homo erectus*. The first discovery

**Java man**   *A scientific reconstruction of Homo erectus.*

**Hands across the millennia**   *In 1998 some 30 paintings made by prehistoric artists were discovered in a cave in Borneo, among them these ghostly silhouettes of human hands.*

of his remains was made at Trinil, in Java, in 1891. His ancestors had probably reached Indonesia by following the trail of their prey – elephants, rhinos and other animals. Java man was sturdily built, with beetle brows and a low forehead, and his brain and voice box were sufficiently well evolved to suggest that he could speak. This would have given him and his fellows a formidable advantage when they went hunting. Mainly, though, they were foragers, living on fruit, nuts, roots and grubs.

## After the ice

The last Ice Age ended some 10 000 years ago, by which time modern man, *Homo sapiens*, had reached the islands. It has not been established whether *Homo erectus* evolved into modern man in South-east Asia, interbred with *Homo sapiens*, or was driven into extinction by competition from a more intelligent creature. Other remains of *Homo erectus* have been found elsewhere in Indonesia and in China, Europe, North Africa and East Africa. Once the land links to the islands of South-east Asia had been swamped by inrushing waters, future immigrants would have had to cross the seas. For this, they needed all their intelligence, along with their basic skills in boat-building, sailing and navigation.

Both before and after the land bridges were swamped, three major groups of immigrants were spreading across the mainland and islands of South-east Asia. The first group consisted of dark-skinned, pygmy-sized Negritos, who moved from India into the Malay Peninsula, the Philippines and Indonesia: isolated pockets of this stock still exist in these countries today. The second were people of Australo-Melanesian origin, who moved into New Guinea. The third group, the Mongoloid proto-Malays, came from southern China. These groups, along with later waves of immigrants, gradually pushed the Negritos into ever more remote areas. With hindsight, their victory in the struggle for existence appears inevitable, for they brought with them the secret of how to grow rice. This opened up possibilities that were denied to simple hunter-gatherers. The conditions for rice cultivation were ideal throughout much of the region, and with good harvests, farming communities could amass the food surpluses needed to sustain growing populations, to build permanent settlements and, above

### Trailblazers of the Bronze Age

During the Second World War, a Dutchman who had been forced by the Japanese to work on the notorious Burma-Siam railway came across what were clearly some prehistoric remains as he swung his pickaxe at the rock-hard ground. After the war, he spoke about his discovery and an archaeological expedition went out to Ban Chiang, in north-east Thailand. The diggers uncovered the burial sites of a community that had entered the Bronze Age a staggering 5600 years ago – 1700 years before it reached Britain. In the graves were bronze utensils, clay pots and vases, decorated with swirling patterns – finds that have been carbon dated to 3500 BC.

**Vietnam in the Bronze Age**   *The Vietnamese trace their origins to the Dong Son culture of the Red River valley (6th-3rd centuries BC). Bronze Age craftsmen decorated their work with patterns and with scenes of daily life.*

*Building a prefab roof*   *A Yao tribesman in northern Vietnam plaits bamboo to make roof panels.*

### Mystery of the jars

The only thing that is not mysterious about the Plain of Jars, in northern Laos, is its name. For it is simply a vast plain, studded with hundreds of stone jars. Nobody knows who built them, or why, or when. Some archaeologists believe that the jars, the heaviest of which weighs 6 tons, may have been used more than 2000 years ago to store rice or rice liquor. This accords with a Laotian legend that tells of the hero Khun Jeuam, who drove out the tyrant Chao Angka, then had the jars made to hold wine so that he could celebrate in style. Another theory is that they were burial jars, used to hold human remains.

all, to engage in trade, instead of devoting all of their energies to staying alive. Farmers, potters, toolmakers and craftsmen could exchange products.

Those with a talent for making useful objects could be freed from the overriding and time-consuming need to grow food and become craftsmen, producing better weapons and tools, and creating artefacts that added to the comfort and enjoyment of life. The large-scale cultivation of rice demands forward planning, irrigation schemes and a well-directed labour force. As society became more complex, kings and a ruling class emerged, as custodians of knowledge and wielders of power. The craftsmen who created the luxuries they enjoyed led the way out of the Stone Age into the Bronze Age. Bronze pots were being cast at Ban Chiang, in north-east Thailand, as early as 3500 BC.

### The spread of civilisation

A steady flow of culture and ideas came from the region's two advanced neighbours – India in the west and China in the north. A Javanese legend tells how writing and an understanding of astronomy and the night sky reached the island from India. Ancient inscriptions of Indian origin have been discovered as far from India as Borneo.

It is thought that the Philippines were originally settled some 30 000 years ago by Negritos, crossing over the land bridges that existed in that era. About 5000 years ago, Indonesian immigrants, braving the seas in outrigger canoes, began to drive the Negritos off cultivable land. Other waves of settlers arrived from Vietnam, southern China and Malaya. This last group brought with them iron tools, the craft of weaving, and the practice of head-hunting.

*Oldest inhabitants*   *More than 250 tribes of the original Negrito stock still follow their ancestral way of life in Irian Jaya, the Indonesian part of New Guinea.*

The early history of Vietnam is hard to disentangle from legend, but excavations have shown that the Red River delta was occupied by Stone Age cave-dwellers some 5000 years ago. In the 6th century BC the Dong Son culture arose in the north, and is regarded as one of the starting points of Vietnamese civilisation. The craftsmen of Dong Son produced bronze drums, jewellery and musical instruments, and their influence spread to Laos, Cambodia and Bali. Burma is separated from its neighbours by mountains. Its earliest known culture, that of the Pyus, who lived in city-states, was overrun by Chinese invaders from Yunnan about 1000 years ago.

15

## Khmers, Chams and Viets

Command of the sea was the key to wealth and power in the early history of Indochina. In an era when sailors felt uneasy if they ventured too far from land, Funan, in present-day Cambodia, was the region's first great maritime power. The port of Oceo, on the Gulf of Thailand, lay on a strategic coast-hugging route between China and the islands of South-east Asia.

Funan's reach extended over much of Cambodia and into Laos, and the profits of trade built temples, palaces and irrigation systems. A Chinese ambassador who visited Funan in AD 225 wrote of royal palaces several storeys high, the king's concubines, and craftsmen who worked in silver and gold. The culture of Funan was a blend of Indian and local spirit worship, symbolised in the legend of the Hindu priest Kaundinya, who shot an arrow into the air, founded the city of Funan where it landed and married a local princess.

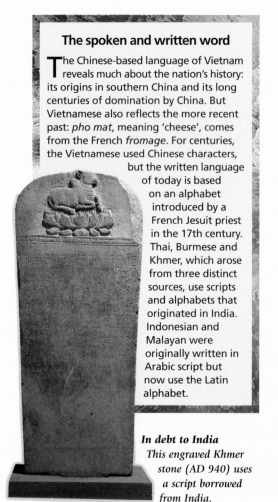

### The spoken and written word

The Chinese-based language of Vietnam reveals much about the nation's history: its origins in southern China and its long centuries of domination by China. But Vietnamese also reflects the more recent past: *pho mat*, meaning 'cheese', comes from the French *fromage*. For centuries, the Vietnamese used Chinese characters, but the written language of today is based on an alphabet introduced by a French Jesuit priest in the 17th century. Thai, Burmese and Khmer, which arose from three distinct sources, use scripts and alphabets that originated in India. Indonesian and Malayan were originally written in Arabic script but now use the Latin alphabet.

*In debt to India*
*This engraved Khmer stone (AD 940) uses a script borrowed from India.*

Funan's days of prosperity lasted from the 1st to the 6th centuries. The decline set in when improvements in ship design and navigational technology meant that ships no longer needed to hug the coastline. The culture was eclipsed by that of Chenla, originally centred on the middle reaches of the River Mekong, and once one of Funan's vassal states. King Isanavarman I of Chenla founded a new capital at Sambor Prei Kok in Cambodia and built Hindu temples. In the 8th century, Chenla was weakened by civil war, and was invaded and annexed by Java.

Javanese rule was overthrown by the Khmer prince Jayavarman II, who had been born in Java but returned to the land of his ancestors in around AD 800 to lead a revolt. He declared himself a god-king, and founded an empire that was to cover Cambodia and large parts of Vietnam, Laos and Thailand.

### Rise of the Cham

In the 2nd century AD, along the southern coast of what is now Vietnam, a warlike seafaring people called the Cham began to build a trading empire that reached its peak

**Vietnam before the 10th century**

some 800 years later. Champa was a Hindu state, ruled by god-kings who built soaring tower temples. It lay across a crucial frontier between the two cultural superpowers of India and China, and was almost constantly at war. In 1177, a Cham army sacked the Khmer capital at Angkor, and nearly toppled the once mighty Khmer Empire. But the Chams had attempted too much. The Khmer king Jayavarman VII, who came to the throne in 1181, rebuilt the Khmer army, established a new capital at Angkor Thom, and forced the Cham to pay tribute as his vassals.

### The first heroines of Vietnam

Vietnam emerged out of the shadows of prehistory in 208 BC, when a Chinese general, Trieu Da, seized power in the north and governed the fertile Red River delta as his own domain, naming it Nam Viet. Independence did not last long: the Han Chinese conquered the region in the 2nd century BC, ruling it through military districts. In AD 40 the aristocratic Trung sisters, Trac and Nhi, raised the people against their occupiers, but were defeated in battle. The suppression of the rebellion

*Vanished glory*   *The temple of Wat Phu was built when the mighty Khmer Empire extended into Laos.*

was the start of a process of 'Chinafication' in Vietnam that lasted for 1000 years. Chinese beliefs, laws and script were imposed on the people, and in 264 the province was named Annam, the 'pacified south'. This was a misnomer: twice the Chinese were driven out by rebellions, and although they conquered Annam for a third time, they frequently had to suppress insurrections.

### The emergence of Burma

In the 8th and 9th centuries AD, a people from the Himalayas migrated into the Irrawaddy valley. The Burmans replaced the original settlers, the Pyus, and absorbed another early culture, that of the Mons. From the resultant fusion of beliefs, customs and technologies was born a remarkably successful Buddhist power – Pagan.

*Indian 'Venus'*   *This statue from pre-Khmer Cambodia shows a strong Indian influence.*

*Temple of a god-king*   *This Hindu temple was built by the Cham, near Nha Trang, Vietnam.*

### The Romans in Burma

Ancient Rome had both trade and diplomatic contacts with the distant Burmese kingdoms of the Mons and the Pyus. A Roman ambassador travelled in the north of the country as early as 128 BC and another envoy, sent by the emperor Marcus Aurelius, reached Burma in AD 166. A little later, the celebrated Greek-Egyptian geographer Ptolemy described a 'land of silver', which appears to have been located in Burma's Arakan mountains. Ptolemy also mentions a region in the vicinity of present-day Moulmein, which was said to be inhabited by cannibals.

## The spread of Buddhism

The kingdom of Pagan burst into the pages of history in 1044, when the warrior king Anoratha came to the throne. Records of the time describe the king and his nobles clad in golden armour and riding at the head of soldiers mounted on war elephants. Anoratha was converted to the Theravada school of Buddhism (which is still followed in Burma today) and became a vigorous champion of his new religion. His political objective was to unify the country and surround it with vassal states. He bent the Chams, the Khmers and the Mons to his will and on his death, in 1077, the entire area was at peace. But the rulers who came after him lacked his drive. The Mons staged a rebellion, and when the Chinese emperor, Kublai Khan, sent his Mongol army to invade in 1283, the once proud empire of Pagan rapidly collapsed.

## Thais on the move

When Kublai Khan's grandfather, Genghis, swept into China with his Mongol hordes early in the 13th century entire populations scattered in terror before their advance. One such displaced group was the Thais of Nan Chao, in southern China. They had already begun a slow movement into land once occupied by Khmers and Mons, and this migration took on a new urgency when the Mongols turned their attention to Nan Chao.

In their new land (known as Siam until modern times) the Thais borrowed religion, systems of government and artistic styles from their new neighbours. But they preserved the social structure of their original homeland, founded on the strong rule of a warrior aristocracy. One of their sovereigns, the multi-talented Ramakamheng, was an outstanding leader in war and peace, a devout Buddhist and a renowned scholar. One of his legacies to the Thais was a script based on the Indian alphabet. By the close of his reign, in 1313, the Thai Empire extended into parts of Burma and as far as Luang Prabang in Laos.

## The maritime empires

From the 10th to the 13th centuries, the trading empire of Srivijaya, based in Sumatra, dominated the Malay Peninsula, the east coast of Java, the west coast of Borneo and the seas that washed their shores. Sriv-

*Peace and power   Seated Buddha in Wat Mahathat at Sukhothai, ancient capital of the Thais.*

ijaya grew so powerful that it sent military expeditions against Cambodia, and its fame reached the Arab world. Its ports were thronged with ships from China, Japan and India, loading cargoes of teak, sandalwood, ivory, tin, camphor and spices. But rivalry with Java weakened this maritime empire and it broke up in 1292.

A new empire arose from its ruins: that of Majapahit, founded by Prince Vijaya. His authority extended over Java, Bali, Sumatra, the coast of Borneo and as far as the south of Taiwan. Majapahit's power rested on holding a near-monopoly of the spice trade. Cloves, nutmeg, pepper, cinnamon, ginger, turmeric and other spices were shipped across the Indian Ocean and up the Red Sea, then transported overland to Alexandria in Egypt, where they were bought by Venetian merchants. The fortunes of Venice were founded on the astronomical sums paid for spices in the markets of Europe, for in the days before refrigeration they preserved food and disguised any bad flavours.

Marco Polo, the Venetian who became an envoy in the service of Kublai Khan, visited Sumatra in 1291, and the following year the Chinese emperor sent a fleet to discipline what he regarded as an upstart rival. Majapahit defeated the Chinese at sea, and continued to flourish for another century.

## The splendour of Angkor

The Khmers were the greatest builders South-east Asia has ever known. Jayavarman VII, who ascended the throne in 1181, rebuilt the Khmer capital at Angkor Thom after it had been destroyed by the Chams. He protected it with walls 25 ft (8 m) high, surrounded by a moat teeming with crocodiles. The triple-towered main gateway was high enough for an elephant with

a covered howdah on its back to protect the divine king from the sun's rays. Parapets, towers, gateways and terraces were covered in carvings of royal triumphs and scenes from Hindu epics. Jayavarman VII raised 20 000 Buddhist and Hindu shrines, among them the temple complex at Angkor Wat. The central pyramid tower, rising above four other towers, represents Mount Meru, sacred to Hindus.

To guarantee the fertility of the rice fields, the Khmers built gigantic reservoirs, canals and fountains. Khmer civilisation has been classified by historians as a 'hydraulic empire'– that is, one based on water management, with the mass of the people carrying out public irrigation works on a huge scale. The Khmer system was good at building up food surpluses, but was vulnerable if the irrigation system failed. In its later years, Angkor was threatened by Mongols from the north and by Thais and Viets from the east. Three times it fell to Thai invaders, and finally its irrigation system was destroyed. In 1434, the capital was moved to Phnom Penh and Angkor was abandoned to the creeping jungle.

**Shiva the destroyer**   Statue at Angkor Wat.

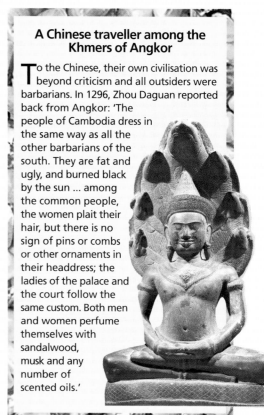

### A Chinese traveller among the Khmers of Angkor

To the Chinese, their own civilisation was beyond criticism and all outsiders were barbarians. In 1296, Zhou Daguan reported back from Angkor: 'The people of Cambodia dress in the same way as all the other barbarians of the south. They are fat and ugly, and burned black by the sun ... among the common people, the women plait their hair, but there is no sign of pins or combs or other ornaments in their headdress; the ladies of the palace and the court follow the same custom. Both men and women perfume themselves with sandalwood, musk and any number of scented oils.'

**Sacred dancers**   Bas-relief at Angkor Wat.

**Deserted city**
Ruined temples at Pagan (left). This ancient Burmese capital was sacked by the Mongols of Kublai Khan in 1287.

**Line of piety**   A patient file of Buddhist monks and novices in Myanmar.

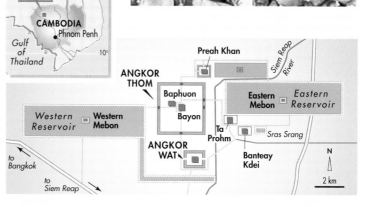

## The strength of religion

Some civilisations and religions spread by conviction, some by conquest, and others by a combination of the two. In South-east Asia, Chinese culture was imposed initially by military conquest, while the beliefs and traditions of India generally spread peacefully. The ancient Hindu beliefs, which supported a society based on a rigid caste system and taught the doctrine of reincarnation, were spread by Brahmins (priests) and absorbed almost by osmosis in Burma, Cambodia, Thailand and the islands of Indonesia. India also gave these lands a style of architecture and

an alphabet that could be adapted to their own languages. There was a ready acceptance, too, for Buddhism, which arose partly as a reaction against the caste system and began to spread through South-east Asia in the 2nd century BC. The new religion taught that suffering is caused by human craving, and that the way to break free from the cycle of suffering and rebirth was to renounce the self and attain Nirvana, or spiritual enlightenment, through meditation.

In the 2nd century BC, northern Vietnam was invaded by the Han Chinese, who believed they were bringing the benefits of a superior civilisation: Chinese art, poetry and architecture, a script based on ideograms, veneration of the emperor, rule by civil servants and the doctrines of Confucius and Lao Zi. Confucianism stressed the importance of social harmony, created by obedience to authority, both in the family and in the state.

The third religion to make an impact on South-east Asia was Islam. Merchants from Persia, Muslim India and the Arab world were lured by the profits to be made from spices, and by the 13th century the Koran and the idea of one God had spread along the trade routes from northern Sumatra to Malaya, Java, Borneo and the Philippines.

***Treasure seekers***
*A Portuguese fleet in full sail for the Spice Islands, early in the 16th century. Painting by C. Anthoniszon.*

***The emperor's envoy***
*Marco Polo (1254–1324) was a Venetian who entered the service of the Chinese emperor Kublai Khan and travelled widely in South-east Asia.*

Marco Polo, who travelled in Malaya at the end of the century, noted that Persian was the language of commerce there. Islam made further headway in Sumatra in the 14th century, and the 15th saw mass conversions in the Malay-Indonesian world. Conversion often began at the top of the social scale. Sumatra's Prince Parameswara married a Muslim princess, accepted the Koran and in 1414 changed his name to Mohammed Iskander Shah. His successors would become maharajahs and sultans.

For several centuries, Arab traders enjoyed a monopoly of the seaborne spice trade with Europe. At one end of this chain of commercial operations was the port of Malacca, on the Malay Peninsula, and at the other was Venice, pouring its wealth into the buildings and artistic treasures that have made it into a city of splendour.

## Defying the Mongols in Burma and Vietnam

Elsewhere in South-east Asia, old empires were falling and new ones rising. In Burma, the kingdom of Pagan came to an end largely because of overconfidence on the part of its ruler. The rising power in Asia during the 13th century were the Mongols, who turned on South-east Asia after sweeping through China. The Mongols sent two missions to the court of Pagan to demand submission, and the Pagan king made the

mistake of refusing to grant an audience to the first and giving orders for members of the second to be put to death. He then made the even greater mistake of advancing into the Chinese province of Yunnan, where he was heavily defeated. The Mongol army invaded Burma in 1283 and set up their own puppet king. The collapse of Pagan's power gave the Mons an opportunity to regain their independence, and Burma fell apart. Three rival kingdoms emerged during two-and-a-half centuries of strife: Pegu, held by the Mons; Ava, kingdom of the Shan; and Arakan.

In the 10th century, the northern Viets finally expelled their Chinese overlords. Successive Viet dynasties pushed south from the Red River delta into territory occupied by the Cham, finally reaching the

***Ancient Buddhas, modern reverence*** *Statues in Ayutthaya are clothed to show reverence.*

Mekong delta. Under the Tang dynasty (1225–1400) they, too, were attacked by the Mongols, but managed to defeat them.

In the valley of the Mekong, the Thais rose against Khmer rule and in 1238 set up the kingdom of Sukhothai. King Ramakamheng, who borrowed an alphabet from the Khmers, pushed out the frontiers, but decline set in after his death and Sukhothai was absorbed into the new Thai kingdom of Ayutthaya. In 1431 the Thais occupied the Khmer capital of Angkor. The Khmer Empire was weakened not only by war with the Thais but also internally by the spread of Buddhism. An emphasis on poverty, meditation and solitude undermined the king's divine authority.

In the early 16th century, a new force erupted into the closed world of dynastic and ethnic rivalries in South-east Asia. The region came into contact with the aggressive nations of the West, and had nothing that could stand up to the superior technology of its ships and fire power.

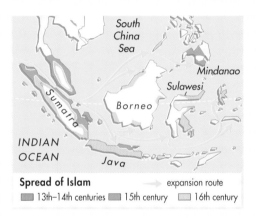

**Spread of Islam**
→ expansion route
▨ 13th–14th centuries  ▨ 15th century  ▢ 16th century

### What is Taoism?

The Taoist philosophy was founded in China in the 6th-century BC by the sage Lao Zi: its name comes from the word *tao*, 'the path'. While Buddhism sought escape from the cycle of life, death and suffering by renouncing desire, and Confucianism put forward the idea of an ordered moral system, Lao Zi was concerned with the relationship between man and nature. Decisions and actions, he believed, should be as natural as water flowing downhill: there would be no need for striving if mankind lived in harmony with nature. Lao Zi saw meditation as a means of achieving *te*, a state of inner harmony and confidence. Later, magical practices were introduced, as a shortcut to *te*. Taosim is a religion, too. Some regard Lao Zi as a god, and the Taoist sage Ngoc Hoang is a god in Vietnam.

***The West goes east*** *The port of Malacca, Malaya, built by the Portuguese in 1512.*

***Recycled pagoda*** *The pagoda of Thien Mu at Hué, Vietnam, was built in 1601 with bricks from a Cham temple. Each of its tiers represents an incarnation of the Buddha.*

NUXMOSCHATA DISSECTA,
*ut appareat a interius putamen durius.*
*b Macis.*
*c Pericarpium.*

2. *Nux Moschata integra.*
3. *Nucleus in duro putam.*
4. *Nux integra.*
5. *Eadem dissecta.*
6. *Nux Moschata oblonga integra.*
7. *Eadem dissecta.*
8. *Opobalsamum.*
9. *Oleum Nucis Moschatae.*

***Wonder spice*** *A 16th-century Italian medical treatise describes the virtues of nutmeg.*

## The spice race

When Columbus sailed west to reach the East, his mission was to find a new route to the Spice Islands and so break Venice's hold on Europe's most lucrative overseas trade: the discovery of the New World was an unexpected consequence. The earliest winners

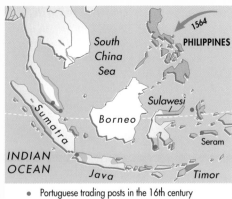

- Portuguese trading posts in the 16th century
**European possessions in the 17th century**
- Portugal
- Holland
- Spain
- → Spanish colonisation

of the spice race were the Portuguese. Since 1416, when Prince Henry the Navigator set up a school of seamanship, they had been pushing around the coast of Africa. They rounded the Cape of Good Hope in 1472 and tapped into the wealth of the East when Vasco da Gama crossed the Indian Ocean to Calicut in 1498. They reached Malacca, in Malaya, in 1511, built a fort and port there, and shipped spices back to Lisbon.

Portuguese ships were powerful enough to break the monopoly of Arab, Indonesian and Malay merchants, but could not keep out European competitors. The Spaniards, hard on Portuguese heels, arrived

### 'As dear as pepper'

Spices became more expensive than ever in the 14th century, when Central Asia was laid waste by the conqueror Tamerlane and the overland supply route was all but blocked. In France, pepper was used as currency. People spoke of costly goods as being 'as dear as pepper', and a pound of nutmeg could change hands for a price equivalent to that of three sheep. Even today, a kilogram of saffron, which uses more than 140 000 flowers, can fetch around £10 000.

in the Moluccas in 1521. The spice race was marked by treaties, broken promises, battles, sieges and massacres – for the stakes were enormous. Only one ship out of five returned from the first circumnavigation of the globe, which set out from Seville under Ferdinand Magellan in 1519. But that ship was laden with cloves from the Spice Islands, and they sold in Europe for 10 000 times what they had cost to buy.

At the end of the 16th century, another European nation joined the spice trade. Dutch merchants found strength in unity. In 1602 they combined their resources to set up the Dutch East India Company. The company subdued local rulers and drove Portuguese and Spanish rivals out of the Moluccas and Java. In 1619 the Dutch founded the port of Batavia (now Jakarta) in Java.

## The first colonies

It was because of spices that Europeans began to colonise the region. The Portuguese installed themselves in Timor after being ousted from Malacca by the Dutch. Magellan claimed the Philippines for Spain in 1521. Missionaries made the islands a Catholic territory, but the Spaniards had to fight a ceaseless war against rebellious Muslims, known to them as the Moros. The Dutch built up their power in Java and Sumatra, and in the wake of the first colonisers came the English and the French, in search of raw materials and markets as well as spices.

***Spice container*** *A decorative bowl made in Delft in the late 17th century.*

***Pepper pickers*** *Gathering pepper in Java, in 1575.*

## Vietnam before colonisation

After throwing off Chinese rule in the 10th century, the Vietnamese pushed south into the Mekong delta, displacing the Cham. But China still regarded the country as a breakaway province, and toppled Vietnam's Ho dynasty in 1407. Popular resistance to the renewed Chinese occupation was led by Le Loi, who founded the Le dynasty, but his successors proved to be ineffective and corrupt. Small peasants were dispossesed by the big landowners, and to add to social unrest, civil war broke out between two clans, the Nguyen and the Trinh. By the middle of the 17th century they had divided the country between them, into North and South Vietnam.

It was reunited in the 1770s by the Tay Son rebellion, a peasant insurrection led by three brothers. One of them, Quang Trung, repelled yet another Chinese invasion in the north in 1788, routing an imperial army of 200 000.

By this time, Western traders and missionaries were active in Vietnam and Prince Anh, heir of the Nguyen clan, escaped execution in the Tay Son rebellion by fleeing to a French mission. With the help of 400 well-armed French mercenaries he won back his family's throne and in 1801 proclaimed himself emperor, taking the name Gia Long, and established a new capital at Hué. One of his first acts was to have the widow and son of the last of the Tay Son brothers torn apart by elephants – a foretaste of the tyranny that was to come.

**Learning from the West**   *Jesuit missionaries show the king of Siam how to view an eclipse of the sun, in 1688, without damaging his eyes.*

During the Nguyen dynasty, emperors and mandarins imposed punitive taxes on the peasants. The Christian missions were forbidden to attempt to convert the population, and the 19th-century emperor Tu Duc ordered the execution of thousands of Vietnamese Christians and 25 European priests.

The French responded by sending naval expeditions to teach the emperor a lesson. They took Da Nang and in 1859 captured Saigon (now Ho Chi Minh City). By 1895 the French were masters of Vietnam. Cochinchina in the south was a colony, while Tonkin and Annam in the north were protectorates under French rule. Laos, threatened by Siam, and Cambodia, riven by internal rivalries, also became French protectorates.

## Britannia rules

India in the 19th century was the 'jewel in the crown' of Britain's empire and any threat to her security rang alarm bells in London. Border incidents in Arakan in the 1820s led to a series of wars with Burma, which ended in 1855 with Britain in uneasy control of a hostile and rebellious country. British rule replaced Buddhist monasteries with Protestant missions: young mission-educated Burmese entered the civil service and formed a middle class, but the peasants still laboured under the burden of debt and took orders from the big landowners.

Britain set up trading posts in Penang and Malacca at the end of the 18th century. Singapore's potential as a counterweight to Dutch commercial influence was spotted by a colonial civil servant, Stamford Raffles, who, without any authority from London, leased the territory from the Sultan of Johore in 1819. It was the start of one of the greatest success stories in the history of commerce. From their base in Malacca, the British expanded trading operations to the entire Malay Peninsula.

Political control followed, with protectorates established over a number of Malay states. Tin had been mined in Malaya for centuries, but rubber was introduced by the British. Seeds of the rubber tree were smuggled out of Brazil to England in 1873, and seedlings were shipped out to Java, Sumatra and Malaya. Indian labourers were imported to work on the new plantations.

**Holland on stilts**   *The town of Dorp, in the Celebes (now Sulawesi), has a distinctly Dutch look in this painting of 1835.*

### The awakening of nationalism

Most European colonists in South-east Asia thought they were bringing the blessings of civilisation to backward nations, but the subject populations saw things differently. The result was rebellion and the rise of nationalist movements. In Java, more than 200 000 died in a rebellion led against the Dutch in 1825-30 by Prince Dipo Negoro. With the rebels crushed, governor Van den Bosch operated a brutal forced-labour regime in Java's sugar and indigo plantations.

Spain had trouble in the Philippines, where a Christian-led independence movement rebelled in 1896. The march to independence was sidetracked by the Spanish-American War, but when that ended in 1898, the defeated Spaniards sold the Philippines to the USA for $20 million. During the Second World War, Japan invaded and occupied the islands, but they were liberated in 1945 and granted independence in 1946.

Japan's victory over Russia in 1905 and the overthrow of the Manchu dynasty in China in 1911 gave hope to independence movements. Some of their leaders found sympathisers and picked up subversive ideas in the West. Ho Chi Minh lived in France as a young man and made several visits to Moscow. In 1920 he helped to found the French Communist Party.

The Second World War gave the colonial system a shock from which it did not recover. The Japanese demonstrated, in an impressive series of early victories, that Asians could defeat Westerners in battle. They entered the war with a surprise attack on the American naval base at Pearl Harbor in December 1941, but were facing defeat by 1945, and Indochina presented a problem for them. It had been left under the control of the collaborationist Vichy government after France surrendered in 1940, but with the Allies victorious in Europe, the French forces in Indochina became a potential threat, so the Japanese disarmed them.

The removal of French power left a vacuum, during which the Vietnamese communist Ho Chi Minh proclaimed independence. Laos and Cambodia soon followed his lead. The Free French, under General Leclerc, arrived back in force to reclaim French Indochina, but found the world had changed: they faced an armed, dedicated and confident resistance movement. The French held the cities, but Ho's Vietminh guerrillas controlled the countryside. Vietnam inevitably became a proxy war in the wider Cold War, with communist China arming and aiding the Vietminh and the USA sending military aid to the

**Doomed hero** *Burmese leader Aung San with British premier Clement Attlee in 1947.*

**French owned** *This brochure laid out French reluctance to give up Indochina.*

**Freedeom fighter** *Ho Chi Minh was leader of the communist Vietminh resistance movement that defeated the French in Vietnam in 1954.*

#### The mysterious death of Aung San

From his student days, Aung San was an active and implacable foe of British rule in Burma. In 1940, to escape a jail sentence, he fled to Japanese-occupied Taiwan, and there, with an eye to the future, he was given military training. When the Japanese invaded Burma, in 1942, they promised independence, and at first they were welcomed. But their harsh rule soon turned the population against them. Aung San, now a general in command of the Burma National Army, helped the British to drive the Japanese out of Burma. After the war, he won London's agreement to independence, but in July 1947 he was assassinated. His killers were never brought to justice.

### José Rizal, hero and martyr

Jesuit-educated José Rizal (1862-96) was a man of many talents – philosopher, poet, novelist, surgeon and Filipino patriot. In 1882, he went to Europe, where he wrote two novels, *Noli me tangere* and *El Filibusterismo* (*The Social Cancer* and *The Reign of Greed* in their English translations), describing the miseries of Spanish colonial rule. His writings were banned, and Rizal was captured on his way to Cuba. Put on trial in Manila for rebellion and sedition, he was shot by firing squad on December 30, 1896 – a day now set aside as Rizal Day.

French. It ended in humiliation for France. At Dien Bien Phu an entire French army was surrounded and in May 1954, after two months of pounding, it surrendered. Peace was signed later that year in Geneva, with Vietnam partitioned along the 17th parallel into a communist North and a pro-Western South and an agreement that nationwide elections would be held on the issue of reunification. Laos and Cambodia won independence in the wake of the French defeat.

In Indonesia, the Japanese had tried to win over the people by putting the anti-Dutch Dr Ahmed Sukarno at the head of a nationalist army. On August 17, 1945, between the Japanese surrender and the return of Allied troops, he declared independence. After a long guerrilla struggle, his dream became reality on August 17, 1950.

Britain, needing the dollar earnings from the tin mines and rubber plantations of a

**French Indochina**

***Wind of change in the East*** *Dr Sukarno is arrested by the Dutch in January 1949 during the struggle for independence.*

friendly Malaya, was ready to grant independence to the Malay States. But the handover of power was delayed until 1958 by the outbreak of a Chinese communist insurrection. They were defeated in the jungle by British and Malayan forces. Singapore, at that date a crown colony, also faced communist threats and had to deal with tensions between its Chinese and Malayan communities. In 1963, Prime Minister Lee

Kuan Yew linked Singapore to Malaya in the Federation of Malaysia, but the union lasted only until 1965, leaving Singapore free to follow its own path and become a model of capitalist wealth creation.

### The 'white rajahs' of Sarawak

In 1839, the adventurous Briton James Brooke helped Muda Hassim, uncle of the Sultan of Brunei, to subdue a Dyak rebellion in Sarawak, a vast territory in the north of Borneo. In gratitude, the sultan made him and his heirs rajahs of Sarawak. Brooke meted out justice personally in his new domain, clamping down on head-hunting, piracy and opium smuggling. Back in Britain, he was made a baronet. He passed Sarawak to his nephew, Charles, second of the 'white rajahs'. The last of the dynasty ceded the territory to Britain in 1946, and in 1963 Sarawak became part of Malaysia.

***Dropping into a trap*** *French paras land in Dien Bien Phu, in the mistaken belief that it was a springboard to victory.*

## Conflicts and confrontations

Independence was not the gateway to peace for South-east Asia. Burma, after the assassination of Aung San, faced insurrections by the Karens, the Chin and other minorities. Indonesia, under Sukarno, embarked on a policy of aggressive expansion, annexing Dutch New Guinea (and renaming it Irian Jaya), clashing with Malaysia and supporting a rebellion in oil-rich Brunei, which was defeated with the help of British troops. Corruption was rife in the Philippines, where the Moros and communist guerrillas were a constant threat. The assassination of opposition leader Benigno Aquino in 1983 caused turmoil which led in 1986 to the flight of President Marcos.

In Vietnam, the promised elections to unify North and South did not take place because of constant stalling by Ngo Dinh Diem, president in the South. Communist demonstrations against his regime were repressed and Viet Cong guerrillas began a campaign of violence. The conflict grew after Saigon called for American officers to train its troops. A handful of military 'helpers' expanded into an army, backed by US sea and air power. Like France before it, the USA had been sucked into the Vietnam quagmire; by 1967 it had 400 000 troops in Vietnam.

The conflict in Vietnam escalated under the presidencies of Johnson and Nixon. Bombing of the North and of Viet Cong

**Vietnam, at the end of 1967**

Into battle  *American forces in Vietnam tried to block the advance of communism.*

### Back to year zero

Like many Cambodians, Saloth Sar went to France to complete his education. But he put more effort into politics than into his studies and failed his course on radio electronics. But one lesson he did learn in the homeland of the French Revolution was the value of a Reign of Terror to those aiming at power. Back in Cambodia, he won the key post of general secretary of the Communist Party and changed his name to Pol Pot. It was a name that came to rank alongside those of Adolf Hitler and Joseph Stalin in the annals of mass murder.

The American bombs that fell on Cambodia during the Vietnam war made good propaganda for Pol Pot in his civil war against the pro-American Lon Nol. His Khmer Rouge army swept into Phnom Penh in April 1975, putting the capital at his mercy. In a psychopathic social experiment, Pol Pot took Cambodia back to year zero. The entire population of the capital was given 48 hours to leave and resettle in the countryside. Anybody who showed signs of being educated, even if it was only by wearing spectacles, was shot or clubbed to death. Some estimates put the total dead, out of a population of 7 million, at more than 2 million. After intervention by Vietnam, Pol Pot was captured in June 1997. He died two months later, allegedly of a heart attack.

bases in Cambodia was added to military operations in the South, but the Viet Cong stood firm. In the USA, opposition grew to what was seen by protesters as an unjust and futile war, and in 1973 Washington pulled out, leaving the South Vietnamese to fight on their own. In April 1975 the

Shelling their own city  *Phnom Penh under Khmer Rouge bombardment, January 1975.*

Viet Cong entered Saigon and a reunified Vietnam passed under the severe rule of Hanoi.

In neighbouring Laos, the communist Pathet Lao won control by 1975 and the monarchy was abolished. Cambodia spiralled into tragedy. The head of state, Prince Norodom Sihanouk, had earned the enmity of the USA by helping the communists in Vietnam. In 1970 he was ousted by a pro-American coup, but the new regime was attacked by the Khmer Rouge led by Pol Pot. He won power in 1975 and began a reign of terror.

### Ordeal of the 'Boat People'

After their victory, the North Vietnamese leaders undertook a vast land reform on the Chinese model. The result was a severe economic setback and widespread food scarcity in the countryside. In the late 70s, hundreds of thousands of Vietnamese, the 'boat people', took to the sea in ramshackle,

*Fighter for freedom* Aung San Suu Kyi, leader of Burma's democratic opposition and winner of the 1991 Nobel peace prize.

### Rebellion in the Philippines

The Moros (Moors), were driven out of Granada, their last stronghold in Spain, in 1492. Later, when Spanish missionaries encountered Muslims in the Philippines, they were given the name Moros. Now this Muslim minority is agitating for secession. Armed rebellion broke out in Mindanao, and in April 2000 an extremist Islamic group took hostages during prayers at a nearby mosque. Riots broke out, churches were burned, and Christians were killed in the streets. The rioting spread to Sulawesi and to the province of Maluku and its capital, Ambon, with hundreds of deaths.

*Armed combat* A Moro fighter in action.

overloaded boats, to escape starvation and political persecution. Frontier conflicts between Vietnam and the Khmer Rouge developed into a full-scale invasion in 1978, when Hanoi sent 120 000 troops across the border to chase out Pol Pot and install a puppet regime. But the people of Cambodia did not welcome occupation by Vietnam and civil war continued until 1990.

In Burma a military dictatorship was imposed in 1962 by General Ne Win, whose 'Burmese path to socialism' turned out to be the path to economic ruin. Thousands of small businessmen of Chinese and Indian origin fled the country, and while ethnic minorities rebelled in the frontier zones, corruption grew in the army.

Ne Win retired in 1988, but demonstrations continued against the junta, and hundreds of citizens were killed in the streets of Rangoon. General Saw Maung, who seized power in September 1988, imposed martial law and changed the country's name to Myanmar. Opposition centred around Aung San Suu Kyi, daughter of the assassinated Aung San, and her party won a two-thirds electoral majority in 1990. But the result was ignored, and Suu Kyi was placed under a house arrest that lasted until 1995.

*Asylum seekers* Vietnamese 'Boat People' refugees in Malaysia, June 1979.

*Day of triumph* Students in Jakarta greet the news of President Suharto's fall in 1998.

In Indonesia, Sukarno's policy of 'guided democracy' sent inflation soaring and stripped opposition parties of their rights. The army took over, removing him from the presidency in 1967. His successor, General Suharto, repaired the shattered economy but his 'New Order' proved to be corrupt. Indonesia's annexation of East Timor in 1976 led to years of oppression, but in the end the islanders won the promise of full independence in 2002. There was ethnic violence, too, in Kalimantan, the Indonesian part of Borneo, where the native Dyaks massacred recent immigrants. In the Moluccas, Muslim fought Christian. Separatists were active in Aceh, Sumatra. The economic crisis in Southeast Asia in the late 1990s hit Indonesia hard and in 1998 Suharto was forced to resign. Megawati Sukarnoputri, the daughter of Dr Sukarno, emerged as a popular political figure and in 2001 became president.

At the dawn of the third millennium, South-east Asia faces a future bristling with problems. With a few shining exceptions, there is rampant abuse of human rights. Corruption marks and mars both political and business life. Ethnic violence has created more than a million internal refugees in Indonesia alone. Asia's economic crisis has sent currencies and stock markets into free fall. Yet there are reasons for optimism, too. This is a region with immense natural resources and a store of proud traditions – and its people have given ample proof down the centuries of their energy, creativity and resilience.

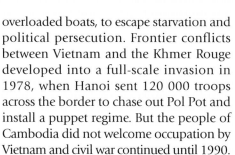

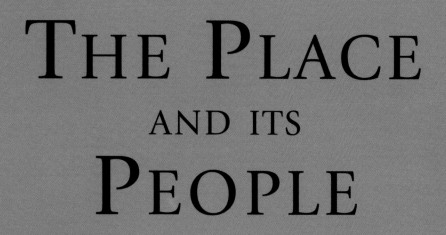

# THE PLACE
## AND ITS
# PEOPLE

With the end of the conflicts that ravaged Indochina into the 1980s, South-east Asia looked forward to an era of peace and prosperity: Singapore and Brunei became Asian mini-tigers; Malaysia and Thailand prepared to join the hi-tech age. Laos and Vietnam introduced elements of free market reform, while Cambodia began to emerge from the Khmer Rouge revolution. But Myanmar suffered under a military regime, and Indonesia and the Philippines were undermined by corruption. People in this part of the world are no strangers to adversity: faced with problems, they find solutions.

CHAPTER 1

# THE POWER AND WONDERS OF NATURE

Nature in South-east Asia operates on the grand scale, whether as destroyer or creator. The forces that devastate can also bring new life. The lava that streams down the slopes of volcanoes is rich in nutrients that will feed tomorrow's crops of rice, pineapples and sugar cane. The monsoons that flood mighty rivers such as the Red River, the Irrawaddy and the Mekong bring down mud that replenishes the fertility of the paddy fields. In the tropical and equatorial rain forests, evolution has gone on a spree and history has in places stood still. Here are the rafflesia, the biggest flowers in the world, and tiny pinhead orchids. Here, too, are Victoria water lilies, whose combination of lightness and strength is said to have inspired the design of the Crystal Palace. And in hills hardly touched by time, people still farm by slash-and-burn methods.

*A quiet moment beside a jungle pool near Luang Prabang, in Laos.*

# Finding a place in the sun

*The sun's rays stream down abundantly in the Tropics, but they are shared out unevenly. Nowhere is the competition for daylight more fierce than in the tropical forests of South-east Asia. Plant growth there is so vigorous, and the tree canopy so dense, that less than five per cent of the precious rays penetrate to the forest floor.*

The tropical and equatorial forests of South-east Asia are the richest in the world, both in the number of trees and the variety of species. An acre (0.4 ha) of forest in Borneo or Indonesia can contain some 200 different species of trees – ten times as many as the same area of a temperate forest in Europe. This exuberant growth is the result of the all-pervading heat and humidity. In such hothouse conditions, plants can grow and produce fruit all year round.

Trees, like most plants, strive towards the sun because they need its energy in order to manufacture food. Every leaf is a solar-powered factory, turning carbon dioxide and water into sugars. The winners in the race for a place in the sun form the top two layers of a tropical forest. The canopy, where tree crowns merge at around 80 ft (24 m), is so dense that it almost forms a roof. But scattered single trees, known as emergents, manage to push through. Rope-like lianas and other climbers tangle around the trees, for this is their only chance of reaching the light. The lianas drop aerial roots that absorb moisture from the air. Even if they lose contact with the soil, they can draw nutrients from water and decaying vegetable matter trapped in crevices in the trees. Strangler figs, germinating in the bark of a tree, send down stems to anchor themselves in the ground and eventually rob their host of light, choking and entombing it.

## Underneath the spreading banyan tree

The banyan, a species of fig tree, is venerated by both Hindus and Buddhists. According to legend, a banyan sprang from the centre of the universe at the moment Buddha was born. A banyan can grow to 130 ft (40 m) or more in height. It spreads by putting out aerial rootlets, which droop to the ground and grow into secondary trunks. These in turn put out rootlets, so that in time a single tree can grow into what looks like an entire grove. Ancient banyans have laced their branches around the stones of sacred sites from Angkor to the temples of Bali.

***Strength in fragility*** *The giant leaves of these Victoria water lilies, floating in a Thailand canal, can support the weight of a child.*

to reclaim land from the sea. The seeds lead the advance by fixing their spear-like shoots in the mud when they fall off the trees.

On sandy beaches, coconuts and other palms are the natural vegetation. Coconut seeds, in their fibrous cases, are carried by the sea and can colonise islands and beaches hundreds of miles away.

*Tropical flowers   Orchids, the largest family of flowering plants in the world, are symbols of purity and fertility in South-east Asia. Many are epiphytes, depending on trees for support but not living on them as parasites. They draw nutrients from material collected in the forks and crevices of the branches.*

*Shaft through the gloom   A rare ray of sunlight reaches the ground in a Javan forest(left). More than 3000 varieties of tree grow in Indonesia.*

## Weird and wonderful plants

Plants that cannot manufacture their own food become parasites or predators. The fungi that grow in trees or on the forest floor live on decaying vegetation. Carnivorous pitcher plants trap and drown unwary insects by forming their flowers into funnels that collect rain. Above 5000 ft (1500 m) mosses, orchids and lichens smother the smaller trees. In Burma, hills that are an extension of the eastern Himalayas are covered by vast forests of conifers, magnolias and rhododendrons. In the mountains of the Philippines, the forest looks like a garden because thousands of orchids have lodged in crevices in tree bark. Butterfly orchids include the *Vanda sanderiana* of Mindanao and the *sampaguita*, the national flower.

The tropical rain forest is a fragile ecosystem. Monsoon rains wash nutrients from the soil. Leaves are under constant attack from animals and insects, and some trees have developed a defence that amounts to chemical warfare, packing their leaves with poison. Population pressures and the demands of the logging industry for hardwoods such as teak have led to the loss of rain forest habitat.

*Nature's botanical garden   Borneo's national park of Kinabalu (right), on the slopes of Mount Kinabalu, is renowned among botanists for the astonishing richness of its ecosystem. It is home to nearly 40 000 species of flowering plant.*

## Mangroves and palm trees

The natural vegetation changes on the margins of land and sea, where the soil is drenched with water. Mangroves grow along muddy shorelines in Borneo and Andaman, on land that is swamped by the sea at high tide. They have evolved to cope with soil that is both liquescent and highly saline. Their roots almost float on the mud: deep roots would be of no value, because nutrients are found only on or near the surface. Some trees anchor themselves in the mud with a spreading buttress of shallow roots. One of the mangrove's most remarkable attributes is the ability

### The threatened mangrove

Schools of fish and a small army of frogs and crabs live in the mud and brackish waters of mangrove swamps, but their habitat is under threat in the modern world. Deforestation is the most serious menace: mangroves are being hacked down because their wood can yield pulp for paper-making. Some swamps are threatened by the advance of pollution, and in others trees have been cut back to make way for shrimp farming.

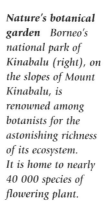

33

# The teeming diversity of forest and sea

**Giant butterfly** *The ornithopter butterfly has a wingspan of up to 8 in (20 cm).*

*The astonishing diversity of animal, bird and insect life in the forests of South-east Asia is most marked in the islands of Indonesia, scattered across a frontier between two worlds – Eurasia and Australasia. In the west of the archipelago are animals of the Old World, such as elephants and tigers, while the eastern islands are home to marsupials.*

A tropical forest provides abundant niches for animal life in its different levels. Fruit, insects and succulent leaves are concentrated in the sun-drenched canopy – food for birds and other flying creatures, and for agile climbers such as monkeys. The hornbill, its head protected by a horny 'helmet', rams its long,

**Dual-purpose bill** *The spider catcher's bill is also useful for sipping nectar.*

tough bill through the tangle of leaves and branches to reach fruit. The comical proboscis monkey, with its quizzical face and long nose, specialises in eating leaves high in the trees. Why they have evolved such a nose is not fully understood: perhaps it gives resonance to their loud, honking calls. Below them gibbons, the smallest of the apes, swing hand over hand through the branches, hooting and shrieking to stake a

territorial claim. Macaques, obsessed with status within the group, share their time between the middle layers of the trees and the ground. The orang-utan of Borneo and Sumatra clambers about the trees looking for fruit, leaves and birds' eggs. In only a few minutes, it can make a nest of sticks in the branches, crudely roofed with leaves to keep out the rain. Its name means 'man of the woods' in Malay, but it looks at its most human when it is a baby.

**Perfect camouflage** *The orchid mantis is almost invisible against an orchid – both to the insects it eats and to the birds that prey on it.*

34

## Nature runs riot

Evolution has gone on a spree in the tropical forests. There are nearly 150 000 species of insects, 1000 species of birds, 250 of reptiles and 90 of frogs. The kalong, a flying fox, is the world's largest bat, with a wingspan of up to 5 ft (1.5 m). The reticulated python, which can grow to 33 ft (10 m), is the world's largest snake. There are water buffaloes, wide-eyed tarsiers, tiny mouse deer, bears, leopards, wild pigs and pig-like tapirs. But some of nature's most impressive creations are threatened with extinction – among them wild elephants, tigers, the monkey-eating eagles of the Philippines, Javan and Sumatran rhinos and anoas of the Celebes, the world's smallest cattle, standing just 3 ft 3 in (1 m) high. Protection measures in the past 25 years have halted a dangerous decline in the population of orang-utans, but their numbers fell severely in forest fires in Borneo and Sumatra in 1997 and 1998.

The rain forest is drenched in colour. Hummingbirds shimmer as they hover by flowers, while multicoloured barbets and parrots perch in branches. Clouds of butterflies make living rainbows; iridescence sparkles from the wings of swarming insects. The green-crested lizard changes colour to suit its mood: it turns chocolate-brown when alarmed, and its throat and lips go crimson during courtship.

***Champion leaper*** *The wide-eyed tarsier, only 6 in (15 cm) long, can jump 6 ft (2 m) between branches. It can also turn its head through 180 degrees, to watch out for danger.*

***'Man of the woods'*** *An orang-utan on Sumatra. Those on Borneo are darker and their faces are less hairy.*

## Colours of the sea

The dazzling spectrum of colours in the forest is matched by that of a myriad darting fish in the seas. As on land, colour is used as an advertisement, for recognition within a species, and for protection. The angel-emperor fish is a flash of black, yellow and blue, while the parrot fish is brilliant green. A species of trigger fish with broken-up patterns of colour has been named the Picasso fish.

The flag fish has a chameleon-like ability to change colour to match its background. The Siamese fighting fish is a warrior in scarlet and blue, so renowned for its aggressiveness that specially bred fighters form the basis of a minor gambling industry in Thailand.

The Philippines are bordered by an ocean trench that plunges to a depth of 7 miles (11 km). Here, in the darkness, lurk swallower and gulper fish, which are little more than huge mouths attached to an elastically expandable stomach. Angler fish use a 'bulb' of bacteria-produced light to attract the smaller fish on which they feed.

***Mark of age*** *The nose of the male proboscis monkey grows as it gets older.*

### Return of the dugong

Dugongs in South-east Asian waters were hunted to near extinction for their hides, meat and oil, but are now a protected species. They are not fish, but mammals, whose ancestors took to the sea aeons ago. Grazing on seaweed, just as, on land, cows graze on grass, they build up a thick layer of blubber and can weigh well over 40 stone (250 kg). This makes it hard to believe the old tales that sailors used to mistake them for mermaids.

# The mighty Mekong

*When a river flows through many countries, it collects many names. The Mekong is 'Turbulent River' in China, 'Mother of Rivers' in Burma and Laos, and 'Great River' in Cambodia. In Vietnam, where it reaches the South China Sea in a nine-branched delta, it is 'River of Nine Dragons'. All the names testify to its power.*

**Life on the water** *Commerce spills over onto the river in one of the Mekong's traditional floating markets. In areas regularly visited by floods, peasants live in floating villages.*

All but one of the great rivers of the world had been traced to their source by the close of the 19th century. One last mystery remained: the source of the Mekong. It was not until April 1995 that a Franco-British expedition established that the Mekong rose not in Tibet, as had previously been thought, but in China, at the head of a 16 400 ft (5000 m) mountain pass in Qinghai province. What begins as a mountain torrent becomes a majestic flow on its 2700 mile (4350 km) journey to the South China Sea. By then, the Mekong has passed through

**Wild waters** *Rapids on the Mekong in Laos show its potential as a source of hydroelectric power.*

### The Mekong

**Sleeping giant** *The Mekong has enormous potential, but plans to tap into this energy were frustrated by the Vietnam War. So far, only one dam has been built, in Laos. The first bridge, the Friendship Bridge, was opened in 1994, linking Laos with Thailand.*

six countries and served both as a frontier and a highway. It has shown many moods, thundering down rapids and meandering through low-lying regions. Its nutrient-rich silt and mud has turned its delta into Vietnam's rice bowl, and it once supported the ancient Khmer civilisation of Cambodia.

### Nature's own flood-control system

The Mekong shifts a prodigious weight of water. Upstream of Cambodia's capital, Phnom Penh, the rate of flow has been measured at 19 000 cu yd (14 700 m³) a second – a figure that can increase fivefold at times of heavy flood. At the delta, it pours 620 billion cu yd (475 billion m³) of water a year into the South China Sea.

In June, when the monsoon rains add their downpour to a river system already swollen by melting snows from the far-off hills, there occurs a rare phenomenon of nature: a river that flows backwards. Cambodia's Tonlé Sap, or Great Lake, is drained in the dry season by the Tonlé Sap River, a tributary of the Mekong. When it is in full flood, water is pushed back up the tributary in a gigantic natural flood-control system and the Great Lake laps over into the surrounding countryside. In the dry season, when the waters recede, the land is enriched by the fertile mud that is left behind.

# Floods, typhoons and monsoons

*South-east Asia is particularly exposed to the caprices of wind and weather. The monsoon can drown people, animals and crops, but it is a creator as well as a destroyer. The curse of the floods becomes a blessing when it spreads fertility over the land.*

**Drowned forest** *Floods submerge a forest in the Philippines. The monsoons, with their torrential rains, bring frequent flooding to the archipelago, which is also hit by typhoons 15 to 20 times a year.*

In 1997 the coastal regions of Vietnam were battered by a typhoon of terrible destructive force. Shrieking winds, floods, and waves whipped up to a height of 20 ft (6 m), left hundreds of people dead. Torrential rain ruined nearly 6000 sq miles (15 000 km²) of rice growing in the fields. Paradoxically, the country was spurred to such a nationwide effort in response to this disaster that it went on to produce one of its biggest-ever rice crops.

Typhoons are unwelcome but regular visitors to the coasts of Vietnam, Thailand, the Philippines and other countries in the region. In the Atlantic, they are called hurricanes; in the Indian Ocean, they are known as cyclones. A typhoon picks up energy from the warmth of tropical seas. Humid air, rising from the surface, condenses into thick thunderclouds, and as more air is sucked in, the whole mass is set spinning into a spiral by the Earth's rotation. Wind speeds can reach 190 mph (300 km/h) or more. When this swirling destructive force reaches the land, it is cut off from its energy supply – but not before it has done its damage.

## In the path of the monsoon

South-east Asia lies between two great oceans, the Indian and the Pacific. The whole region is in the path of monsoon winds that blow from the south-west in summer and drench the land with moisture they have picked up from the warm seas. In Borneo, Sumatra and eastern areas of the Philippines, there is no dry season. More than 118 in (3 m) of rain can fall in a year: rivers burst their banks and

homes are swept away. During periods of flood, the countryside becomes a waterworld, with the earth a sea of mud. If the rains last for more than a month, the big trees disappear from the landscape, toppled by the wind because their roots have no anchor to hold them firm. Over the centuries, people have learned to turn the flooding to their advantage, growing crops on the fertile mud left behind when the waters recede. But in modern times the desperate need of a growing population for land is forcing people to live in areas that were one once thought to be uninhabitable. This can mean encroaching on the rain forest, chopping down trees whose roots bind the soil and so making floods even more devastating than in the past.

**Drowned city** *A flooded street in Phnom Penh, Cambodia, after the monsoon of 1992.*

**The survivors** *Flood victims wade to safety during floods in central Vietnam in December 1999.*

# Giants of fire and flame

*A 'ring of fire' encircles the Pacific, marking places where pressure beneath the Earth bursts through its crust. The Philippines and the the Indonesian islands, lying along frontiers between tectonic plates, have long suffered from the terrifying power of volcanoes.*

***Volcanic harvest*** *Gathering sulphur on Kawah Ijen, Java.*

In August 1883 the island of Krakatoa, between Java and Sumatra, blew up, bringing death to 36 000 men, women and children. The shock of exploding gases, which flung white-hot rocks the size of wagons high into the air, was felt 9000 miles (14 000 km) away in California. Huge clouds of volcanic dust rose into the upper atmosphere and circled the Earth, causing vivid red sunsets. But the eruption, spectacular though it was, was not the direct cause of the deaths. The victims, for the most part peasants and fishermen, were drowned by tsunamis, giant waves set in motion by the explosion. Nine of them swept over the shores of Java and Sumatra. Two huge waves in succession picked up a gunboat on the coast and flung it like a toy miles into the rain forest. At the northwest tip of Java, the highest of the tsunamis reached 130 ft (40 m).

## Afloat on molten rock

The lithosphere, the outer shell of the planet, is split into rigid 'plates' that float on a sea of molten rock. Both volcanoes and earthquakes occur along the boundaries between shifting plates – as people in Indonesia and the Philippines know to their cost. Entire cultures have been wiped out by volcanic eruptions. In the 9th century the kingdom of Mataram, in the centre of Java, was abandoned suddenly and mysteriously. The mystery was not solved until 1000 years later, when the Buddhist temples and terraces of Borobudur were discovered beneath a thick layer of volcanic ash.

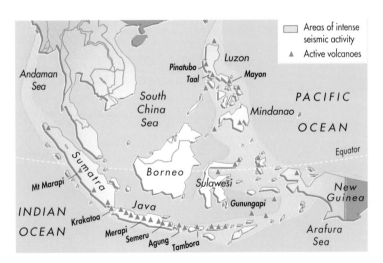

***Smouldering giant*** *Steam rises from the sea at the foot of Krakatoa, Java. Its last major eruption, in 1883, caused 36 000 deaths.*

## After the terror – fertility

In 1815 the eruption of Tambora, in Indonesia's Lesser Sunda Islands, killed 10 000 and at least 50 000 more perished as a huge cloud of ash blocked out the sun for months, bringing famine and disease. In 1991, at Mount Pinatubo in the Philippines, the largest eruption of the 20th century hurled more than 2 cu miles (8 km³)

of ash and millions of tons of sulphur dioxide into the stratosphere. Nor have the fires beneath Krakatoa died down: Anak Krakatoa, 'Child of Krakatoa', erupted in 1969. When a volcano erupts, streams of lava and mud roll down its slopes, annihilating crops and homes. But the villagers always return, for they know that the lava will weather into fertile soil. They grow rice, cabbages, maize, beans, coffee, tea, loofah-yielding gourds, cloves, sugar cane, pineapples and tobacco. Volcanoes produce good building material, too. In Java, volcanic rock was used to build the temples of Borobudur and Prambana.

***Colour in the craters*** *The lakes of Keli Mutu, Indonesia, change colour as the years go by.*

## Abodes of the gods

Volcanoes can cause death and destruction, but they also bring fertility to the land. It is small wonder that in ancient times they were associated with angry and vengeful gods who needed to be appeased, sometimes with human sacrifice. Gods and spirits still haunt these mysterious landscapes. Invisible phantoms are said to visit the desolate summit of Lawu, in the centre of Java. The almost perfect pyramid of Mayon in the Philippines invites stories of the supernatural because its eruptions often produce 'glowing clouds' – a suspension of incandescent gas and white-hot lava that streams down its sides. Mount Agung in Bali is so sacred that the temple complex of Pura Besakih has been built on its slopes.

### Sacrificing to the volcano gods

After a violent eruption the central cone of a volcano can collapse, creating a depression known as a caldera. One of the most impressive calderas in the world is Bromo, in the east of Java. Rising to 7848 ft (2392 m) from a desolate sea of sand, the summit is often obscured by mist. Sulphur-laden fumes above the volcano create spectacular sunsets and sunrises. In the 1970s, a lake of boiling water filled the caldera. Following an eruption, the water evaporated in seconds.

Once a year the caldera, which is 5 miles (8 km) in diameter, becomes the gigantic stage for a ceremony known as the *kasodo*.

At midnight, thousands gather to throw offerings of flowers, cloth, silver and chickens into the crater, to placate the god Brahma, from whom Bromo takes its name. According to an ancient legend, Prince Joko Seger and his wife Roro Anteng, ancestors of the Tengger people, lie at the bottom of a cave in the caldera. Roro Anteng gave birth to 25 children and the last one was thrown into the crater, sacrificing it to the god Brahma. Volcanoes throughout the region are associated with sacrifice. In the Philippines, the ancient Bagobas tribe threw people into the craters to turn away the wrath of the gods.

# Life in the misty hills

*Below the snowcapped peaks of South-east Asia, semi-nomadic people farm by the slash-and-burn technique. The cash crop is a deadly one – opium.*

**Mountain homes** *A village of the Akha seminomads in northern Thailand.*

Rain forests, often wrapped in mist, clothe the lower and middle slopes of highland regions in South-east Asia; higher up, plant growth is stunted and trees give up the struggle altogether. Temperatures fall 1 °C for every 500 ft (150 m) of extra altitude, and the force of the wind increases with height. The soil, with no protection against rain and frost, becomes thin and lacking in nutrients, making life hard for plants, animals and humans. From Burma to Vietnam, the pattern is the same: the people who are pushed into the highlands are the newcomers and those who belong to ethnic minorities.

## Farmers and lawbreakers

In Thailand, the highlands traditionally belonged to the king, who offered the use of them to the people known as *montagnards*. With no property rights and no way of producing the abundant rice harvests of the deltas and plains, the mountain people became semi-nomads, turning to one of the world's most primitive forms of agriculture: slash and burn. Trees and undergrowth are chopped down and burned, and cereals and vegetables are sown in the ashes, which smother weeds and

add minerals to the soil. The system is called *ray* in Thailand and Laos, *taungya* in Burma, and *ladang* in Malaysia. After two harvests, the soil is exhausted and the farmers move on to build another village and raise new crops on another hillside.

Some farmers and peasants fall back on a crop that is illegal but lucrative. In the area known as the 'Golden Triangle', where Laos, Thailand and Burma meet, hill tribes such as the Hmong, the Yao and the Lahu cultivate the opium poppy, *Papaver somniferum*. It

flourishes on the poor soil of steep hillsides above 5000 ft (1500 m) and produces both opium and its derivative, heroin. The crop may be illegal, but smuggling, controlled by warlords based in Burma, is easy. The brown gum of opium and the white powder of heroin are readily portable.

**Digging the dirt** *Hmong women in Vietnam scratch a living from the mountainside.*

## The opium warlord

In the turmoil that followed the Second World War and the 1949 communist victory in China, the warlord Khun Sa established himself as a key figure in Burma's opium trade. Part Chinese and part Shan (the largest of Myanmar's ethnic minorities), Khun Sa won a three-cornered war against Burmese communists and Chinese Nationalist troops who fled to Burma after their 1949 defeat. He broke the Nationalist hold on smuggling routes into Thailand, buying opium from the Shan and other hill tribes and selling it to China, Thailand and Laos. He joined forces with Shan rebels against Myanmar's military regime and in 1992 declared the Shan state to be an independent nation.

**Farming with fire** *Land is prepared for crops in Laos, using the slash-and-burn method.*

# Indonesia, a nation of islands

*With an official tally of 13 677 islands, Indonesia is the world's biggest archipelago. The islands are scattered in a graceful curve, across 3000 miles (4800 km) – the distance between the Rock of Gibraltar and the Urals.*

Indonesia has the fourth largest population in the world, after China, India and the USA. But only 6000 of its islands – less than half the total – are populated. An extraordinary mosaic of peoples makes up its population of more than 210 million, among them Javanese, Chinese, Malays, Balinese and Dyaks – whose not-so-remote ancestors were head hunters.

## A jigsaw of islands

Some of the islands are little more than specks of rock; others, such as Borneo and New Guinea (both shared with other countries), are so huge and so thickly covered with impenetrable rain forest that their interiors have never been fully explored. On the map, the islands look like a series of doodles on a page. The archipelago of Sulawesi (formerly the Celebes) resembles a huge jellyfish, its fronds waving in the sea. Pulau Peleng has the shape of a sea bird with outstretched wings. Halmahera, main island of the Moluccas, is a starfish skewered across the Equator.

Mangrove swamps cover the coastal fringes of many islands. The tangled roots of the trees provide a home for crabs and molluscs – and for the crab-eating monkeys that prey upon them. Other islands have sandy beaches where turtles scramble from the sea to lay their eggs. Once the baby turtles hatch they race to the sea, as crabs, lizards and sea birds gather to feast upon them.

Some 3-4 million turtles a year are gathered to be exported to gourmet restaurants in the Far East. In Bali, there was a time when no wedding was complete without turtle on the menu, but it has now been recognised that this vulnerable marine reptile is threatened with extinction. Even the uninhabited islands of Indonesia face a threat as trawlers looking for new fishing grounds enter their waters, and tour operators bring in visitors whose very presence destroys the idyll they are seeking.

***The dragon's lair*** *The island of Komodo, surrounded by coral reefs.*

### The living 'dragons' of Komodo

The Komodo dragon looks like a survivor from the time of the dinosaurs, but in fact it is a lizard, the largest in the world. It evolved in isolation on Komodo and nearby islands to the west of Bali, and with no competition or natural predators grew to an enormous size: a fully grown adult can reach 10 ft (3 m) long, including the powerful tail it uses as a weapon. This giant lizard is a meat-eater that can move fast enough in short bursts to take a deer, wild pig, monkey or stray dog. It is also a cannibal, and will use its sharp claws and dagger teeth to attack smaller members of its own kind. Its chief food is carrion: a remarkable sense of smell enables it to detect a potential meal from several miles away. Komodo and the islands of Rinca and Padar are a national reserve for the 5000 or so surviving Komodo dragons.

***Ready to attack*** *The Komodo dragon has an extra weapon – poisonous saliva.*

***Paradise island*** *Rice grows beside palm trees on the island of Lombok, one of the Lesser Sunda group to the west of Bali.*

# Where danger lurks

*Noise is a constant companion in the rain forests of Sarawak and Sabah, two Malaysian states on the island of Borneo. The forests are loud with the honking of proboscis monkeys by day and with the roaring of orang-utans by night. Danger lurks there, too, among the tree ferns and giant flowers – from silent killers such as the panther, and from a wriggling host of deadly snakes.*

**State bird** *The hornbill, symbol of Sarawak.*

So dense is the Borneo rain forest that there are only two practicable ways to explore Sarawak and Sabah – by aeroplane or by riverboat. Those who travel by boat find themselves, at some stages of the journey, gently gliding through dark green tunnels where vegetation from both banks meets overhead; in other places, they find themselves battling against foaming rapids.

### Deadly snakes

As well as the thrills of the river trip, the rain forest offers an ever-changing procession of sights and sounds. Trees can grow to 200 ft (60 m), their topmost branches entwined in a canopy where the occasional orange-and-black flash of a hornbill may be seen. The forest abounds with snakes, venomous and nonvenomous, cobras, kraits and pit vipers are among the species to avoid. Minerals and vitamins are washed out of the soil by drenching rains, and some plants have made good the deficiency by evolving into insect-eaters. The pitcher plant can hold up to $3^1/_2$ pints (2 litres) of water, which is turned into a thin soup by the decaying bodies of trapped insects. Deforestation by loggers has brought some animals close to extinction, but the forest is still home to monkeys, gibbons, orang-utans, panthers, porcupines, tapirs, deer, bats and a multitude of birds.

### Vanishing hunter-gatherers

The forest is also home to a few rare tribes, notably the Penans, who have learned to live in harmony with the natural world. They know how to repel mosquitoes with lemongrass oil, and how to choose roots and bark that will cure anything from a skin infection to stomach ache. In today's world, some Penans are beginning to turn away from their old way of life as hunter-gatherers and to hire themselves out as loggers, or as guides in the national parks. Despite the advance of logging, and the development of a flourishing oil industry, Sabah still has its virgin rain forests.

The slopes of Mount Kinabalu are a paradise for botanists, with giant mosses that grow 3 ft (1 m) high, ferns that can tower above 30 ft (10 m); several species of the insect-eating pitcher plant; the largest flower in the world, the rafflesia; and the world's smallest orchid, the pinhead. Streaks of quartz in the granite of the mountain are said to be the tears of a grief-stricken woman whose Chinese lover never returned to her. The summit looks down over sandy beaches and offshore islets in a sparkling sea. But at sea level, all is not as peaceful as it seems, for the waters farther north are used by smugglers, and pirates sometimes operate in the Sulu Sea.

**Warrior race** *The Iban of Sarawak, formerly known as Sea Dyaks and feared as head-hunters, are noted for their tattoos.*

**Communal living** *The traditional long houses of Sarawak are now a popular tourist attraction.*

### Life in a long house

Deep in the interior there are places where life still follows a centuries-old pattern and the long house fulfils the role of an entire village. Families and communities live, sleep, work, carry out religious rites and ceremonies, and raise their children, all in the same building. The Iban, the largest ethnic group in Sarawak, with a population of 500 000, raise their long houses on stilts alongside rivers. They were head-hunters, as were rival tribes, and a long house has obvious advantages for defence. However, the younger generation is forsaking the long house for the attractions offered by towns.

# In the primeval forest

*Every country in South-east Asia has realised that its scenic wonders, its forests and seas, animals and plants are priceless assets. They have created national parks where this heritage can be preserved, both for its own sake and for the benefit of botanists, naturalists and tourists.*

The National Park of Taman Negara in Malaysia contains the oldest rain forest in the world: it has survived for 130 million years. Its 1677 sq miles (4343 km²) are well supplied with hides from which visitors can watch the wildlife. In Sabah, Mount Kinabalu Park has magnificent views from its 13 455 ft (4101 m) summit, the highest in South-east Asia. It is particularly rich in monkeys, bird life and carnivorous plants. The Bako National Park contains many varieties of the brilliantly showy hibiscus, as well as mischievous macaques that will swoop down from the trees to steal food from a picnic.

## Open-air 'zoo'

At Khao Yai in western Thailand, the country's oldest park, established in 1961, covers 839 sq miles (2172 km²) of primeval rain forest. Carefully concealed viewing balconies have been built so that visitors can observe, at heart-stoppingly close quarters, elephants, lemurs, gibbons, wild pigs, deer, Asiatic black bears and even, if they are lucky, an occasional leopard or tiger drinking at a pool or pausing at a salt lick. At the Bau Ka Chong park, in Thailand's extreme south, a nature study centre has been set up in the heart of the rain forest. An

enclosed open-air 'zoo' allows visitors to observe and study binturongs (long-haired members of the civet family), gibbons (the only primates that regularly travel by swinging hand over hand through the trees), kites and other rare creatures.

The park at Cuc Phong in the north of Vietnam is a prehistoric world, with giant ferns and orchids. Naturalists have identified nearly 500 species of medicinal herbs and plants, and counted 137 species of birds, 36 families of reptiles, 17 varieties of frogs and toads, and 67 species of mammals, among them langur monkeys, leopards, tigers and wild boars. Every March, great clouds of brilliantly coloured butterflies appear. They bring a strange halo effect to the forest, fluttering, darting, separating, then coming together again in obedience to some law of nature that is imperative to them but incomprehensible to humans. Mankind inhabited this Eden more than 12 000 years ago, for prehistoric human remains and fragments of stone tools have been found in mossy caves in the park.

**Under threat** *The gibbon of Thailand is among the animals whose numbers are decreasing.*

**Emblem of a nation** *The banga ray, Malaysia's national flower.*

## The struggle to preserve the wilderness

For millennia, rain forests were places where humans lived in harmony with nature. In modern times, they became an arena where nature was exploited. Now, with the spread of ecological awareness, the balance is beginning to tip back. In Asia generally, the struggle is hampered by lack of funds, lack of technological resources and lack of a public opinion demanding conservation. Both the Khmer Rouge in Cambodia and the military regime in Burma have allowed teak forests to be cut down for political and financial gain.

**The biggest** *At 3 ft 3 in (1 m) across, the rafflesia is the world's biggest flower. It may also be the smelliest: to pollinate it has to attract flies.*

**Haven for a tiger** *The rare white tiger is now under protection in the national parks of Sumatra.*

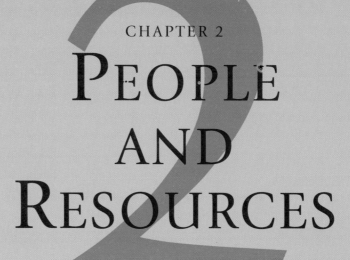

CHAPTER 2

# PEOPLE AND RESOURCES

South-east Asia still has a long way to go if it is to catch up with the economic giants of the West, but it has formidable assets in its natural resources and in the energy of its people. Singapore and the tiny oil-rich sultanate of Brunei led the march to prosperity in the 1980s and early 1990s, becoming Asian 'mini-tigers' in the style of Japan, South Korea and China, the big tigers to the north. The world economic crisis that began in 1997 was an undoubted setback, but the response so far has been a bold one. ASEAN (Association of South-east Asian Nations) has set itself the aim of capturing a competitive edge in a rapidly changing world, giving priority to the development of telecommunications, e-commerce and information technology. China has proposed making itself and the ASEAN countries into a single vast free trade zone: if this came about, the potential for growth would be staggering, for it would create a market of more than 1.8 billion people.

*Harvesting tea in the hills of the Cameron Highlands, Malaysia.*

# A bowl of rice

*Rice is grown throughout South-east Asia on the plains and deltas, and even in the hill country. Its production requires hard work and efficient organisation. It is the staple food of the region, and countries such as Myanmar (Burma) and Thailand are major exporters.*

'Too much water and the rice rots; too much sun and it withers.' 'Rice in the barn is money in the bank.' These traditional sayings draw attention to the importance of rice as the staple food of millions of people in South-east Asia, and to the skill and hard work needed for its production. There are ceremonies and noisy festivals at every stage of the cultivation process, from sowing to harvest, to win favour with the rice goddess.

### 'Dry' and 'wet' rice

In hill country, 'dry' rice is grown without irrigation canals, on land that has been prepared by the slash-and-burn technique. The 'wet' rice method of the plains and deltas, with their year-round warmth, rainy seasons and sophisticated irrigation systems, is far more productive.

In mainland regions, the rains begin around mid May. In June, on fields that were ploughed in the dry season, often using bullocks, the farmer starts a nursery for young plants. Rice seeds are pushed into the fertile mud and after about 30 days they have become delicate green seedlings, ready for transplanting. Then comes the back-breaking job of planting the seedlings in rows in the flooded paddy fields.

As the rains continue to pour down, the ears of the rice must stay above the rising water, otherwise they will rot. The plants grow taller as the water around them rises, but the water level has to be regulated by opening and closing sluice gates in the irrigation dykes. And the water in the paddy fields must constantly be changed, to avoid a build-up of bacteria and toxins that could transform a fertile field into an acidic swamp.

Towards the middle of October comes the flowering season, when the growing plant demands plenty of sun. With rainfall decreasing and the water level falling, the rice soaks up several weeks of sunshine. Finally, with the fields completely drained, the paddy (rice that has not been husked) is ready for harvesting. Then comes threshing, to separate the grain from the straw. In most villages of South-east Asia this is still done by hand, as is the winnowing that throws off the chaff (the husks). Polishing, to produce white rice, is done with the aid of traditional machines, operated by foot or by water power. It removes the outer brown

**The old way** *Growing rice is as back-breaking a task today as it has been for thousands of years. But modernisation has arrived, with the use of chemical fertilisers and pesticides.*

**Watery slopes** *Women of Vietnam's Dao minority plant seedlings on flooded terraces.*

*On the way back up* Rice fields at the foot of the Shan hills, Myanmar. Exports slumped in the 1970s, but are now rising again: by the mid 1990s Myanmar ranked sixth in the world for the export of white rice.

*The volcano's gift* The soil of Bali is so packed with nutrients that rice can grow to well over 3 ft (1 m) tall – like this giant crop on the terraced slopes of a volcano.

## Waste not, want not

In Malaysia, Indonesia, Thailand and Vietnam, rice is generally cooked so that the grains are fluffy and will separate easily. In Cambodia and Laos, they prefer rice that is slightly sticky – not as congealed as rice pudding, but cooked until the grains take on a pearly sheen. Apart from being served in bowls as part of the daily diet, rice can be processed to produce flour and starch, or used in the manufacture of cakes and noodles. At harvest time, the peasants set aside part of the crop to make rice wine or a fiery spirit called arrack, that can reach around 40% proof. Nothing goes to waste with rice. Bran and straw are fed to farm animals, and the straw can be plaited to make the conical hats worn by labourers in the paddy fields.

*Temptation on the table* Rice balls are a favourite in northern Vietnam.

coating that is rich in proteins and minerals, and unless these are provided by other food items, a white rice diet can lead to the debilitating disease beriberi, once the curse of South-east Asia. Miracle rices, developed in recent decades, give a higher yield of proteins as well as permitting up to three crops a year.

*Threshing time* Newly harvested rice is threshed by hand in the traditional way, to separate the grain from the straw.

## Three great rice bowls

The deltas of the Mekong in Vietnam and the Irrawaddy in Myanmar (Burma) and the central plain of Thailand are the great rice-growing regions, with Thailand the biggest rice exporter in the world, followed by the USA, then Vietnam. The fecundity of the Mekong delta, which produces more than 5 million tons of rice a year, was largely created by digging 900 miles (1500 km) of canals for drainage and irrigation. In Thailand, in the plain of Bangkok, irrigation canals were dug in the 19th and 20th centuries. The Chao Phraya project, consisting of a huge dam and four great canals, feeds reservoirs that supply the paddy fields in the dry season, allowing extra harvests. The Irrawaddy delta benefits from exceptionally heavy rainfall, which compensates to some extent

for the fact that cultivation methods there are less advanced than in the other great rice-producing regions. In the 1970s, politics interfered with rice production in Myanmar. With prices strictly controlled under the military junta, farmers held back their produce and exports slumped to one-twentieth of the pre-Second World War figure. But high-yielding varieties, foreign aid and higher prices reversed the decline.

*Great expectations* *Young Vietnamese boys go fishing.*

# Fish sauce, today and every day

*In South-east Asia, where paddy fields are far more likely to be encountered than pasture land, fish is the main source of protein in the diet. It comes from rivers, open seas, fish farms and even from the paddy fields themselves, when they are in flood.*

After the end of the Vietnam War, areas in and around many villages in the north of the country were pockmarked with enormous craters, the legacy of raids by American B52 bombers. Instead of filling them in, the villagers turned them to advantage by stocking them with fish and ducks.

## Fish in the rice fields

Fishing is a necessity for peasants throughout the region. Despite the advice of nutritionists, polished rice is preferred in many areas to brown rice, though this can lead to deficiency diseases, as protein and vitamins are removed in the polishing. Balance is restored to the diet by fish, and by the brownish fish sauce that is served with meals. In Vietnam, this sauce is called *nuoc mam.* In the Philippines, it is *patis;* in Thailand, it is *nam pla.* The recipe includes fish, chilli peppers, garlic and sometimes anchovies, fermented for months to produce a pungent mixture that most Westerners regard as an acquired taste.

Ramakamheng, an early king of Thailand who is claimed to be the founder of the Thai nation, is said to have written, in the 13th century: 'There are fish in the water and there is rice in the fields'. This Asian version of the Biblical 'land flowing with milk and honey' draws attention to the fact that when the paddy fields are flooded, they are full of small fish. These 'rice fish' are the basis of the ubiquitous fish sauce, and when they are in short supply, shrimps make an excellent substitute. Fish and shrimps can also be turned into paste, a dish that is a great favourite in Cambodia, a nation that consumes an impressive 80 lb (36 kg) of fish and fish products per head each year.

## Harvest of the sea

In hollows where it is difficult to grow rice, peasants make fishponds, for subsistence fishing is vital for them. But it cannot compare in scale with sea fishing, which for many countries in the region is the basis of a valuable export trade. In the Philippines, for example, there are 200 busy ports, serving a fishing fleet of 3000 trawlers and 250 000 smaller boats. They bring in some 2 million tons of fish a year, and Japan is their major market. The fishing industry in Vietnam, with its long coastline facing the South China Sea, and 270 000 sq miles (700 000 km$^2$) of territorial waters, has enormous potential to expand.

But the future is not entirely rosy. Stocks are falling in some areas because of overfishing and pollution in rivers and bays. Some fishermen use illegal methods, such as dynamiting. Inland, the paddy fields from which fish are taken are increasingly contaminated by chemical fertilisers. Thanks to the eco-movement – and to plain economic logic – governments are aware of the need to tackle these problems.

*In the net* *Catching 'rice fish' in an irrigation canal in northern Thailand.*

*Who'll buy?* *Fresh fish on a market stall in Jakarta.*

*Day's work done*
*Cleaning the nets in Da Nang Bay, Vietnam.*

# Straits of peril

*The recent discovery of offshore oil reserves in South-east Asia has added a new cause of potential conflict to a region whose seaways have long been made hazardous by pirates and by political instability.*

The Spratly Islands, between Borneo and the coast of Vietnam, were, until a few years ago, obscure specks of land in the South China Sea. Now they are the cause of international tension, with conflicting territorial claims being made by Brunei, Malaysia, the Philippines, Vietnam, China and Taiwan. The reason for this sudden rush of interest is simple: promising oil reserves have been discovered beneath the surrounding seas. So far, the dispute has simmered rather than boiled over. In 1999, at an ASEAN (Association of South-east Asian Nations) meeting in Manila, a code of conduct was drawn up to prevent outright conflict between members over the issue. China refused to accept the code, but announced that it would 'never seek hegemony' in the region.

## Pirates, separatists and terrorists

Disputes over oil reserves are not the only problem threatening the seaways of the region. Piracy is so great a menace in the South China Sea that, in February 2000, the governments of Malaysia and Indonesia agreed to pool their resources in combating it. Separatist movements, such as that of the Moros (Muslims) in the Philippines, threaten the stability of the region. And following the USA's declaration of a global war on terrorism and the bombing of targets in Afghanistan, in response to suicide attacks on New York's World Trade Center and on the Pentagon on September 11, 2001, a new threat has appeared. Indonesia is the biggest Muslim country in the world, and though the vast majority of its 175 million Muslims are far from being extremists, there are groups among them who seem prepared to commit terrorist acts. The most feared is Lascar Jihad, which since 1999 has been waging war against Christians in the Moluccas. It is suspected of having received money, weapons and training from Osama bin

**The straits**

Laden's Afghanistan-based terror group al-Qaida. In the Philippines, the Abu Sayyaf group, a breakaway from the Moro Liberation Front, has turned to kidnapping for ransom.

These troubled seas are a highway for one of the most valuable cargoes in the world. Japan and South Korea depend predominantly for their energy supplies on oil from the Middle East. The Strait of Malacca between Malaysia and Sumatra, and the Sunda Strait between Sumatra and Java, are vulnerable points on the journey.

***Menace on the high seas*** *Even in the 21st century, pirates still operate in the seas around Malaysia and Indonesia.*

***Shipping galore*** *Tankers, fishing boats and other vessels crowd the seafront at Singapore.*

# Oil, the key to prosperity

*Oil has been like manna from above for the tiny sultanate of Brunei, making it one of the richest countries in the world, with an annual GDP averaging US $4850 million. It is also one of the mainstays of the economies of Indonesia and Myanmar, and could transform the fortunes of Vietnam, too.*

***Exploiting resources*** *Drilling for oil in central Sumatra.*

***Past and present*** *An oil tanker crosses a line of Vietnamese fishing boats in the South China Sea.*

A mong South-east Asia's abundance of natural resources, one of the most pivotal has been the deposits of oil and natural gas. Indonesia and Myanmar (Burma) have been exploiting this 'black gold' for more than a century, and Brunei struck oil in the 1920s. Vietnam, with an annual production of 12.5 million tons of crude oil, is a newcomer to this high-profit business. Thailand also has reserves of oil and natural gas.

### A state within the state

Indonesia's first oil fields in northern Sumatra were the basis for the formation of Royal Dutch Shell in 1907. After Indonesia became independent, the country created its own company, which in 1968 became the all-powerful Pertamina, operating as a state within the state. Exploration, drilling, refining and transporting all demand heavy investment. The company took 85 per cent of the profits, but what was left was sufficiently tempting for foreign investors. A combination of inefficiency and corruption drove Pertamina into bankruptcy, but petrochemicals still account for one-third of Indonesia's exports.

In Burma's colonial days, Burmah Oil was a power in the land, and today the state-owned Myanmar Petrochemical Enterprise is one of the country's most profitable companies. Brunei, which in 2001 put out to international tender three exploration blocks in its territorial waters, is looking ahead. 'Suppose that after 25 years we don't find any more oil or gas resources,' a government spokesman said. 'That is the biggest challenge for us.' What they plan to do is to invest in hi-tech industries and financial services.

### A bonanza shared

B runei, an enclave of only 2226 sq miles (5765 km²) in the north-west of Borneo, coped with the economic downturn at the end of the 1990s reasonably well, because of its revenues from oil. Sultan Haji Hassanal Bolkiah is one of the world's richest men. He owns 50 per cent of Brunei Petroleum, the country's leading company in the exploitation of oil and natural gas reserves. But the people have shared in the oil bonanza. Brunei is a welfare state, with free education and a free health service. The sultan even went so far as to buy an Australian cattle ranch, bigger than his entire country, to provide beef for his subjects.

***Black gold*** *Oil installation in Kalimantan, Indonesian territory that covers two-thirds of Borneo.*

▲ Oil fields

# Tin and rubber, essential raw materials

*Global demand for tin and rubber has expanded at a phenomenal rate with the growth of the food-canning and car-manufacturing industries. South-east Asia has abundant reserves of these two essential raw materials.*

**Tapping a tree** *Latex is gathered from a rubber tree.*

The value of tin to the food-canning industry is that it can give a rustproof coating to iron or steel. It has become of key importance in the world economy, and the richest deposits in the world are found in South-east Asia, especially in Malaysia and Indonesia.

Rubber was brought to the West in 1823, when the Scot Charles Macintosh sandwiched naphtha-treated rubber between two layers of cloth to make the raincoats that still bear his name. The rubber in those first mackintoshes became brittle in cold weather, but this problem was solved in 1841 by the American Charles Goodyear, who invented the process of vulcanisation – treating the rubber with sulphur and heat to improve its strength and elasticity.

## A nation born of tin

The existence of Malaysia as a single country is closely linked to tin. Late in the 19th century the British, who had arrived as traders, were made nervous by rioting between native Malays and Chinese settlers working in the tin mines. They took the disturbances as an excuse for establishing political control. Perak, Selangor, Pahang and Negri Sembilan were united in a single federation, with Kuala Lumpur as their capital, and British residents were appointed to 'advise' their sultans. By 1930, Britain had control of the entire Malaya Peninsula. After the Second World War and the Emergency (a communist insurrection) Sarawak, Sabah and, briefly, Singapore joined the Federation of Malaysia.

## Rubber from Brazil

Rubber, obtained from the milky sap or latex of the *Hevea braziliensis* tree, was used by Amazonian Indians before the time of Columbus to make waterproof shoes and clothing. Brazil grew rich on its monopoly of rubber, but in 1876 the explorer Sir Henry Wickham smuggled some seeds out of the country to add to England's botanical collection at Kew Gardens. From there, rubber seeds reached Ceylon, Java, Sumatra and Malaya, where the heat and humidity provided ideal conditions. The new source of supply coincided with the invention of the motor car, which runs on rubber tyres – a 19th-century invention that conquered the world in the 20th. By the end of that century, Thailand, Indonesia and Malaysia were producing three-quarters of the world's supply. Brazil is still a producer, but the days when fortunes could be made are a distant memory.

**Family business** *Processing latex in Thailand.*

### From tree to tyre

The rubber tree, which can grow to 50-65 ft (15-20 m) high, is planted in clay or sandy soil. Its milky sap, called latex, is bled out drop by drop by making an incision in the bark. Once filtered and allowed to coagulate, the latex dries into sheets of crepe, the name given to rubber that has not been vulcanised. Synthetic rubber can be made from coal, oil or alcohol.

**Scooping it up** *A worker gathers cassiterite, or tinstone, at an open mine near Ipoh, capital of the Malaysian state of Perak.*

# The overseas Chinese

*Chinese immigrants in South-east Asia number a little over 20 million, among a total population of more than half a billion. Only in Singapore do they constitute a majority. But their impact has been immense: yesterday's coolies have become today's bankers and business tycoons.*

**Final resting place** *An ethnic Chinese cemetery in Thailand.*

South-east Asia's ethnic Chinese can trace their origins almost entirely to the two southern provinces of Guangdong and Fujian, and to the island of Hainan. In Indonesia, ethnic Chinese account for less than 3 per cent of the population, but they dominate business life. Singapore, one of Asia's outstanding success stories, is more than 75 per cent Chinese.

## Where they settled

The major waves of Chinese immigration came in the 19th century, when Dutch, French and British colonialism was at its height and a work force was needed for the tin mines, the rubber plantations and the fields. But South-east Asia was sparsely populated, so the missing manpower was supplied by coolies from southern China, where life for the peasants had always been grindingly hard. These economic migrants initially had the aim of making money, sending funds home if possible, then returning to China

to marry and raise a family. Later immigrants married local women and settled down. The Cantonese, from Guangdong, tended to settle in Vietnam, the Malay Peninsula and Singapore and to go into trade, open restaurants or become craftsmen. The Hokkiens, from Fujian, went to the Philippines, Indonesia and mainland Malaya. They often became merchants or bankers. The Hakka, one of China's many minority groups, spread widely and made their mark through personalities as different as General Ne Win, who ruled Burma after a 1962 military coup, and the novelist Han Suyin, author of *A Many-splendoured Thing*.

Many of the overseas Chinese live in Chinatowns in the ports or big cities. For the most part, they have integrated with the local communities: *mestizos* are Chinese-Filipinos, *minh huong* Chinese-Vietnamese, *baba* Chinese-Malays, *peranakar* Chinese-Indonesians and *luk-jin* Chinese-Thais. But success can breed resentment, and the ethnic Chinese have been a tempting target at times of political instability. Thousands were massacred in Indonesia after the crushing of a communist coup in 1965. In Cambodia the Chinese minority were victims of some of the worst atrocities perpetrated by the Khmer Rouge.

**Ready for the feast** *The* minh huong, *Vietnam's ethnic Chinese, still preserve many of the religious and folk traditions of their ancestors, such as displaying flower-bedecked pigs, to be roasted for the Chinese New Year.*

## Success stories

Despite all the setbacks, their political and economic journeys have been impressive. Sun Yat Sen, the revolutionary who toppled the Imperial Manchu throne, came from Guangdong, while Cory Aquino, who overthrew the regime of President Marcos in the Philippines, was of Chinese descent. During Hong Kong's years under British rule, its

### 2000 years of immigration

Traces of Chinese immigration dating to the 3rd century BC have been discovered in Vietnam. But it was not until some 600 years later that they began to reach South-east Asia in any numbers. Under the Tang dynasty (618–906) trade was encouraged and Chinese ships brought silks and porcelain to the islands of the southern seas, to be exchanged for such luxury items as ivory and spices. Gradually, Chinese settlements grew up round the ports. But the expansion of the Middle Kingdom's influence was brought to an abrupt halt in the 16th century by the eruption into its market of Spanish and Dutch traders. Then, in 1644, the Ming dynasty was overthrown by the Manchus, fierce warriors from the north. The new dynasty prohibited all emigration from China, so those who left later did so at their peril. There was danger, too, in the lands where they settled, with anti-Chinese pogroms in the Philippines, Java and Vietnam in the 17th and 18th centuries.

Major settlements of overseas Chinese

CHINA

MYANMAR
LAOS
THAILAND
CAMBODIA
VIETNAM
PHILIPPINES
PACIFIC OCEAN
South China Sea
MALAYSIA
BRUNEI
SINGAPORE
Sumatra
Borneo
Sulawesi
INDONESIA
INDIAN OCEAN
Java
EAST TIMOR

**The new way** *Chinese newlyweds follow a new tradition – a drive through Ho Chi Minh City.*

***After the riot*** *Indonesia's ethnic Chinese, whether communist or Christian, have suffered from mob violence. Here, a Chinese Catholic covers her face as she hurries past a church that was attacked during the 1998 riots in Jakarta.*

Chinese inhabitants made an immense contribution to the colony's prosperity, and the overseas Chinese have invested massively in building the new China.

There is more to their success in business than a capacity for hard work. The common origin of the vast majority, in southern China, means that they share the same language – Cantonese – and that they are bound together in close-knit families and clans.

Community feeling has been strengthened by persecution and is reinforced by cultural and religious ties. Members of Chinese professional and social groups help one another. Former schoolfellows keep in touch through their associations, and even groups of friends who meet regularly to gamble or to play *mahjong* are reaffirming what they have in common. In financial life, forms of credit have evolved that make the overseas Chinese independent of conventional banks. Loans can be arranged within the community. Lotteries are popular, and so is the tontine, a form of life insurance under which members pay money into a common pool and the total fund is inherited by the last surviving member.

The overseas Chinese have shown a marked capacity for adaptation and integration. As Lee Kuan Yew, Singapore's first prime minister, put it: 'We are ethnic Chinese, but at the end of the day our fundamental loyalties are to our home country, not to China.'

## The richest tycoon in Hong Kong

In the 1940s a Chinese orphan fled the Japanese invasion to seek refuge in Hong Kong. He found little security there, for Hong Kong surrendered at the end of 1941. But at the age of 17 he eked out a precarious living by selling plastic flowers. Today, Li Ka-Shing is a tycoon, head of the giant property and communications conglomerate Hutchison Whampoa. In the city of the mega-wealthy he became the richest of them all, combining both economic and political power. He took into partnership the son of the Chinese leader Deng Xiaoping and helped to negotiate the return of Hong Kong to China in 1997.

***Free to celebrate, at last*** *A boutique in Jakarta prepares for the Chinese New Year. So strong was anti-Chinese feeling in Indonesia that it was not until 2000 that the government repealed a law prohibiting any celebration of traditional Chinese festivals.*

# Dreams and despair

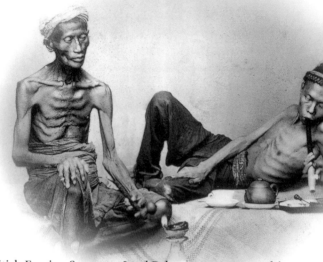

*Opium has come to be associated in the West with Imperial China at its most dissolute; with the image of addicts pursuing their dreams in smoke-wreathed dens, but finding only despair. In fact, China's emperors tried to abolish the opium trade. South-east Asia is still paying the price of their failure.*

The respectable directors of Britain's East India Company were the drug barons of the early 19th century. British society at that time had an obsession with Chinese silk, porcelain and, above all, tea. But the Chinese emperors, secure in the belief that their Middle Kingdom was the centre of the universe, felt no need for imports from Britain that would pay for such valuable exports.

## The Opium Wars

Their subjects, however, were open to the temptation of opium, a drug the Imperial Court banned, describing it as 'foreign filth'. The chief source of supply was the poppy fields of Bengal, where Britain's East India Company had a monopoly. Two Scots, William Jardine and James Matheson, established a trading company in Canton (now Guangzhou), buying tea and luxury goods with the money they made from smuggling opium into Chinese ports. By 1831, 'John Company', as it was known, was drawing one-sixth of its revenue from opium. Emperor Daoguang, angered at the defiance of his commands, acted decisively. His commissioner seized 20 000 chests of opium from British warehouses in Canton. So began the first Opium War (1839-42).

The British Foreign Secretary, Lord Palmerston, sent warships to defend the principle of free trade and force China to make reparation by ceding Hong Kong. A second Opium War (1856-60) brought further concessions, and the drug continued to spread its false dreams and its all-too-real misery across China and beyond.

In the 1880s, when France was colonising Indochina, she followed the British example and took over the monopoly of opium. French sales offices, bearing a yellow flag with the initials RO (*Régie Opium*) stayed in business until as late as 1948. The ethnic minorities in Laos and Vietnam, the Hmong, Lahu, Akha and other hill tribes, were encouraged to make money by growing the opium poppy instead of rice. That was why, in the Vietnam War, the *montagnards* (mountain people) often sided with the French, and later the Americans, against the Vietminh and Vietcong.

## Alternatives that failed

Although growing the opium poppy for anything other than medicinal purposes is outlawed in South-east Asia, it has so far proved impossible to wipe out its cultivation. International organisations have tried to persuade the hill tribes to grow other cash crops, among them flax, strawberries, camphor, mushrooms, sesame, coffee and mulberry trees. But none of these can promise the same high cash returns as opium and its derivatives,

---

### The 2000-fold price hike

The opium poppy is planted in June, in fields that have been cleared of stones and weeds. Harvesting is done by women and children, between December and February. An incision is made in the seed head and the liquid, which hardens into a brown gum, is scraped out. The opium is then processed in laboratories, first into a morphine base, then into heroin. The price paid on the streets of London, Frankfurt or Paris for a shot of heroin, mixed with lactose, is 2000 times what the peasants earned for the original opium.

**Sinister beauty** *The opium poppy and its dried seed head.*

**Seeds of peril** *The poppy's narcotic resin lies in its seed head.*

heroin and morphine, for none has such a seemingly inexhaustible world market. Surprisingly, perhaps, opium is relatively little used by those who grow the crop, although there are addicts among them. The Hmong and other hill tribes also keep aside a small amount of the crop for use as a painkiller, and as a means of easing the last days of villagers enfeebled by age. In a similar way, opium in the form of laudanum was widely used as a medicine and as a restorative in Europe and the USA in the 19th century. As late as the 1920s, heroin was being legally promoted in the West as a wonder cure for such complaints as asthma and tuberculosis.

The growers are poorly paid in comparison with the middlemen, the smugglers and drug barons. Britain and France may have played a key role in the trade in the past, but in modern times other governments have profited unofficially from the drug. Afghanistan is the world's biggest producer, followed by Myanmar (Burma) and Laos. The Burmese military regime, faced with Shan and Karen separatist movements in the northern hill regions, has an uneasy relationship with the poppy-growers. In 2000, when the government made a start on resettling 50 000 peasants from one of the Shan regions, in order to eradicate poppy-growing, the result was an increase in guerrilla activity.

*Starting young   It is tobacco, not opium, in the pipe of this young woman of Thailand's Kaleung minority. The tribes who grow opium use it sparingly.*

### The Golden Triangle

Twenty years ago, the Golden Triangle in the border territory of Laos, Burma and Thailand was one of the most dangerous places on Earth. Guerrillas professing loyalty to half a dozen causes, and warlords with loyalty only to themselves, disputed the control of the immensely profitable opium trade. The opium poppy is still grown there, but this once forbidden zone is now the haunt of tourists. *Montagnards*, the mountain people, sell cheap trinkets, and allow themselves to be photographed at their work. The big drug barons stay out of sight in their luxurious houses: their money persuades the authorities to leave them alone.

*Deadly harvest   Opium, in the form of brownish gum. The next stage is heroin.*

*Cash crop   A young boy of Thailand's Hmong minority in a field of opium poppies.*

# When the mini-tigers lost their footing

*It was a black day for economic stability in South-east Asia when, on July 2, 1997, Thailand announced that its national currency, the baht, had collapsed under an onslaught of speculation. Other currencies caught a cold from Thailand's 'sneeze'. Had the good times come to an end?*

The 'Asian miracle' of the 1970s and 1980s was held up as a model for the world. South-east Asia, with its teeming resources and its enviable location on the go-ahead Pacific Rim, appeared to be destined for astronomic growth. For a while, progress was dazzling, but in 1997 came a shock: boom turned to bust with alarming rapidity.

## A frenzy of construction

Taiwan, Japan and Hong Kong were among the first to see the possibilities of a region that had a large population of skilled workers, but not enough jobs to go round. Businesses switched some of their production to South-east Asia to take advantage of the cheap labour. Nations that had previously exported mainly food and raw materials began to enjoy a manufacturing boom. Factories in Indonesia turned out sports shoes and furniture. Cars, lorries and electronic goods rolled off the assembly lines in Thailand, where the annual growth rate reached 13 per cent in the late 1980s. Singapore's economy, under the firm leadership of Lee Kuan Yew, grew by around 9 per cent a year, every year for two decades. Vietnam, emerging from the devastation of war, was prepared to welcome foreign investment.

Capital cities throughout the region went into a building frenzy. Tower blocks, their glass sides flashing like mirrors, punctuated the skyline, while at street level newly built freeways were crammed with shiny new cars. The resultant pollution and traffic snarl-ups were regarded as prices worth paying for such an unprecedented leap forward.

## The day of reckoning

The reckoning came on July 2, 1997, when the Bank of Thailand announced that it could no longer defend the national currency, the baht, against speculators. Loss of confidence in the nation's finances was blamed on the government's lax approach towards financial regulation and to a rush by overseas investors, worried by the recession in Japan, to call in their short-term loans. By the end of the year the baht had halved in value. Panic swept through the stock exchanges of the region. Share prices went into free fall, especially in the overvalued finance and property sectors. A string of bankruptcies followed and

### Diamond studs in the welfare state

Brunei, with its vast resources of oil and natural gas, emerged relatively unscathed from the economic downturn. It was even able to invest in diversifying the economy, against the day when the wells might run dry. Haji Hassanal Bolkiah, sultan of this 2226 sq mile (5765 km²) country, has used oil revenues to build a welfare state for his 350 000 subjects. The sultan does not offend against Brunei's sober Muslim dress code. When he attends a state dinner, his simple clothes can be disconcerting at first. But closer inspection will reveal that the buttons on his plain black shirt are diamonds.

**Hail to the heir** *The Sultan of Brunei at a sumptuous dinner on August 10, 1998, when his son was proclaimed heir.*

**The wealth of Islam** *The gilded domes and minarets of the mosque in Bandar Seri Begawan, capital of oil-rich Brunei.*

currencies collapsed. In 1998, Thailand's projected growth was minus 7 per cent. Indonesia saw the rupiah fall by 80 per cent in six months. By 1999, inflation in Laos was running at 150 per cent. Even the people of Singapore had to accept a wage cut.

Political problems added to the economic misery. Indonesia was torn apart by ethnic violence and by separatist movements, such as that in East Timor, which finally won independence. Corruption scandals shook Malaysia and Thailand. In Vietnam, foreign investment was reduced to a trickle because overseas companies wanting to do business there were dismayed by the number of bureaucratic hurdles put in their way.

There were, nevertheless, some glimmers of hope. ASEAN accelerated its timetable for creating a free trade area, setting 2004 as the starting date. Ambitious plans were laid to expand tourism. However, in an increasingly complex world, the prospects of economic recovery for the nations of South-east Asia depended as much on markets in the USA, Japan and China as it did on their own efforts.

### The long agony of Myanmar

In September 1998, the World Bank severed ties with Myanmar (Burma) because of its failure to keep up repayments on loans. Isolation is not a new experience for the military junta that has imposed an iron rule in Myanmar. It was only in the face of protests that Myanmar was allowed to join ASEAN, the organisation set up to foster economic and social development in South-east Asia. The country's economy improved when oil deposits were discovered offshore and big international oil companies scrambled for the right to exploit the new-found wealth. In the end, the contract went to Total. But despite the profits from oil, the future looked bleak. Doctors and engineers emigrated to Europe, the USA and elsewhere. Growing numbers of refugees crossed the border into Thailand, to escape forced labour. According to UN figures, 40 per cent of Myanmar's children do not attend school. Aung San Suu Kyi, Nobel peace prize winner and charismatic opponent of the regime, resists in the only way she can – by refusing to go into exile.

*Trainers galore*   *Factory workers in the suburbs of the Indonesian capital, Jakarta, making sports shoes for Reebok.*

*Business, but not as usual*   *Even the bustling city-state of Singapore did not escape the economic crisis. In 1998, for the first time in a dozen years, its budget ran into deficit.*

**Founding father** *Stamford Raffles surveys Singapore.*

# Singapore: a vision of prosperity for all

*Apart from its fine deep-water harbour, Singapore has no natural advantages. It is so lacking in resources that it has to pipe in drinking water across a causeway from Malaysia. Yet this tiny island state has become a stupendous success story.*

The astonishing economic growth of Singapore is the product of the vision of two men, separated in time by more than a century and in origin by half a world – Sir Stamford Raffles and Lee Kuan Yew. When Raffles, an Englishman in the service of the East India Company, first hoisted the Union Jack there in 1819, Singapore was little more than a huge mangrove swamp, uninhabited apart from a handful of Malay fishermen and occasional pirates who used the harbour. But Raffles realised its potential: lying at a crossroads between the Indian and Pacific Oceans, it was a base from which to challenge the Dutch

**Times past and present** *A thrift-conscious Singaporean, dwarfed by an advertising hoarding for luxury goods.*

grip on trade in the region. He paid an annual rent to the Sultan of Johore in exchange for trading rights, and Singapore began its march towards prosperity.

Being part of a trading empire was not entirely a novel experience. In the 14th century, Singapore belonged to the Javanese empire of Majapahit, and the name Singapura (Lion City) was bestowed on it late in that century by a Sumatran prince. But then came centuries of decline. Chinese merchants, silversmiths, goldsmiths and other craftsmen were quick to take advantage of the more settled conditions under the British, who took over full sovereignty in 1824. Half a century later, 77 000 Chinese were living in Singapore, and by 1909 their number had grown to 654 000. Many of the immigrants married Malay women, giving rise to an ethnic mix that

developed, among other things, Singapore's unique cooking style *nyonya*, a mouth-watering blend of Chinese ingredients and Malayan spices.

## Affluence and justice

Tiny Singapore prospered from the export of Malayan tin and rubber and from the presence of a British naval base. But one of the greatest humiliations suffered by Britain in the Second World War came when 'fortress Singapore' fell to the Japanese in February 1942. Its guns had been facing the wrong way, out to sea, and the Japanese attack came down the Malay Peninsula. Internal self government came in 1959, under Lee Kuan Yew, leader of the People's Action Party, as prime minister. Like Raffles before him, Lee had a vision for Singapore, summed up in his own words as building 'an affluent and just society'. With full independence, in 1963, Singapore joined the Malaysian Federation. But its intention to remain a free port clashed with Malaysia's economic ambitions, and it was expelled from the Federation in 1965.

### Singapore: mini-state with a giant's strength

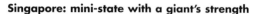

**A legacy of empire** *As an outpost of the British Empire, Singapore acquired a taste for one of England's more enduring exports – cricket. A knockabout game is played under menacing clouds at the Singapore Cricket Club.*

## Five firm foundations

Lee Kuan Yew came from a Chinese family, which helps to explain why the society he played a key role in shaping is so heavily influenced by Confucian ideas of duty. Singapore became one of the cleanest, safest, most prosperous and corruption-free states in the world, but there was a price to pay. 'When you are hungry, when you lack basic services, freedom, human rights and democracy do not add up to much,' said Lee. Elections might be free, but when Lee gave up the premiership in 1990, there was only one opposition MP. Trade unions were tamed by a government-sponsored National Trades Union Congress. Radio and television were censored, and newspapers muzzled by a licensing system. Anybody who dropped litter, crossed the street in the wrong place, smoke or chewed gum in a designated public place was fined. Drug smugglers faced death. Under Lee's successor Goh Chock Tong, some of the more draconian rules were relaxed, but Internet providers must still report to the government any user who accesses a prohibited website.

Singapore's economic success is based on five firm foundations. First, spending on education increased from US $600 000 in 1960 to US $10 million in 1963, and today Singapore has three universities. Second, there is the almost frenzied activity of its port, which is one of the busiest in the world. Recovering rapidly from the loss of the Royal Navy base, Singapore increased the quantity of goods shipped through its port from 69 million tons a year in the 1970s to more than 169 million tons annually in the 1990s. The third foundation is the encouragement of heavy industry, mainly shipbuilding and petrochemicals. An Economic Development Board, set up in 1961, fostered export industries through offering low taxes and tax holidays, and a Development Bank gave long-term loans. Fourth is the manufacture of textiles, and fifth the development of a dynamic electronics and micro-processing industry.

*Named by the founder* So many Chinese immigrants settled on the south bank of the Singapore river in the 19th century that Sir Stamford Raffles gave this bustling area the name it has kept since – Chinatown.

### A nation of homeowners

By the end of the 1950s, the population of Singapore had passed 1.5 million. Today, it stands at more than 4 million, making this tiny island state one of the most densely populated places on earth. It has a staggering 15 700 people per sq mile (6060 per km²), with almost 90 per cent of Singaporeans owning their own homes. Architects and town planners have performed near miracles in reclaiming an area of 23 sq miles (60 km²) from the sea, remodelling enire districts and building a dozen new towns. So great has been the pressure on space that housing development has encroached on such picturesque areas of old Singapore as Chinatown. In order to improve the quality of life for citizens, ponds, lakes and streams have been cleaned up, and a 163 acre (66 ha) wildlife refuge as well as a 49 acre (20 ha) park have been sited in the middle of an industrial zone. The refuge is home to some 300 species of animal. Care for the environment is seen in the details of everyday life. Singaporeans try to economise on water, even when cleaning their teeth, knowing it has to be piped in from Malaysia.

*Ancient and modern* Skyscrapers looming over a Chinese temple.

*The towers of trade* Sir Stamford Raffles dreamed of Singapore as a great trading centre, and so, more than 100 years later, did Lee Kuan Yew.

# The mighty microchip

*The first computers were room-sized monsters, needing thousands of valves to perform their calculations. Miniaturisation was the key to the unprecedented expansion of the electronics industry – and when it came there were skilled workers, eager entrepreneurs and alert governments in South-east Asia poised to take full advantage.*

**Robot insect**   *On display at a Singapore fair – a robot claimed to be the world's smallest.*

The world has been transformed by the microchip, a tiny crystal wafer that can be used to perform calculations and relay instructions about anything from a car's engine to a payroll system. And in no part of the world has the chip had a greater impact than in South-east Asia. Singapore, Thailand and Malaysia saw their electronics industries take off in the 1970s, and other countries in the region were quick to follow. The region's new hi-tech industries benefited from the fact that the amount of computing power that can be condensed onto a chip virtually doubled every year for several decades, opening the way to the single-chip or multichip microprocessor. This is the 'brain' that controls not just computers, but most of the devices used in everyday life in the modern world – central heating systems, industrial processes, metering equipment, railway systems, air traffic, televisions, videos and a host of domestic appliances.

The multinational electronics companies, most of them based in the USA, saw immediate advantages in locating some of their production in South-east Asia. The region had a long tradition of skilled workmanship, but labour was much cheaper than at home. Trade unions, if they existed at all, were relatively weak, and governments, eager to provide employment and boost exports, were relaxed about working practices.

## Into the information age

The production of microprocessors was the springboard from which South-east Asia launched itself into the information age, manufacturing both hardware and software. However, following another tradition of the region, much of the software was pirated.

The entire world was given a fright when computer analysts predicted the coming of the millennium bug. Since their built-in calendars recognised years only by the last two digits, it seemed that computers had no way of differentiating between 1900 and 2000. When the new millennium arrived, the analysts said, computers would crash, causing havoc around the world. In the event, the predicted computer chaos did not happen.

**Logging on to a tuk-tuk**   *A passenger boards the first tuk-tuk (three-wheeler taxi) in Bangkok to be connected with the Internet.*

### Hacking as a political weapon

In August 2000, the official website of Myanmar, a propaganda arm of its military regime, was 'turned round' by computer hackers. They replaced the opening page of the site with a quotation from Gandhi, whose campaign of passive resistance helped to win independence for India, and added slogans in favour of human rights, pacifism and democracy. They also set up links with human rights websites active in attacking the record of the ruling junta. In the previous year, Jose Ramos Horta, winner of the Nobel peace prize in 1996, had warned the Indonesian government: 'A group of information pirates can cause more damage in Indonesia than battalions of insurgents, deployed throughout the entire country.'

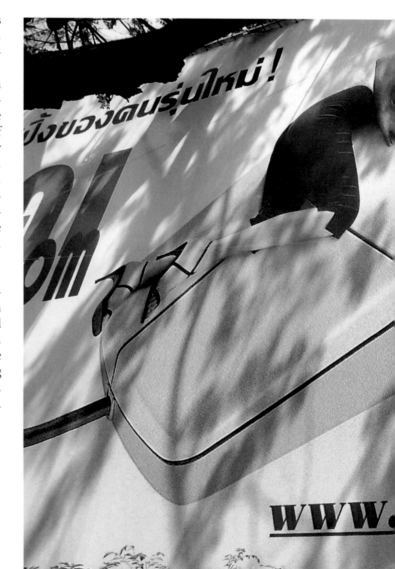

**Shopping, Bangkok style**
*The message of this street advertisement in bustling Bangkok is that would-be shoppers have no need to go farther than the nearest modem to place their order.*

## Scourge of the hackers

But serious problems have been caused by computer hackers, who break into other people's systems and programs for gain, from bravado, for political reasons, or simply out of malice. Sometimes, a hacker will leave a 'calling card' in the form of a virus that will damage or disrupt a system, then reproduce itself and spread to other computers. One of the most devastating of these, the 'Love Bug', originated in the Philippines. It was released in May 2000, by an e-mail carrying the message 'I Love You'. Once the mail was opened, the virus destroyed the user's files, but not before mailing itself to all the names and addresses

*Sci-fi factory* Microprocessors are assembled in a Philippines factory that looks more like a laboratory.

in them. The virus, which caused millions of dollars' worth of damage, was created by a failed college student, who claimed, successfully, that it had been released by accident.

Hacking is an international problem. In the USA, the threat is taken so seriously that the CIA has announced a 'cyberwar center' to protect government websites, air traffic control systems and

international financial dealings. The problem is taken seriously in South-east Asia, too. A computer laboratory in Singapore has created a competition on the 'to catch a thief' principle, with prizes of up to US $10 000 for hackers who can penetrate systems thought to be inviolable, and so expose their weaknesses.

In 2000, the Asia Pacific region, which covers India, South Korea and Taiwan as well as South-east Asian countries such as Singapore, was the fastest-growing microchip market in the world. It was valued at US $52 billion, and was forecast to reach US $85 billion by 2003.

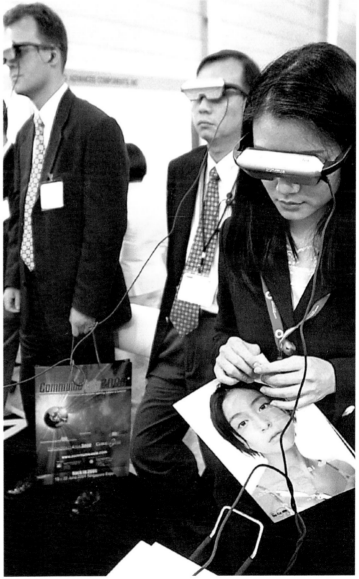

*Virtual customers* Potential buyers at a Singapore trade fair sample virtual reality for themselves.

# Hopes and pitfalls of the tourist trade

*South-east Asia has an unspoiled paradise to offer the tourist: virgin forests, wildlife in a natural setting, spectacular scenery, ancient temples, traditional crafts, lonely beaches and cities that are pulsatingly alive. Yet the central paradox of tourism is inescapable: the greater the number of people attracted to any paradise, the less unspoiled it becomes.*

**Photo opportunity** *Young Thai girls, in traditional costume, prepare for tourists to take their photographs – for payment.*

Most countries in South-east Asia were latecomers to the tourist trade. They were too dangerous, too remote or too primitive to attract large numbers of visitors. Romantic Bali, with its temple dancers, brilliant green forests, sparkling blue seas and miles of beaches, was an exception. Another was Thailand, which escaped the wars that ravaged so many other countries in the region. And in the Philippines, which had a long relationship with the United States, a thriving industry was dedicated to catering to the American tourist. Elsewhere, tourism took second place to such activities as fighting wars or laying the foundations of industry.

## A high-earning business

A hundred years ago, it took more than a month to reach Indochina from Europe. Today, the journey can be completed in a matter of hours. It was jet travel, as well as the return of peace, that opened the 'forgotten' beauty spots of South-east Asia to tourism.

For some countries it was a high-earning business. In the late 1990s, Thailand was making US $7 billion a year from tourism, Singapore was pulling in US $5.79 billion a year, Indonesia more than US $4 billion a year, Malaysia nearly US $3 billion and the Philippines US $2.53 billion. To earn such sums, the ground had to be prepared, and in this Thailand led the way. It welcomed investment by Japanese, overseas Chinese, Taiwanese, Malaysian and American companies in high-prestige stores and in luxury hotels belonging to such groups as Hyatt, Hilton and Meridien.

## Tourist attractions

At the other end of the scale, Myanmar, under military rule, declared 1996 the 'Year of the Tourist', but managed to attract only US $35 million from tourists. Malaysia was the top tourist attraction in 2000, with 12 million overseas visitors. Vietnam, following a policy of *doi moi* (renewal) in the years of peace, attracted 2 million

## Myanmar: to go or not to go?

Myanmar (Burma) is in the iron grip of a military junta that has ignored a democratic vote, harassed opposition leader Aung San Suu Kyi and allocated to itself tough emergency powers. To some liberal-minded people in the West, anybody who visits Myanmar as a tourist is supporting the regime by making a contribution to its economy, or even by giving the impression, albeit unintended, of tacit approval. Against this, it is argued that exposing the regime to scrutiny by people from overseas can only act as a curb on its unacceptable activities, and that Western contacts with ordinary Burmese will let them know they are not alone in their struggle.

**Philippines paradise** *A sea of turquoise and blue, a drowsy beach ... such is the unspoiled beauty of Palawan Island.*

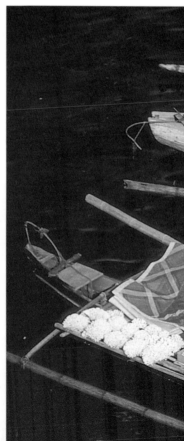

tourists in the same year – more than visited the Philippines. Tiny Singapore welcomed 7.69 million visitors in 2000, and although not all of them went primarily for tourism, most needed somewhere to unwind after a round of business meetings, exhibitions and conventions.

At present, more tourists in South-east Asia come from Japan than from any other country, but tour operators are looking ahead to the vast potential of China as a source of visitors. For visitors from the West, the region has a host of exotic sights, sounds and tastes to offer. Apart from relaxing on unspoiled beaches, bargain-hunting in street markets and experiencing the hectic night life of the cities, there are Hindu, Buddhist and Chinese temples to visit, each one a work of art. On a rain forest trail there is the chance to see and photograph elephants, tigers, acrobatic gibbons, orang-utans and a multitude of colourful birds.

It was in search of spices, to improve the food on the tables of Europe, that Western adventurers first voyaged to South-east Asia, and eating there can still be an adventure. The cuisine embraces the traditions of China and India, as well as a few that are home-grown. For those prepared to experiment, there is barbecued grasshopper in Thailand, bird's nest soup in Malaysia, and the durian of Laos – which smells foul but is reputed to be the most delicious wild fruit on earth.

Brunei, as befits a small and wealthy country, is aiming at the affluent end of the tourist market, but some other countries have mass tourism as their objective. In Thailand, for example, people are hired to pose in traditional costumes and

*All this … and massage too!* Well-heeled Westerners, on a beach in Bali, add to their feeling of well-being with a massage.

put on a show when a tourist coach pulls to a halt. In Bali, temple dancers have been required to perform in front of tourists festooned with cameras.

## Plans to create an Angkorland

Cambodia has thrown open to tourists its most stupendous attraction, the temples of Angkor. Since their discovery by the French naturalist Henri Mouhout, in 1860, the temples have been pillaged by visitors, leading to fears of a cultural disaster should these glories of Khmer architecture be exposed to mass tourism. A Malaysian finance group has come forward with plans to create an Angkorland, with a US $80 million hotel complex, complete with son-et-lumière effects, on a site close to the temples. The promoters say it will draw in another US $1 billion's worth of investment and attract 250 000 visitors a year. UNESCO was horrified by the proposal.

*Jumbo journey* An adventure trek in Thailand.

*Performers at rest* Even while waiting to perform for guests at a luxury hotel these young Balinese dancers cannot help but fall into graceful poses.

*Selling with a smile* In the Philippines island of Mindanao, the shops come to the tourists. Traders bring their goods to market on outrigger canoes.

# Pirates on the pavements

*Four out of every ten items of computer software that come onto the world market are pirate versions, made without fee or licence in South-east Asia. A powerful black economy, unconstrained by the laws of copyright, threatens the livelihoods of legitimate traders.*

South-east Asia, with its reservoir of skilled craftsmen, has a history of illegally copying luxury products – Louis Vuitton suitcases, Lacoste sports shirts, Cartier and Rolex watches – all bearing the trademark or logo of the original and all of them fakes. It also has a history of piracy, and pirates still operate in the South China Sea. But the traditional definition of piracy, as robbery and violence on the high seas, has been extended to cover the theft of intellectual property. South-east Asia's new pirates ply their nefarious trade in the shopping malls, in the warehouses and on the pavements of city streets.

### Changing fashions in fakery

There are fashions in fakery, just as there are in the genuine article, and at one stage there was even a kind of inverted snobbery among some Western visitors about fake goods they bought in Asia. A counterfeit 'Made in Thailand' Gucci handbag was a badge of status, because it made the owner seem more dashing. Today, though,

***Bargain boutique*** *Imitation Lacoste sportswear on sale in Singapore.*

flaunting make-believe luxury items is no longer in style. The market has switched to copying less expensive, more everyday, articles that have established a name in the marketplace – Stanley knives or Swiss Army knives, or Mattel toys. Naturally, they do not have the quality of the originals: a blade might snap, or a teddy bear might have easily exposed wires that make it dangerous to children.

### From accomplice to victim

The buyer of fake copies is no longer an amused accomplice, but an angry victim. Modern inventions such as the CD, the video and computer software, all of them products of human ingenuity and expensive research programmes, have brought vast profits to the modern pirates. They have been almost as profitable as the drugs trade, and the penalties, if caught, are far less severe. The economic crisis that hit South-east Asia in 1997-8 was a boon for the counterfeiters of such items, for they were able to undercut the prices of legitimate goods. Even in Singapore, where the law is generally held in high respect, the proportion of illicit software on sale rose from 10 per cent to more than 50 per cent. In Thailand and Indonesia, as high a figure as 90 per cent of the computer programs in use were illegal copies. One shopping centre in the heart of Bangkok had 300 outlets, all selling nothing but unlicensed software at bargain prices.

Illegal copying of music, films and video games has reached such proportions that American companies calculate it is costing them around US $11 billion a year. When the blockbuster movie *Titanic* was released in 1997, as many as 50 million pirate copies went on sale throughout Asia,

***Quick profit, no frills*** *A street trader in Manila lays out his 'salvage' wares on the pavement. All are bogus brand-name goods, at bargain prices.*

***The China connection*** *A street market in Hanoi sells illicit CDs from China at less than US $1.50 each.*

selling at the equivalent of less than US $1.50 a copy. A number of legitimate picture houses, unable to meet this cut-throat competition, were driven out of business.

## The fight against piracy

In some countries, pirated goods are sold openly. In others, shops put licensed items on display but hide their illegal items behind partitions. A similar principle is followed when illegal goods are exported. Ships leased or owned by pirate syndicates are fitted with detachable underwater storage tanks that can be as much as 50 ft (15 m) long. If customs officials intercept the ship and decide to make a search, the tanks can be jettisoned. They are linked to satellite-controlled guidance systems, so they can be recovered once the customs officials have gone on their way. This type of primitive submarine was originally developed for drug smugglers. The use of such an expensive subterfuge shows how profitable the trade in pirated items has become.

*Caught red-handed* A masked and bleeding looter is led away under arrest in Jakarta in 2000. The reaction to police raids on shops selling fake goods in the city was an outbreak of rioting and looting.

In the face of the piracy menace, the major producing companies, such as Warner, Sony, EMI and Universal, are combining forces to trap the pirates. They have taken on lawyers, private detectives and former FBI agents, and they have the cooperation of local police. But raids and seizures rarely lead to the arrest of the big dealers. In Malaysia, for example, the police mounted 1464 raids during 1999. They used armoured vehicles, helicopters and elite squads, but all of this effort produced not a single conviction.

### The great *Star Wars* robbery

Motion pictures can be duplicated at great speed. *The Phantom Menace*, the fourth film in the *Star Wars* saga, directed by George Lucas, was copied in the USA on the very day that it was released in 1999. The pirates smuggled a DVD camera into a cinema and stole the movie straight from the screen. The video master tapes were flown to Asia, where they were transferred to laser discs in less than 24 hours. The quality did not match that of legitimate copies, but the reputation of the director and of the earlier *Star Wars* movies meant there was a ready market for bargain-price copies.

*Under the crusher* Pirate CDs are crushed under a bulldozer in Thailand. In 2000, some 320000 contraband items were destroyed by the authorities.

65

# Populations in search of living space

*In the 19th century, South-east Asia was so sparsely populated that coolies had to be imported from China to work on the rubber plantations and down the tin mines. Today, from the overpopulated plains and deltas of Vietnam to the despair-ridden shantytowns of Manila, the cry of the poor goes up: 'Give us the space to live!'*

**Kalimantan bound** *Unenthusiastic Javanese on their way to a new life.*

The population of the Philippines has doubled since 1975. Java has more than 2000 people to a square mile (800 per km²). The deltas of the Mekong and the Red River in Vietnam, and the plain of Luzon in the Philippines, are human ant hills. Indonesia, with 212 million inhabitants, is the fourth most populous country in the world and 60 per cent of its people live in Java, which takes up only 7 per cent of its territory.

## A green revolution

To feed, house, educate and find employment for all these people is a Herculean challenge for countries still in their early stages of development. Governments are trying to boost employment, increase the food supply and earn foreign currency by developing industry, improving agriculture and fostering tourism. Vietnam has undertaken a 'green revolution' with the aim of growing more rice. Through intensive farming and the extension of rice cultivation to new land on the margins of the rain forests, it has so far kept pace with its growing population and produced a surplus for export.

## In the land of the Dyaks

But producing more food does not add more space for the people to live in. Indonesia has led the way in tackling this problem by a mass transplanting of families from overcrowded Java to remote and thinly populated areas – the so-called 'lands of abundance' – in Sumatra, Irian Jaya and Kalimantan, the Indonesian part of Borneo. Nearly 8 million Javanese have been resettled in this way, taken from their homes and allocated patches of newly cleared land in the rain forest. Apart from the culture shock of such a move, the newcomers in Kalimantan have faced bitter hostility from the indigenous people, the Dyaks, whose ancestors were head-hunters. Some settlers have been massacred by Dyaks, who feel that their way of life is threatened and that they are in danger of losing their identity.

**Shantytown shopping** *A street market on the fringes of a shantytown in the Philippines.*

### Make way for youth

Half the population of South-east Asia is under 25 years old – and the dynamism of youth has proved to be a force that can change society. Only in Singapore, where for many years families were limited to two children, do the over-65s amount to more than 7 per cent of the population. Half of those living in Vietnam today were not born when the Vietnam War ended in 1975. In Cambodia, the birth rate is 4.6 per 1000; in Laos it reaches 5.75 per 1000.

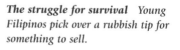

**The struggle for survival** *Young Filipinos pick over a rubbish tip for something to sell.*

# Hope for a threatened heritage

*Blessed with a landscape of surpassing natural beauty, the people of South-east Asia have lived for centuries in harmony with nature, but runaway increases in population have rudely disturbed the balance.*

When an underdeveloped country is in a hurry to catch up, care for the environment can be low on its list of priorities. Nature has been so prodigal with its gifts to South-east Asia that the environment has survived relatively intact the kind of treatment that would have caused long-term ecological disaster in many other parts of the world. To bombing, Agent Orange and other defoliants in times of war have been added logging, the growth of industry, natural disasters such as forest fires, and the growing use of pesticides and insecticides on crops in the years of peace.

## Help from overseas

Conservation got off to a slow start in South-east Asia. The big landowners have often been more concerned with profit than with preserving the environment. And with populations rising at an uncontrolled rate, the main concern of most farmers is the scarcity of cultivable land. But there are growing signs that the infant conservation movement is beginning to make an impact. The spread of national parks in South-east Asia indicates that governments are prepared to allocate resources to preserving the natural heritage. Often, the initial impetus comes from overseas. The Society for Ecological Restoration, based in the University of Wisconsin, has fostered a project under which villagers in coastal areas of Thailand are planting mangrove trees along the shoreline to create nurseries for fish. Schemes such as this have a good chance of success as they combine conservation with feeding the people.

## Trees and animals under threat

Information and research play a key role in allocating resources effectively. In 1999, the International Union for the Conservation of Nature and Natural Resources published a Red List of plants threatened with extinction. There were 33798 species on the list and nearly 9000 of them were trees. The rain forests of South-east Asia are protected by their vastness, but one of their glories is the variety of tree species they contain. Animals are under threat, too. Conservation International, a private charity based in Chicago, has calculated that a third of the threatened species live in tropical regions. Among them are the rhinoceroses of Sumatra, Java and Vietnam, the orang-utan, the Komodo dragon and the forest tiger.

*Natural disaster Smoke pollution during the forest fires that ravaged Kalimantan.*

*Man-made disaster Another giant falls victim to the chainsaw massacre that is sweeping through the forests of Indonesia.*

### Forest fire that turned night into day

In 1997 and 1998, forest fires in Borneo and Sumatra raged over an area more than half the size of Scotland. The flames, whipped up by the wind, created a pall of smoke that hung over Singapore, parts of Malaysia and Indonesia, Thailand and the Philippines, darkening the sky in the daytime and threatening the health of 70 million people. In Malaysia, the pollution index topped 800, on a scale which rates 500 as indicating an 'extreme health hazard'. In the all-pervading murk, an airliner crashed in Sumatra, with the loss of all 234 aboard. The orang-utan population of Borneo suffered terribly, both from the fires and through loss of habitat: the Kutai National Park in Kalimantan, a haven for orang-utans and gibbons, was gutted. Only the monsoon season brought the giant conflagration under control.

*The blighted rain forest A Sumatran rain forest, ravaged for the paper industry.*

CHAPTER 3

# LIVING IN SOUTH-EAST ASIA

Few places in the world can match South-east Asia for its peoples' veneration of age. This feeling is rooted in religion, and in a devotion to the family that includes ancestors. Through all the turmoil of recent decades – wars, economic successes and downturns – the people have held fast to their religious beliefs and practices.
The Balinese keep altars in their homes, on which to lay offerings to the gods and spirits. Muslims pray five times a day, facing Mecca, the birthplace of Muhammad.
Such habits reinforce the idea of an ordered society in which rights are balanced by duties and obligations.
But a new wind is beginning to blow through this society: the middle classes own computers and log on to the Internet, and women are making an increasingly valued contribution to the future.

*Buddhists pray at the magnificent Shwedagon pagoda in Rangoon, capital of Myanmar (Burma).*

# Rites and ceremonies for all seasons

*In a culture imbued with a profound sense of the sacred, and one in which life can be threatened by flood, famine, volcano and storm – or transformed by a good harvest – ritual is a trusted way of keeping the gods on one's side.*

***The protectors*** *After the death of a family member, the Torujas of Sulawesi raise a stone or carve a wooden statue that will join others protecting the household from harm.*

In a typical Vietnamese or Thai home, a statue of Buddha sits on a shelf or a piece of furniture. In front of it will be smouldering sticks of incense and offerings of flowers, fresh mangoes or mandarin oranges, even of alcohol. The Buddha is sometimes accompanied, or replaced, by the female figure of Quan Am, who represents compassion and lies in repose on a lotus flower, symbol of fertility and purity. In another part of the house is an altar to the ancestors. Photographs of deceased members of the family are displayed, going back four generations to great-great-grandparents. They, too, are venerated with incense, flowers and fruit. The dead, in return for these marks of respect, watch over and protect the living.

If the family is Chinese in origin, the arrival of the New Year is the occasion for a special feast. The head of the household, having paid his outstanding debts for the old year, welcomes the new one by inviting the gods of wealth and fertility into the home and sitting down with his family and the spirits of his ancestors to a celebration meal of duck, other meats, rice and traditional cakes. Outside the house, just by the doorway, will be a small altar with offerings to Tho Cong, protector of the household, lit by candles or by little electric bulbs. In a Christian household, or even if only one member of the family is Christian, a Virgin or a Holy Family will look on from an alcove or a shelf. Buddhism, Christianity, Taoism, Confucianism, and the veneration of ancestors all live side by side.

Many overseas Chinese in South-east Asia follow the teachings of two early sages: Lao Zi (6th century BC), who stressed the importance of being in harmony with nature, and Confucius (551-479 BC), who emphasised the importance of duty, respect between rulers and ruled, and the proper performance of rites. His disciples are represented in the house in the form of statuettes or coloured images. Another strong influence in Chinese households is that of geomancy, or feng shui: in order to channel good influences and

***Altar in the home*** *A place of honour, set aside in a Bangkok house for statues of the Buddha and a photograph of royalty.*

***The end … and the beginning*** *A Buddhist cremation at Kuta, in Indonesia. According to the doctrine of reincarnation, the soul of the deceased is being released to start a new life.*

### The house of the spirits

Every house in Thailand has next to it a tiny 'house of the spirits'. In towns and cities, it is made of cement; in the countryside, the materials are wood or straw. It shelters the guardian spirits, to whom pious householders make daily offerings of jasmine flowers, wine, incense or cigarettes. If the main house is extended, so, too, is the spirit house.

*Crowning moment   A Thai couple are crowned at their wedding.*

ward off evil ones, the orientation of furniture, rooms, houses, tombs, offices, even entire cities must be in harmony with that of the surrounding landscape.

## Temple rituals and rites of passage

Chinese temples are busy places, where people go to pray and ask the gods for favours, or to consult priests skilled in the arts of divination. For this, the priests may use the *I Ching*, an aid to decision-taking said to have been compiled by Confucius; or they may use lengths of bamboo representing yin and yang, the female and male principles. Good fortune follows when the two are in balance. The temples in Myanmar, Laos, Thailand, Cambodia and Vietnam, where Buddhism is strong, are full of activity, too. The faithful offer gifts to the monks and buy sheets of very thin gold leaf that they can rub onto statues of the Buddha. Veneration of the Buddha does not prevent people making small offerings to various spirits, thanking those that are benevolent and appeasing those that are malicious. Any communication with the supernatural world can lead to good fortune and a better life.

The most important rites of all are those associated with the passage from life to death, from the known to the unknown. Muslims, who form the majority religion in Indonesia, Brunei and Malaysia, bury their dead in a simple ceremony with prayers from the Koran. Buddhists cremate their dead, sending them on to reincarnation and a new life. But the funeral rites of other beliefs can be complex. The Torujas of Indonesia's Sulawesi archipelago (formerly the Celebes) go through a complex ritual to conduct the dead to the next world. In the first stage, the dead person stays in the house and is regarded as being ill, rather than dead. Pigs or oxen are sacrificed, and offerings are brought before the corpse. When the due time arrives, the ancestor is carried in a coffin to a cliff, and an effigy is made or a stone erected as a memorial. Not until there has been ceremonial dancing and the sacrifice of further animals does the ancestor move into the spirit world and meet the gods. If the offerings have been generous enough, the departed spirit will become a protector of the household.

### Calling back the spirits

An ancient belief in Laos is that everyone has 32 guardian spirits, which leave the body on death and have to be called back by means of a special ritual, the *baci*. The ceremony is conducted by a holy man, the *mohphon*, who begins with offerings of flowers and wine to the gods. Then the mourners tie strands of cotton around the dead person's wrists, to protect and strengthen them against the perils of the journey to come. When the cotton bracelets disappear through decomposition, the guardian spirits will return.

*Buddha's flowers*
*An offering at Bali.*

71

# Buddhism, a religion without a supreme god

*Buddhism was born in the 6th century BC, partly in reaction to the rigid caste system of Hinduism. Its founder pointed the way to spiritual enlightenment, and his teachings became the dominant faith of South-east Asia.*

*Pose for meditation   Vietnamese Buddha, in the lotus position.*

The founder of Buddhism was the Indian prince Siddhartha, who lived in the 6th century BC. He was born into the high-caste Gautama family and was brought up in luxury by a father who wanted to shield him from the sight of human suffering. The tradition tells how one day the young prince encountered in succession an old man, a sick man, a corpse and a holy man. The first three embodied the sorrows that afflict mankind: age, illness and death. But the fourth had reached a state of serenity.

### The Eightfold Path

For the next seven years the prince went on a quest for spiritual truth through fasting and extreme self-denial. But asceticism did not bring the enlightenment he sought: that came when he was meditating beneath a peepul, or bo, tree. There, he entered a state beyond the reach of life, death, suffering and change, and became the Buddha, the Awakened or Enlightened One. Buddhism inherited from Hinduism the idea of reincarnation, but rejected its rigid caste system. The Buddha taught that since life is inseparable from suffering, and no happiness lasts for ever, the cycle of birth, death and rebirth (*samsara*) is a curse, not a blessing. Suffering arose out of human desire, the craving for self-identity and for permanence. Such cravings could be defeated by following the 'Eightfold Path'

to the state of enlightenment known as Nirvana: right understanding, right thinking, right speaking, right action, right livelihood and, when meditating, right effort, right attention and right concentration. Those who followed this path to Nirvana were freed from the cycle of reincarnation.

Unlike other major religions, Buddhism does not worship a supreme creator god. It teaches that the Buddha is a model to be imitated, rather than a god to be prayed to, that there have been several Buddhas, and there will be more to come.

### Cao Daï: an eclectic faith

Buddhist beliefs were modified as different schools developed. The two most important are Theravada Buddhism (also called Hinayana, the Lesser Vehicle) and Mahayana (the Greater Vehicle). Theravada lays emphasis on the monastic life and on the pursuit of wisdom, while Mahayana Buddhism stresses the value of compassion. It embraces the doctrine of the bodhisattvas, who renounce their own hopes of attaining Nirvana in order to help

**Happiness is giving things up**   *Young novice monks in Myanmar. To be accepted as trainees they have to have their heads shaved and to give up fashionable clothes in favour of simple robes.*

*Venerating the Buddha*   *Monks in a temple in Laos.*

*Receiving alms*   *A monk at Phnom Penh, Cambodia, waits for his daily portion of rice, which is given as charity by the faithful.*

others to break free of the cycle of rebirth and suffering. As it spread, Buddhism absorbed existing belief systems and recognised gods and goddesses as incarnations of cosmic forces.

Around 90 per cent of the populations of Burma, Thailand and Cambodia, and 60 per cent in Laos are Theravada Buddhists. In Vietnam, where nearly half the population practises Mahayana Buddhism, the religion is sometimes intertwined with Taoism, Confucianism and Cao Daïsm. This last faith, founded by the civil servant Ngo Minh Chieu in 1928, when Vietnam was under French colonial rule, is eclectic: it ranges the world to combine Buddhist teachings with those of several other major religions. Cao Daï flourishes particularly in the south, and not only takes spiritual care of its congregations, but is also firmly anchored in everyday life, educating children, organising festivals and bringing people together for collective projects. Its priests are expected to be models of virtue and poverty: they must renounce smoking and alcohol, do no harm to their fellow humans, take nothing they have not been given, never tell a lie and never speak ill of anyone.

In Myanmar, Buddhism is the state religion. Around Pagan, the first Burmese capital, lie the greatest collection of Buddhist monuments in the world – the ruins of 5000 pagodas. Many are kept in excellent condition and are still used. In 1975, an earthquake destroyed a number of major temples, but they were restored by the pious nation.

### The marketing monk

All young men in Thailand are expected to spend part of their life as a monk, living on the charity of the faithful. One young man who became a monk for life had a talent for raising money. After a number of mystical revelations, Dhammachayo decided he had been called to build a huge temple to the Buddhist faith. So successful were his efforts that he raised nearly US $200 000 towards building costs. In 1999 Thailand's National Association for Marketing presented him with an award for the best marketing campaign of the year. The idea of a monk who was a master of marketing sent a shudder through the government and the Buddhist hierarchy, who hinted that he might be derobed. The essence of Buddhism is to eradicate thoughts of the self and show compassion to others, but some monks were so adept at drawing in offerings that they were amassing fortunes. The government objected not so much to the unorthodox nature of these practices as to the fact that the profits from them were not taxable.

*Remembering his words*
*Monks at a festival celebrating one of the Buddha's sermons.*

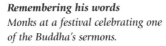

# Hinduism in Bali

*Bali is a last outpost of Hinduism in the predominantly Muslim Indonesia. The tradition dates back to the 14th and 15th centuries, when the trading empire of Majapahit moved its centre there from Java. It has absorbed other faiths, including vestiges of animism and ancestor worship.*

**Flower for a demon**   *An offering made in hope.*

Religion is present in every aspect of life in Bali. Even the lie of the land has a religious significance. The high ground, moving upstream along the rivers, is the home of all that is good and holy. The downstream direction, through lower-lying land, leads to the ocean, the abode of demons and evil spirits. A shipwreck or a drowning are interpreted as signs of their ravening hunger for wickedness. When two Balinese meet they do not ask 'How is it going?' but 'Upstream or downstream?' The Balinese perform complex rituals to propitiate the gods and fend off the demons. On the sacred slopes of the volcano Gunung Agung, at 10 338 ft (3150 m) the highest mountain on the island, stands the temple of Besikah. Here families, and sometimes entire clans, gather to pray and make offerings which will, they hope, bring good fortune. There are offerings to the demons, too, but these are left on the ground, whereas those to benevolent spirits are given places of honour, on high altars wreathed in incense smoke.

## Castes, but no untouchables

Hindu beliefs have been adapted to suit the Balinese way of life. For instance, there are castes in Bali, but no bottom caste of untouchables. Village life takes place in and around temples built for the worship of the three supreme gods of Hinduism: Brahma the creator, Wisnu (Vishnu) the preserver, and Siva (Shiva) the destroyer. Gods and humans come into contact in the sacred enclosure of the *pura*, where handbells are rung and the smoke of incense rises in front of a stone altar. Long processions of women, bearing pyramids of fruit, cakes and dried rice on their heads, wind their way to the *pura*. The priest, clad in white, blesses their offerings, sprinkles holy water over the worshippers and recites mantras (sacred phrases) to win the favour of the gods. There are altars in the homes, too, where reverence is paid to ancestors.

## Balancing good and evil

The Balinese move constantly between the worlds of good and evil, trying to keep them in balance. The goblin, witch or demon that has to be appeased is treated with as much respect as the god, benign spirit or ancestor whose favours are sought. This calls for a kind of mental and spiritual gymnastics at which the Balinese have become masters. In every rice field stands a shrine to Dewi Sri, the goddess of fertility, but the farmers also make offerings to the spirits that might destroy their precious harvest. Whether it is a matter of going to the market, starting a small business, opening a nightclub, painting a bridge, acting as a tourist guide, or erecting a sign at a crossroads, the balance has to be maintained. For this world is an echo of the unseen world.

**Devotees at prayer**   *Women in Bali, an island of devout Hinduism in a sea of Islam, at a ceremony of purification.*

## Rites of passage

The major crossroads of life are marked in Bali by rites of passage, beginning at the moment of birth, when the placenta is ceremonially buried beneath a stone. A baby is regarded as holy and is not allowed to touch the 'unclean' ground until its first birthday. The onset of puberty, regarded as entry into the adult world, is marked by filing the front teeth into a straight line. Prominent canines have too close a resemblance to the fangs of demons. Marriage is either conventional or by elopement. In the first, *mapedik*, the young man's family visit the girl's family bearing gifts and make a formal proposal. A more dashing couple will choose *ngrorod*, or elopement. The young man will 'kidnap' the girl and spend a three-day honeymoon with her, in a place that is supposed to be secret but is known to everyone. A religious ceremony follows the elopement, but a civil ceremony precedes the honeymoon.

The whole village is involved in the cremation that marks the passage from life into death. Sumptuously decorated effigies are made in gilded paper, bamboo or other wood and the coffin takes the form of an animal. Cremations are very expensive. If a family cannot afford one, the corpse is buried, to be disinterred later for a cheaper mass cremation.

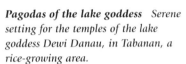

*Pagodas of the lake goddess   Serene setting for the temples of the lake goddess Dewi Danau, in Tabanan, a rice-growing area.*

*Outdoor altar   The Balinese are among the most religious people in the world, with altars in temples, in homes and outside the house, ready to accept offerings and prayers.*

### Daybreak banishes the demons of the night

In a world full of contrasts – between good and evil, upstream and downstream, gods and demons – the sun represents for the Balinese all that is positive and the night is a time of danger. The sun is honoured as the material form of the god Surya, and from the moment it rises, the household comes to life. The women brush the floor, cook rice for the day, and make offerings of flowers and small gifts for the gods and for the ancestors. It is just as essential to lay out on the ground *ngejot* – offerings to the evil spirits. The women look after the pigs and chickens and go to market to haggle for bargains. With sunset come the hours of peril. Only if a woman remembered the *ngejot* will her family be able to sleep easily in their beds.

*Festival day in Pejeng*
*Offerings for a festival at Pejeng's Temple of Penataran Sasih, home of an ancient 10 ft (3 m) bronze drum, the Moon of Pejeng.*

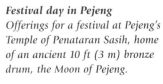

# Islam, South-east Asian style

*Islam, an Arabic word meaning 'submission to the will of Allah', lays down strict rules about belief and unbelievers. The form that has developed in the religious melting pot of South-east Asia has learned to live with Hinduism and Buddhism, but anti-Christian riots broke out in Indonesia in the late 1990s, revealing tensions beneath the surface.*

**Learning the Koran**  *Two young Muslim brothers at their most important lesson.*

Indonesia has nearly 190 million Muslims, amounting to around 90 per cent of its total population. Malaysia has 13 million followers of the Prophet Muhammad, the Philippines 3 million, Singapore 400 000 and Brunei around 200 000. The Muslim faith was brought to South-east Asia in the 13th century by Arabs, Persians and Muslim Indians who sailed across the Indian Ocean towards the coasts of present-day Sumatra, Java and Malaysia in search of the fabulous wealth of the spice trade.

## Trade and the Koran

In the busy ports of the Java-based Hindu empire of Majapahit, merchants spread the new religion. By the start of the 16th century, Islam had made converts in the Malay Peninsula, Sumatra and the north coast of Java. The Majapahit Empire had retreated to Bali, which is still mainly Hindu. As the Muslim merchants extended their trading routes, they took the Koran with them and powerful converts set up sultanates. Islam reached Borneo and the south Philippines, where the arrival of the Spaniards and of Christianity in the mid century brought an end to this phase of expansion.

## Riots in Jakarta

Islam has two main branches: Shiite and Sunni. Most South-east Asians are Sunni Muslims. They tend to take a more tolerant attitude towards other faiths than do the Shiites. They are devout, answering the call to prayer five times a day, giving alms to the poor, observing the fast of Ramadan and trying, at least once in their lifetime, to make the pilgrimage to Mecca. The women wear the veil and the children chant the Koran at school. In South-east Asia, Sunni Islam has rubbed up against Hinduism, Buddhism and animism, and has relegated

them to the background rather than making sustained attempts to eradicate their influence. During General Suharto's 32-year rule in Indonesia, resentments between Muslims and Christians were held in check. But in November 1998 they erupted to the surface in Jakarta, after Ambonese guards refused to close a gambling hall during prayers at a nearby mosque. Riots broke out, churches were burned and Christians were killed in the streets. The rioting spread to Sulawesi and to the eastern province of Maluku, with hundreds of deaths. The American bombing of Afghanistan in 2001 further whipped up anti-Christian feeling in several Muslim countries in the region.

**The faithful at prayer**  *Muslims pray, facing Mecca, in the Istiqlal mosque, Jakarta.*

**Let the feasting begin**  *The end of Ramadan, in Jakarta.*

### The fasting is over – and it is festival time!

Ramadan, the ninth month in the Islamic year, is held sacred by Muslims because it commemorates the first revelation of the Koran to Muhammad. For 30 days, they take neither food nor water from sunrise to sunset. The end of Ramadan, and of the fast, is greeted by an explosion of festival joy. Towns and villages in Indonesia ring with triumphant cheering and truckloads of young men pour into the city centres for a night of festivity. On the morning of the first day of the tenth month (the *shawwal*) crowds assemble for collective prayers. In the week that follows, thousands of people return to their villages. Parents and children, grandparents, aunts and uncles, brothers, sisters and cousins wear new clothes, exchange presents, apologise for the faults of the past nine months and make resolutions to do better.

# The submissive society

*Despite the turbulence and revolutions of modern times, Cambodia and Thailand are still monarchies. Malaysia has a paramount ruler as its head of state, and in Brunei the sultan is also the prime minister. South-east Asians have a profound respect for authority, and the reasons lie in their history.*

From their very beginnings, the civilisations of South-east Asia were authoritarian. A ruler who had to organise peasants to dig canals and maintain irrigation systems for rice needed to have his commands obeyed. Contact with India and China, the two great civilisations to the west and north, reinforced the idea that rulers should rule and the people obey.

## The mandate of heaven

India passed on to the Burmese, the Cham, the Angkoreans and the Thais the concept of a god-king and of a stratified society, close to the Hindu caste system. Northern Vietnam, subjugated by the Chinese for around 1000 years, became a cultural colony and Confucianism, with its rigorous insistence on rights and duties, set the rules for an ordered, hierarchical society. A wife was expected to obey her husband, a son to obey his father, a widow to defer to her eldest son, a servant to carry out the orders of his master. Youth should respect age, and the living should venerate their ancestors. At the top of the pyramid of power was a virtuous and enlightened emperor, who held a mandate to rule from heaven. Rebellion against the emperor was a rebellion against heaven itself.

When Islam arrived in the region, it reinforced and in some places introduced the concept of male domination. It demanded submission to religious leaders and high respect for those who had made the pilgrimage to Mecca. During the colonial era, authority was imposed from above. Britain, Holland, France and other Western powers forced obedience ultimately, and on occasion directly, at the end of a gun. Finally, during and after the long anticolonial wars, Marxism imprinted its iron heel on Vietnam, Cambodia and Laos. Insisting on duty to the socialist state, it found fertile ground in a Vietnam already imbued with the principles of Confucianism. The Vietnamese have a dozen words for 'I' and as many for 'you'. Which personal pronouns are chosen depends on the relative social positions of the two speakers: parents and children, old and young, superior and social inferior. In Cambodia, the communist Khmer Rouge made submission the only alternative to death – and even then, the choice might not be offered.

*The king and us   Two respectful Thai girls hold the portrait of their king, Bhumibol Adulyadej.*

### The monarch and the movie

In 1956 a Hollywood musical, *The King and I*, starring Yul Brynner and Deborah Kerr, brought to the screen the story of a 19th-century king of Siam (now Thailand) and the English governess appointed to educate his 67 children. In 2000, a remake of the film, *Anna and the King*, was banned in Thailand on the grounds that it gave a false impression of the country's history and that, even though based on historical events, the film was 'offensive to the Thai people'. In reality, to suggest there may have been romantic feelings between King Mongkut and a foreigner was to commit *lèse majesté*, the crime of insulting the crown.

*Order of worship   A service at the Istiqlal mosque, Jakarta. The military take the front rows, male civilians are behind them and women at the back.*

# Last days of the hill tribes

*In the competition for security and a reasonable share of material rewards, the ethnic minorities of South-east Asia have never stood in the ranks of the prize winners. In past centuries they were pushed into the mountains and rain forests, where the soil is thin and the living is hard. Today, the march of progress challenges their traditional way of life.*

To walk through an Akha village in the hills of northern Thailand is to wander into the past. The houses, perched on stilts, are made of bamboo and straw. Beneath them is an accumulation of jars, baskets and tools. Black pigs snuffle and grunt, hens cackle and lean dogs, devoured by fleas, scratch themselves vigorously. Barefooted children, wearing rags decorated with badges advertising American fizzy drinks, play with old tyres. The women make headdresses out of feathers, beads and silver ornaments; the men, back from the fields, mend guns and baskets. The village is unlikely to have electricity or running water. A surgery and a school have been promised for a quarter of a century, but have not yet arrived.

### The vanishing paradise

The Akha live, and look, like the political refugees they are. Originating in Tibet, they became caught up in a swirling movement of peoples, and more than 1000 years ago enjoyed a brief golden age, when they created city-states in Yunnan, China. A second phase of migration began when large numbers were forced out of Yunnan, and today there are perhaps half a million Akha, spread across southern China, Burma, Laos and Thailand.

The Akha see the spirit world as being just as real as the material world. Everything in their lives is governed by taboo and ritual: when, where and how to clear and burn the forest; when to plant and harvest rice; when to visit punishment on those who offend against the law; even when to conceive a child. But the old ways are being abandoned as large tracts of their forest paradise are destroyed by logging companies and new roads bring the modern world into their hillside fastnesses.

**Wearing her wealth**  *An Akha woman, wearing a headdress set off by feathers, silver coins and ornaments.*

**Village that time forgot**  *Life in an Akha village in northern Thailand has changed little down the centuries.*

As with the Akha, so with the Hmong of Thailand, south-west China, Laos and Vietnam. They number nearly 6 million, but history has left them behind, for they date from an era before nation states were formed, when frontiers were unknown. The opium poppy provides their biggest cash crop, and they cannot understand why today they are blamed and harassed for growing it, whereas a few decades ago its cultivation was actively encouraged. In French Indochina it earned profits and tax revenues for the colonial power, and it was condoned during the Vietnam War because the Hmong were valued allies of both the French and the Americans. Since the war, attempts to wean the Hmong away from opium-growing by providing them with a substitute cash crop have generally ended in failure.

In Myanmar, Thailand, Laos and Vietnam the most fertile land is found in the deltas, the valleys and flood plains, where rice can be harvested twice or three times a year. It is not by chance that such lands are populated by the ethnic majorities. Over the centuries they have used their superior strength to keep out minority groups – or to drive them out. In the Philippines and Indonesia, too, ethnic minorities have been pushed into remote and economically unattractive regions. Not only were they in competition for land, they could also be a very real threat to their neighbours. The Kalinga of northern Luzon in the Philippines call themselves the Tagu, human beings. The word Kalinga means 'enemy' and was given to them, understandably enough, by the villagers they raided when they wanted to add to their stock of human heads.

### The Iban, 'saved' by tourism

The Iban of Sarawak were once head-hunters, too. During the paternalistic rule of the 'White rajahs' (the Englishman Sir James Brooke and his successors) they held a favoured place as a warrior nation and were used to stamp out piracy and, even though it was an Iban tradition, the taking of human heads. Like other ethnic minorities, they lived by hunting, gathering and slash-and-burn farming. Head-hunting apart, they have managed better than most to keep their old ways. This is partly due to money earned from tourism, for with their feathered headdresses, tattoos, long houses and fearsome reputation they are a compelling attraction. Even so, the younger generation are abandoning the long houses and settling in towns.

*Hill tribe* Dao children, in north Vietnam.

**Main ethnic groups**

- Tibeto-Birman
- Thai-Kadai
- Hmong-Yao
- Mon-Khmer
- Malayo-Polynesian

### Gypsies of the sea

It used to be said of the Badjao that the only time they ever set foot on land was when they were buried. If that claim was ever true, it no longer is, but they still spend almost their entire lives on boats, sailing from island to island between the Philippines, Sulawesi and New Guinea. They dive for pearls and sea cucumbers and fish with lines, nets and spears. Babies are taken on their first swim by their fathers when they are just three days old. For hundreds of years, the 'sea gypsies' have followed this way of life, selling the sea's bounty to Chinese traders so that they can buy their staple food, cassava. Some have built houses on coral reefs, raising them above the waves on stilts.

*Finery for all ages* Three generations of Hmong women in Vietnam, proudly wearing their sumptuously embroidered clothing. The pride is justified: it can take three years to make just one costume.

# Days of challenge for the traditional family

*Society in South-east Asia is firmly based on the extended family. Parents and children, grandparents, aunts, uncles and other family members will work in the same fields, live in the same villages, sometimes in the same households. The customs of the countryside have lived on in the towns, but even in the most traditional of societies, times are beginning to change.*

**New-style family** *Cambodian parents and children, out for a spin.*

Ever since rice-growing was introduced to South-east Asia, more than 3000 years ago, the basic unit in society has been the patriarchal family, close-knit and working to a common end. For the cultivation of rice demands collective labour and there is no more productive unit than the family. Changes may be on the way, but they are coming slowly.

### Authority that comes with age

Families are grouped into clans, and authority within both clan and family rests with the oldest male member, the patriarch. He personifies their dignity and prestige, and is deferred to on all matters of importance. Peasants, who are increasingly moving from the villages into the towns, from the fields to the factories, take with them a profound loyalty to the family. In Vietnam, where families are modelled on the Confucian system, the patriarch ensures that reverence is paid to the ancestors, for the worth of individual family members is determined by where they stand, in relation both to preceding generations and to those that will follow.

The ideal family, following the Chinese model, houses four generations under the same roof. When a girl marries, she joins her husband's family and owes obedience to her mother-in-law. Even in countries such as Myanmar and Cambodia, where Chinese Confucian ideas have never put down firm roots, the family plays a key role.

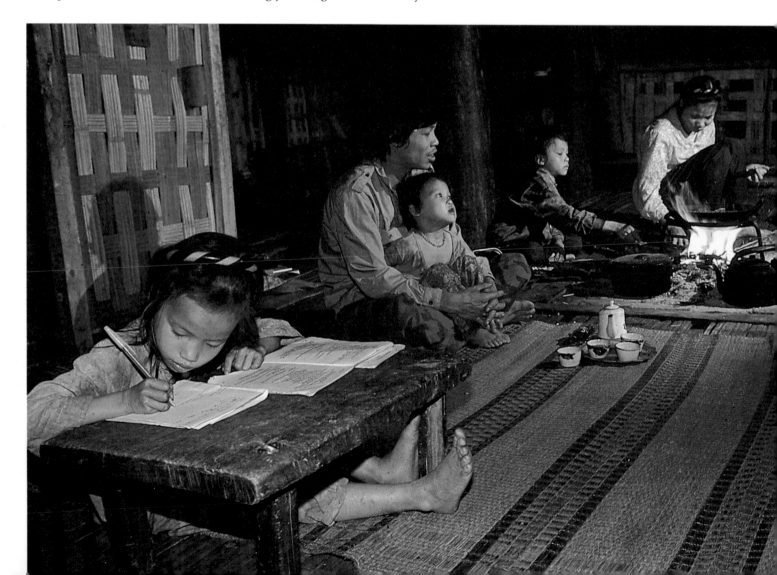

## The emancipation of women

South-east Asia cannot be isolated from the changes that have taken place in the rest of the world. Ideas spread rapidly in the age of television, radio, movies, books and magazines, and the Internet. Modern-minded women in Bangkok and Jakarta, Singapore and Ho Chi Minh City, have challenged male domination and argued for the right of women to be regarded as individuals, not simply as dutiful wives and mothers.

In the West, earning a living, rather than depending on husbands as the only breadwinners, has been one of the main motors of change for women. In South-east Asia, working women are held back by 3000 years of history. They are normally paid less than men and their work is often casual, with no job security; promotion to the managerial ranks is relatively rare. As Mme Nguyen, one of the few Vietnamese women to occupy a high government post, put it: 'The poverty of the country prevents women from enjoying equal rights.' As it happens, Vietnam is at the forefront of the emancipation of women. Women can hold land there in their own names, and a fair number have been elected to positions of leadership in cooperative enterprises. In Indonesia and Malaysia, the traditions of Islam uphold the dominance of men. A husband can dismiss his wife for adultery,

***Body beautiful contest*** *The cult of the individual, rather than of the family, is starting to make an impact in South-east Asia.*

barrenness or disobedience simply by telling her that he wants a divorce. A woman seeking a divorce, on the other hand, has to prove her case in front of a judge.

From the outside, South-east Asian society appears to be puritanical. The ideal conduct for a woman, especially one from a poor family, is to be shy and submissive to her husband and to her boss. In Indonesia there is even a word for this behaviour – *malu*. But underneath, attitudes are changing. Newspapers, books, television and radio all tell of a different society, one of steamy love affairs, and one in which the individual, not just the family, has a right to be heard.

***Old-style family*** *Three generations of a Dao family in Vietnam.*

***A family affair*** *A Confucian wedding party on the Mekong, Vietnam.*

***Just married*** *Newlyweds in Ho Chi Minh City. Vietnam has been a pacesetter in the liberation of women.*

### The rights of man in 19th-century Vietnam

A husband could divorce his wife for any of the following reasons:
1. Gossiping, slander and uncontrollable jealousy.
2. Barrenness.
3. Repellent illness (eg leprosy).
4. Misconduct.
5. Theft that discredits him.
6. Lack of respect to his parents.
7. Attacking him with violence.

There were three defences to these accusations:
1. If the wife had no parents to take her back.
2. If she was in mourning for either parent-in-law.
3. If the husband was poor when they wed, but became rich after marriage.

# The virtues of traditional medicine

*Assessed in terms of their access to modern medical care, many nations in South-east Asia belong to the Third World. But Western doctors are increasingly recognising the value of the traditional therapies of the East.*

**Road to happiness** *This poster in Singapore urges young couples to limit their families to two children.*

With the exception of Singapore, Brunei and a number of big cities elsewhere in the region, there are far from enough trained doctors in South-east Asia, and even where they exist, modern drugs and medicines are too expensive for most people. They are produced overseas, in laboratories belonging to the big international companies, which spend billions on research and jealously guard their patent rights. The expectation of life in Singapore is 76 years for a man and 82½ for a woman; at the other end of the scale, the figures for Cambodia are 51 and 55 years.

### Traditional healers

In the villages, in the rain forests, in the mountains and generally among the ethnic minorities, people who fall ill rely on traditional remedies, based on centuries of trial and error. In Laos, for instance, when somebody falls ill, they send for the *mo ya* (healer), who has a deep understanding of the curative properties of plants and minerals. The healer will prepare infusions, decoctions, draughts, potions, soothing creams and poultices. The patient's family may also send for a *mo phi phay* or a *mo thevada*, both of them a kind of shaman or medicine man, who is believed to be able to identify the presence of evil spirits that have attacked the victim. Mingling Buddhist prayers, incantations and weird chantings, these healers make use of an array of objects that are held to contain magical properties, and whether it is due to the power of suggestion or to something more mysterious, their patients remarkably often find that they are cured.

There are also methods grounded in the medical wisdom of ancient China. Acupuncture, acupressure, cupping and moxibustion (treatment by placing burning leaves of the moxa plant near the patient's skin) are all part of the pharmacy at the disposal of traditional medicine. Such methods have been taken up in the West, to the extent that what was once termed alternative medicine is now known as complementary medicine.

Another group of medicines whose origins can be traced back to ancient China includes powdered snakeskin and sexual stimulants and aphrodisiacs, based on the use of rhinoceros horn or deer antlers. Such preparations can be easily bought in the Chinatowns of all the big cities.

### The struggle to keep numbers down

For several generations, the populations of South-east Asian countries have been increasing at an explosive rate. In 1940, Indonesia had 71 million inhabitants; today the figure is over 212 million. The populations of Vietnam and the Philippines are both approaching 80 million. One obvious response has been birth control campaigns. Almost everywhere in Vietnam, advertisements urge couples to limit the size of their families. Posters show a mother and a father with a single child, making it clear that family limitation is the key to a happy and comfortable life. In Thailand, a doctor named Mechai Viravaidya has become famous for his publicity campaigns. Apart from setting up a large number of family planning clinics and promoting his ideas on television, he has organised the release of millions of condoms, blown up like balloons as a publicity stunt. He even arranged for them to be blessed by monks. But the weight of tradition counts heavily in a

### Acupuncture

The theory of acupuncture is that energy, or chi, moves to the vital organs along invisible channels in the body, known as meridians. Illness is a sign that these channels are blocked, causing a lack of balance between the body's yin and yang (feminine and masculine) energies. The acupuncturist examines the patient carefully, then inserts needles into acupuncture points – traditionally there are 365 – along meridian lines and gently vibrates them. The therapy is said to help in cases of asthma, migraine, arthritis and muscular pain, and to be an effective anaesthetic.

**Massage parlour** *A South-east Asian way of balancing the body's energies.*

region where having a large family is for many people the only guarantee that there will be somebody to look after them in their old age.

### The scourge of AIDS

For a number of years, the spread of sexually transmitted diseases, and AIDS in particular, has been causing alarm in many countries. Thailand has been severely hit, especially in the capital, Bangkok, but few large cities are free from the scourge. The authorities point out that the victims are usually drug users and prostitutes, both male and female, and blame sexual tourism by Westerners.

*The new way* A visiting doctor vaccinates a baby in rural Vietnam.

*The old way* Traditional medicine, hygienically prepared in Laos.

*Dentists at work* Medicine men on the Indonesian island of Siberut, off the coast of Sumatra, prepare a potion of locally gathered herbs to cure a bad case of toothache.

# A place to live – for people and gods

*A house in South-east Asia is more than a place to live and raise a family: it is a refuge from danger from wild animals, human enemies, storm and flood – and a place of religious significance.*

According to the Toruja people of Sulawesi (formerly the Celebes) in Indonesia, a house should reflect the three levels of existence. The upper level is for the gods and ancestors, the middle section is where human beings are born, live out their lives and die, and the lower part is the abode of malevolent spirits and the forces of darkness.

## Space for the gods

A traditional Torujan house, the *tongkonan*, has space for the gods in a massive, curving roof that rises dramatically to form the shape of a pair of buffalo horns. The house stands above the ground on thick piles, and the heavy beams that support the roof and the rest of the structure are slotted so that they fit together without the need for metal nails. The walls are decorated with buffalo horns and with colourful designs in which red stands for humanity, white for purity and

**Cramped but cheerful**  *A Muong house in Vietnam.*

yellow for divine power. Only families descended from the old nobility are allowed to build a *tongkonan*, and nobody is allowed to sell one to outsiders, for its ownership is a mark of high status. Building one is an important event in the life of a family, marked by a feast and by the ceremonial sacrifice of pigs, chickens or even a buffalo. Wealthy families who have forsaken the traditional home for a more comfortable modern house will often keep the *tongkonan* in good repair, expensive though this is, so that it can be used for family gatherings and ceremonies.

The Torujan belief that a house should take account of the unseen forces that regulate the universe is shared by the Hindu people of the Indonesian island of Bali. The Balinese look to the mountains and volcanoes that dominate their island as the homes of the gods and the source of all that is good. The uphill or upstream direction is *kaja*, while downhill, leading to the realm of demons, is *kelod*, and humans inhabit the space between mountains and sea. The village houses are aligned to point uphill, particularly to the three sacred volcanoes of Agung, Batur and Batukau.

**A roof for the gods**  *A traditional* tongkonan *house in Sulawesi, with its great upcurving roof where the gods and the spirits of ancestors are believed to dwell.*

**Built to last**  *Hardwood pillars support the roof of a family home on Sumba island, Indonesia.*

*The simple life* Fishermen's huts beside the River Mekong in north-east Thailand.

### Inside a shophouse

The paraphernalia of business life has a way of invading the living quarters in the Chinese shophouses of Malaysia. Inside the house, which is reached through the shop, a fan stirs the warm night air, lifting the corners of bills stacked under a heavy paperweight, shaped like a tortoise. Resting his elbows on a marble table, the master of the house is finishing his accounts for the day on an abacus. Meanwhile, his perspiring brothers and uncles are noisily flinging down mah-jong pieces. The night will be a long one for them, but not for the children, who are already drowsy and have been put to bed. A woman pushes sticks of incense into a bronze vase in front of a little red, black and gold altar on which stand two oval-framed portraits of family ancestors alongside a statuette of a protecting goddess. Old and new sit comfortably together, with modern life represented by a refrigerator, a motorbike standing in one corner, and a large wall calendar that carries the photograph of a fashionable singer.

Like traditional houses in many parts of the region, the homes of the Batak people of northern Sumatra stand on stilts. This improves ventilation in a climate that can often be oppressively humid, and gives some protection against floods and wild animals. Dogs, goats, pigs and chickens occupy the space below, where food scraps will fall down to them through slats in the floor above. Traditional building materials are bamboo, wood, straw and palm leaves, but corrugated iron is increasingly used for roofs. The outside walls of a Batak house are decorated with mosaics and carvings of geometric shapes, animals and monsters, but there are no internal walls: privacy is obtained at night by letting down rattan mats.

Stilts can be a useful defence measure against human enemies, too. The Melanau of Sarawak, in the Malaysian part of Borneo, live in an area that was once notorious for pirates. Their houses were miniature fortresses, on stilts some 45 ft (14 m) high, and from that height they would pour scalding water on attackers. The Iban long houses of Sarawak and Sabah were also raised on stilts, though their main defence, in the era of head-hunting, came from their reputation as warriors, and from their numbers, for a longhouse is shared by several families.

### The lost charm of yesteryear

In the colonial period, houses were built to overawe the ruled and to remind the rulers of home. They were solid, imposing edifices, with eaves, archways, pillars and verandahs. In the 1920s Bangkok had a love affair with the European Art Deco style, and it still has a fine collection of Art Deco buildings.

Many Chinese who emigrated to Malaysia, Singapore and other parts of the region were traders and craftsmen, used to living 'above the shop'. Chinese shophouses, as the name suggests, are fronted by a shop, and the family lives above it – or, if the building has only one storey, behind it. The front opens onto a public arcade or covered walkway.

In the big, overcrowded cities of the region, the public and commercial buildings may be spectacular, but the houses of ordinary people have in many places lost the charm of yesteryear. More and more districts are being taken over by apartment blocks, which have none of the warmth and communal spirit of traditional dwellings. But the most brutal contrast with the past is in the shantytowns that fester around the fringes of many of the cities. They have no electricity, no running water and no proper sewerage system. Home, in the shadow of a gleaming skyscraper, may well be nothing more than an assembly of cardboard boxes, roofed with rusting corrugated iron.

*The grand life* French colonial-style building in Ho Chi Minh City.

# Flavours and aromas in the lands of spice

*The aromas from the kitchens of South-east Asia hint at a prodigious variety of spices, herbs, sauces, fruits, vegetables and meats. There is a mouth-watering variety, too, in national cuisines, which gloriously combine the culinary traditions of China, India and France with those of native ethnic groups.*

**When appearance counts** *Preparing salad vegetables, Thai-style.*

The social customs that develop around so apparently simple a matter as eating a meal can reveal much about the character of a people. At the end of a banquet given by a family of Chinese origin, it is customary for the host to offer the diners another helping of rice, but accepting it would cause the host to lose face, since it would indicate that the diner was still hungry. In several South-east Asian countries, it is considered good manners to leave a little food on the plate, as a sign that the host has been more than generous. In the Philippines, if a stranger passes by while a family is eating, it is customary to invite the newcomer to join them. It is polite to decline graciously, and claim that one has already eaten. Such conventions hint at a time when hunger was more widespread than it is today.

## The rules of etiquette

Different rules of etiquette apply in the different countries of South-east Asia, but the aim is always to put people at their ease. Peasants in Asia often take their midday meal in the fields, and when they eat at home often follow the style of their grandparents and manage without a table. In the cities, many of the cheaper eating houses offer only low tables at which people kneel or squat to eat. In rural areas and among the ethnic minorities it is quite common for people to eat with their fingers or with a spoon. Knives are not used at mealtimes in South-east Asia. In the eyes of a Vietnamese hostess, cutting up meat is work for a butcher, not for a guest. If there are forks, they are never used to ferry food from plate to mouth, but to push the food towards the spoon. Putting a fork into the mouth would be as crude an action in Thailand as eating with a knife would be in a Western country.

**Soup with extras** *A travelling soup seller lays out her wares in Hanoi.*

At a banquet thrown by an overseas Chinese family, husband and wife are never seated apart. The colour of the porcelain changes according to the occasion: red or pink for a fashionable wedding; yellow for an anniversary. The hostess will offer warm napkins for guests to wipe their hands before serving them appetisers and cold hors d'oeuvres. The main meal does not begin until the host serves chosen morsels to his most honoured guests. Toasts are proposed and drunk throughout the course of the meal, but neither water nor tea is drunk before the soup that marks the end of the banquet.

## Food with eye appeal

A meal must be pleasing to the eye as well as appeal to the palate: South-east Asian cooks take great care to mingle tastes, colours and smell. In the West, four basic tastes are recognised – sweet, bitter, sour and salty. The Far East recognises at least four more – piquant, astringent, sharp and fatty. A subtle appreciation of flavours has long been characteristic of the region's cuisine. About a century ago, a Burmese named U Bho Hlaing listed tastes that were 'by nature incompatible', among them crab and mushroom, pigeon and ginger, and, more exotically, fish and rhinoceros.

***Fast food in Vietnam***
*The Vietnamese follow the Chinese tradition of holding their rice bowls close to the mouth and scooping in the contents with the help of chopsticks.*

### The correct way to use chopsticks

In many South-east Asian countries, chopsticks are used only for eating noodles and a few other dishes. But in Singapore, Vietnam and other countries where the Chinese influence is strong, they are in general use. Every diner has a bowl of rice, and instead of being served as separate courses, all the other dishes are placed in the middle of the table. People use their chopsticks to pick up a sliver of duck or a tiny chunk of salt pork. The way chopsticks are handled reveals how a person has been brought up. Children are taught not to fidget with them, or to rummage through the central platter, searching for a tempting morsel. Only at funerals is it permitted to pass food from chopstick to chopstick, or to place them on the bowl at the end of a meal.

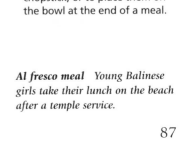

***Al fresco meal*** *Young Balinese girls take their lunch on the beach after a temple service.*

Rice is a staple food throughout the region, often boiled until it is glutinous. Sometimes it is rolled into balls for dipping into a sauce. An ubiquitous sauce, called *nuoc mam* in Vietnam, is made by fermenting anchovies with layers of salt in barrels. The variety of dishes to go with the rice is stunning. From Indonesia come nasi goreng (rice fried with shrimps, meat and spices), sweet-sour fish and peanuts in palm sugar; from Thailand, beef and chicken salads, and sizzlingly hot dishes spiced with chillies; from Malaysia, satay (barbecued meat on skewers, served with peanut sauce); from Vietnam, spring rolls (pancakes stuffed with pork and served with fresh leaves of lettuce and mint).

Fish, from rivers and the sea, is the main source of protein. There is a vast range of fruit, from strawberries and avocados to mangoes, papayas, bananas, guavas and the durian, which most Westerners find an acquired taste at best. For rich gourmets there is shark's fin soup, or birds' nest soup, made with the nests of swiftlets from caves in Sabah, Malaysia. Gathering the nests is a dangerous occupation that involves climbing rickety ladders and swaying poles nearly 200 ft (60m) from the ground. There are some dishes, found wherever China's culinary influence has spread, that are unappealing or even unthinkable to Western appetites – sea slugs, bear's paws, roast dog, fried insects or the lips of orang-utans.

## Spirits of Asia

***For that relaxing moment***
*Rice wine and cigars, rolled in palm leaves, in Borneo.*

There is a saying in South-east Asia that 'a meal without alcohol is like a flag without a breeze'. Despite the fact that Islam prohibits alcohol, it is tolerated for non-Muslims, even in countries that are predominantly Muslim, such as Indonesia. The beer may be local or European, while wine and spirits are based either on rice or on the coconut palm. In Thailand and Laos there is a potent spirit distilled from rice, called Mekong, said to be powerful enough to counteract the polluted waters of the river of the same name. Some ethnic minorities drink rice alcohol direct from the jar, through a straw.

***Pavement artistry*** *In Rangoon, even food sold in the street is set out with a watchful eye on its aesthetic appeal to potential buyers.*

***A night on the town*** *Dinner and a glamorous show in one of Bangkok's biggest Chinese restaurants.*

# The sporting life

*Wherever the British go, they take their sports with them. Football has won hundreds of thousands of fans in South-east Asia, and cricket has caught on in Singapore. But the region has its indigenous sports, too. Thailand, for example, has the fearsome* muay-thai, *known to the West as kick-boxing.*

Despite Rudyard Kipling's claim that East is East and West is West, and never the twain shall meet, a number of Western sports have won large and enthusiastic followings in South-east Asia. It is not surprising that cricket, born on the village greens of England, should have a devoted following in Singapore, since the settlement was founded by an Englishman. More remarkable, perhaps, is that the quintessentially French sport of boules should have spread beyond Indochina. It is played in Singapore and Thailand, as well as in Cambodia, and the standard is so high that in 1988 and again in 1990 the Thai women's team were world boules champions. Football, introduced by the British, has made giant strides since an Asian Football Confederation was founded in 1954. At first glance, badminton may look like another colonial import, for its name and its rule book come from 19th-century England. But in fact the game was played in both ancient China and ancient India.

The American influence on the region's sports and pastimes is most obvious in the Philippines, where pool, basketball and tenpin bowling are widely popular. They were taken there, and to Vietnam, by generations of GIs. In the year 2000, the world champion at pool was a Filipino.

One result of the popularity of bowling is that it provides employment for a small army of Filipino children, picking up and replacing the fallen pins, for the bowling alleys in the Philippines are not always automated.

**The heroes** *Cut-outs of kick-boxers in Bangkok.*

**At the net** *Fast reflexes and natural litheness have produced a host of skilled badminton players and a number of world champions in South-east Asia.*

## The lethal sport of Thai boxing

Many of the indigenous sports of South-east Asia had their origins in the days when skill in hand-to-hand combat could mean the difference between life and death. *Muay-thai*, or kick-boxing, has at least 100 000 practitioners in Thailand, and many times that number of fans. Its rise to popularity began in the 15th century, after a *muay-thai* contest was fought to decide which of two rival princes should inherit the throne. Its greatest hero is the 18th-century boxer Mai Kwanom. He was captured in battle by the Burmese, and to impress their king he offered to fight a dozen of their best warriors. Mai Kwanom defeated them all, and the king, in awe and admiration, gave him his freedom.

In earlier centuries, boxers protected their fists by wrapping horse hair around them. Then came strips of cotton, soaked in glue, and reinforced with powdered glass if the fight was to be to the death. In 1921, some of the Marquess of Queensbury rules for boxing were adopted. Padded leather gloves were introduced, the boxers were classified according to weight, and fights were split into rounds. *Muay-thai* permits blows with the foot, the fist, the elbow and the knee, and it is these last two that usually do most damage and win fights. Before a match, the boxers carry out a ritual dance, wearing a *mongkon*, or headband, which has been blessed by a monk. They kneel to pray before the bout, and take off the headband before entering the ring. With excitement whipped up by frenzied drumming and clashing cymbals, the fans pay little heed to the fact that officially gambling is illegal.

**No blows barred** *A Thai boxer kicks for the head, in a bout at Phuket.*

89

**Preparations**  *A Malay and his kite.*

# A passion for gambling – and for violence

*Whether the sport be as violent as kick-boxing, as cruel as cockfighting, as terrifying in its impact as two water buffalo charging each other head-on, or as gentle as a game of cards, the people of South-east Asia have a simple guideline: if it can have more than one outcome, it is worth a gamble.*

Many of the traditional sports and pastimes of the region had their origins in the days when violence was part of everyday life. Even a sedentary game such as chess has obvious affinities with war, since the object is to threaten the opponent's king. *Amis de mano*, the stick-fighting of the Philippines, began as a method of self-defence against armed robbers. The kick-boxers of Thailand and Myanmar are doing for fame and for cash what their ancestors did for survival. *Krabi kabong*, another Thai speciality, is a combination of boxing and fighting with clubs, spears and swords that was lethal in former days. Today the sport is ceremonial, with punches pulled, thrusts stopped short of the target and marks awarded for skill. Traditional sports among ethnic groups can be particularly robust. Bullfighting in the Philippines is a matter not of pitting man against bull, but of setting bull against bull, to charge one another head-on. In Mindanao, a mare on heat will be tethered to a stake and two stallions be set to fight for possession.

## Open-air chess

Whether the stakes be large or small, money changes hands when the cards are brought out. A game called *to tom* is especially popular in Vietnam, where it is said that a man of taste and discernment needs three accomplishments: the ability to appreciate a tea of quality, the knowledge to quote from the celebrated 18th-century novel *Kim Van Kieu*, and the skill to excel at *to tom*. Throughout the region, draughts and chess are played in the open air, on street corners or on benches that are shaded from the sun. Mah-jong, which originated in China, combines some of the elements of poker, bridge and dominoes, uses 144 counters and is played indoors.

## Battles on land, on water and in the air

Young men in Laos, Cambodia and Myanmar perform amazing acrobatics at *takraw*, a game played with a wickerwork rattan

ball, which has to be kept in the air without using the hands. In the most common version of the game, the players pass the ball to one another in a circle. The Vietnamese version, also known as *chinlon*, is played across a net, like volleyball.

Kite-flying is as popular among adults in South-east Asia as it is with children. The kites are generally enormous, meticulously made and brilliantly decorated. In April, enthusiasts in Thailand stage competitions in which 'male' and 'female' kites – the *chula* and the *pupkao* – fight battles in the sky. The field below is divided into two halves, and the objective is to grapple the rival kite or entangle its string so that it crashes to earth in one's own territory.

Nowhere in the region is water very far away, and passions run high at the canoe races on great rivers such as the Mekong. The canoes are gorgeously decorated and the crews, wearing their team colours, are spurred on by a frenzy of drumming and by the cries of spectators crowded on the river banks.

Gambling, along with striptease and prostitution, is among the allurements on offer in the sleazier nightclubs of Bangkok, Manila and other big cities. It finds an eager clientele among those who

**Asian song contest**  *A songbirds competition in Thailand. The birds, in cages suspended high on poles, are trained to break into song when their owners whistle.*

have become newly affluent through business deals. Even in communist-ruled Laos, where the government takes a puritanical view and bans its own citizens from gambling, a huge new casino has been built near Vientiane, where foreigners can make – or lose – their money in slot machines, or at roulette or blackjack. In Vietnam, the sons of the well-off have discovered a new thrill, a hazardous game of 'chicken' in which they race one another on motorbikes while blindfolded. They are gambling, not with money, but with life and limb, and there have been a number of serious accidents.

***Teamwork on the river*** *A canoe race on the Mekong, in Cambodia.*

***Place your bets*** *Open-air cockpit in Na Trang, Vietnam. With all bets committed to memory, and nothing written down, the gambling fever can rise to a frenzy. Fights and scuffles are not unusual after a match.*

### Cockfighting in the noisy pit of death

Gambling has such a hold on the people of South-east Asia that any living creature is liable to become a contestant in a fight to the death: insect against insect; fighting fish against fighting fish; even, in Singapore, fly against fly. In the noisy and brutal sport of cockfighting, the birds fight in a pit, surrounded by gamblers placing bets and yelling for their favourites. Champion birds are fed a special diet high in vitamins and are cosseted with baths and massage to keep them in peak condition. Before a fight begins, the birds are fitted with vicious metal spurs and held head to head to work them into a fighting rage. Fights often end with the death of the winner as well as the loser, so single-mindedly are the birds bred to fight, and so lethal the weapons with which they are armed.

***A cool hand*** *A tense moment, calling for steady nerves, in a card game between fishermen at Hoi An, in Vietnam.*

CHAPTER 4

# CITIES OF THE PAST AND OF TOMORROW

Cities have always attracted people looking for fame and fortune, and South-east Asia is no exception. When the monarchs were god-kings, peasants flocked in from the countryside to work on building and engineering projects. Artisans beautified the temples and provided luxury items for the courts; other newcomers became soldiers, traders and merchants, or served the needs of fellow citizens: all added to the wealth and renown of their city. Cities such as Angkor in Cambodia, Hué in Vietnam and Pagan in Myanmar overflow with the splendours of the past and have become living museums. Others, such as Manila in the Philippines, Ho Chi Minh City in Vietnam and Kuala Lumpur in Malaysia, are successful manufacturing and commercial centres. Their success is based on the same foundations as those of the ancient cities: by offering the prospect of a better life, they attract people of creativity and energy.

*Skyscrapers and temples of commerce tower over the Masjid Jamek mosque in Kuala Lumpur.*

# The capital that time forgot

*Set dramatically against an encircling green backdrop of tree-covered mountains, Luang Prabang was the first capital of ancient Laos. The 'City of the Golden Buddha' became a centre of religious devotion, as well as of royal power. Today, it is a sleepy provincial market town, bypassed by the flow of history. But the glories of the past live on in its temples, its steeples and the former royal palace.*

Early in the morning, files of Buddhist monks and novices, clad in saffron robes, walk through the quiet streets of Luang Prabang, each carrying a metal bowl to hold offerings from their fellow citizens of a few handfuls of rice, vegetables or fruit. Although the bowls are commonly referred to in the West as 'begging bowls', the monks are not regarded as beggars, and giving them food is an act of devotion, not simply charity. Luang Prabang is a Sleeping Beauty of a town, where dilapidated French colonial villas and the gleam of gold from temple roofs make the past a part of everyday life. Even war and revolution seem to have created only temporary interruptions in the town's long slumber.

## Glories of the past

It is possible to cover the entire town on foot in 20 minutes without hurrying, for it consists of no more than five or six main streets crossed by narrow roads, some of which are little better than tracks. The busiest

**Riverside shopping** *Riverside stalls along the Mekong. The surrounding countryside is a vast market garden.*

thoroughfare in town is the River Mekong, which is used to transport market garden produce from the surrounding countryside. Climbing the steep walks that lead to the Dala market, peasants bring in fish, poultry, rice wine and bitter-tasting pumpkins. The stalls are laid out with varying items of ironmongery, or with pastries containing such tempting fillings as mincemeat spiced with peppers. In their brilliantly coloured clothes, ornamented with embroidery, women from the Hmong, Yao, Lahu and Lisu minorities sell silver trinkets and splendid examples of their needlework. A handful of small businesses, a sports stadium that doubles up for cultural events and political rallies, and a few hotels catering to tourists complete the tally of commercial and public activity. The entire population numbers fewer than 20 000 today, but the chief glory of Luang Prabang lies in the past, in its ancient (and not so ancient) palaces, temples and pagodas.

**Sleeping Beauty** *Rice pancakes, held in wooden frames, dry in the sun on a Luang Prabang street.*

**Ethnic bargains** *Hmong women lay out a bright display of embroidery in the Dala market.*

94

In the turbulent 14th century, General Fa Ngoum conquered a vast area of northern and central Thailand, which he named Lan Sang, 'The Kingdom of a Million Elephants'. He chose as his capital a settlement on an easily defended peninsula where the River Khan runs into the Mekong. Fa Ngoum, who had been brought up in the Khmer court at Angkor, made Buddhism the religion of his new kingdom and was presented by his Khmer allies with a golden statue of the Buddha, the Pha Bang, from which the name Luang Prabang is derived (Luang means 'Great').

***Fit for a king … and for a nation*** *The royal palace, on the banks of the Mekong, was turned into a museum following the 1975 revolution.*

The city remained the capital for two centuries. More than 60 temples were built and the Golden Buddha became an icon of the Lao nation. In the mid 15th century it was abandoned in favour of Vientiane. The Kingdom of a Million Elephants embarked on a path of conquest that extended its frontiers, but at the end of the 17th century internal tensions led to a break-up and Laos fell under the domination of Thailand and Vietnam. With the arrival of the French, it was absorbed into French Indochina. The monarchy survived the years of French colonial rule, the Second World War and the first two decades of the country's independence, but was abolished in 1975 when the communist Pathet Lao came to power. King Sisavang Vatthana and his queen died mysteriously in exile.

## *Moon rock in the palace*

The Golden Buddha that gives the city its name stands in the former royal palace, which was built as late as 1904 and is now a museum, the Haw Kham. The main entrance is particularly impressive: ambassadors from foreign nations, and other important visitors, would be brought up the Mekong in boats, disembark on the river bank and walk up a broad flight of steps directly into the palace. The splendours of the East meet the wonders of the West in the Haw Kham Museum. The royal apartments are furnished in the European art deco style of the 1920s and 1930s. And along with the Golden Buddha and a display of sumptuous silk screens, elephant tusks, traditional friezes, murals and mosaics, the museum contains a curious but fascinating collection of gifts offered to the monarch – a collection that includes not only Sèvres dinner services but also the model of an American spacecraft and a lump of moon rock, presented after the Apollo moon landings.

## A city of temples

In the 18th century, Luang Prabang had 65 temples. The ravages of war, fire and time have reduced this number by more than half, but the temples that remain are of compelling interest. The most magnificent is Wat Xieng Thong, the Golden City Temple, built in 1560. The rear wall is decorated with a mosaic based on the tree of life, and one of its chapels contains a fine reclining Buddha, as old as the temple itself. Another chapel houses a 40 ft (12 m) high royal funeral chariot and urns holding the ashes of dead princes and princesses.

Wat Vixoun lays claim to being the city's oldest working temple, for it was originally built in 1513, though it had to be rebuilt after being put to the torch by Chinese raiders in 1887. It holds a number of wooden Buddhas in the 'calling for rain' posture, and one of its domes is known as the 'watermelon stupa' because of its extremely bulbous shape.

A number of temples adorn the

***Temple treasure*** *The reclining Buddha of Wat Xieng Thong.*

slopes of Mount Phu Si, including one that is said to be on the site of a footprint of the Buddha. The view from the top of the mountain is breathtaking. Reflecting the last rays of the sun among a blaze of frangipani and banyan trees, like a jewel in its casket, lies Luang Prabang, 'the city that time forgot'.

95

# Jakarta, between affluence and poverty

*Overcrowded, sprawling, polluted, always on the brink of being brought to a complete halt by traffic snarl-ups, but nevertheless a city pulsating with energy, the capital of Indonesia is in many ways a microcosm of the entire country. It is a melting pot of languages, cultures and ethnic groups, brought together by an 'accident' of history – the fact that they were all once under Dutch colonial rule.*

**Strong man** *Huge street poster of General Suharto, dictatorial head of state until 1998.*

In 1945, at the end of the Second World War, Jakarta had a population of 900 000. Today, the figure is rapidly approaching 10 million. The city, for all its slums, its pollution, its crimes and its traffic problems, has a magnetic attraction for impoverished peasants. Shantytowns spread their wretchedness alongside canals and railway lines, resulting in a city where great wealth and abject poverty exist side by side. Jakarta entered the pages of history because of its strategic location, on the northern coast of Java.

When the Portuguese arrived, in 1522, it was a major port, under the Pajajaran kings, the last Hindu dynasty to rule West Java. Its name then was Sunda Kelapa, and behind the various name changes it has undergone since, there lies a tormented story of sieges, massacres, plagues, conquests, revolutions and liberations.

### The tide of Islam

The Portuguese tried to win a foothold in the spice trade at Sunda Kelapa, but in 1527 they were driven out by the rising tide of Islam. The Muslim conquerors renamed the city Jayakarta ('Victorious') and so it remained for nearly 100 years, until the arrival of the Dutch. Faced with a hostile population, the newcomers built a fortress, which they named Batavia, and from this base, in 1619, they stormed Jayakarta and set it ablaze. Batavia was to become the capital of the Dutch Empire in the East Indies. When the Japanese invaded, in 1942, they changed the name to Jakarta, to appeal to nationalist sentiment. The old port of Sunda Kelapa, however, kept its name. It is remarkable today as a showcase of the age of sailing ships. Dozens of brightly painted Macassar schooners are on display there, some of them still in use. Old Batavia, now the Kota district, still has a cobblestoned Dutch charm. The 18th-century City Hall is now the Jakarta History Museum. As well as being the seat of government, it housed the courts where lawbreakers were put on trial and the dungeons where they were imprisoned.

### The city expands

The first major expansion of Batavia came after a massacre of its Chinese residents by the Indonesian population in 1740. The Dutch prohibited the surviving Chinese from living within the city walls, and moved them out to Glodok, which is now Jakarta's bustling Chinatown. Epidemics of cholera, malaria and dysentery in the port area in the 19th century led to a second phase of expansion.

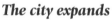

**City that never sleeps** *Night or day, the traffic in Jakarta flows nonstop, beneath skyscraper towers and around well-lit national monuments.*

Imposing residences for rich merchants and officials were built along wide, shady avenues in what were then the outskirts of the city. With Indonesia's independence, declared in 1945 and conceded in 1949, President Ahmed Sukarno embarked on a grandiose plan to make Jakarta the greatest city in South-east Asia. His 450 ft (137 m) Monas (Monumen Nasional) Tower, topped by a giant flame, brought gleamingly to life by 77 lb (35 kg) of gold leaf, dominates the city. Modern Jakarta is an urban ant hill, a jumble of skyscrapers, market stalls, street hawkers, supermarkets, luxury stores, big hotels, well-patronised little restaurants and traffic bottlenecks. A lake in the Taman Mini Park contains a model of the entire archipelago, so that visitors can row around Indonesia in miniature. In the same park are 27 full-scale traditional houses, one for each of the country's provinces. Much the same point has already been made by the city itself, for it is a melting pot for all the peoples of this immense nation.

*The living past*   Brightly painted schooners at the old port, Sunda Kepala, bring cargoes of wood from Borneo, as they have done since Muslim traders first sailed around the islands of Indonesia.

*Bird market*   Pigeons for sale at Pasar Burung.

### Pleasures and perils of a trip through Jakarta

Taking a trip in Jakarta can be an adventure. The heat, noise and crowded footways make walking a poor choice for many visitors, but the alternatives have drawbacks, too. A taxi? If there happens to be a meter, it is not likely to be working, so the traveller must expect an exhausting session of haggling. A bus? On an ordinary *bis biasa*, the journey will be uncomfortable and hot, with passengers packed like sardines and pickpockets a menace. A *bis patas*, an air-conditioned bus, is a better option, though it will still be a frustrating stop-start journey through traffic jams. It is easier, though not for those of a nervous disposition, to weave through the traffic on the back of an *ojek*, a motorbike. For those who enjoy close-ups of life in the streets there is the *bajaj*, a motorised tricycle, or the *bekak*, a bicycle-rickshaw – though these have been banned from busy main streets. Most of these forms of transport involve haggling over the fare – a tradition which, along with the pollution, may account for the famous *pusing*, the Jakarta headache.

### Villages in the city

Skyscrapers, supermarkets, grandiose monuments and the office blocks of multinational companies dominate the skyline of Jakarta. But in their shadow, a jumble of little streets can lead into an alternative city. Here are tiny houses built higgledy-piggledy, with the streets no more than trodden-down earth. The inhabitants spend much of their time gossiping on their doorsteps, because there is nothing more productive to do. They generally come from the same ethnic groups, for they moved to the city from the same villages in search of work, in most cases without success. Despite the hardships of daily life, there is a strong feeling of community and laughter comes easily – as it did in the villages they left behind.

**Lords of the dance**  Dancers portrayed in the National Museum, with their sumptuous headdresses and heavily embroidered costumes.

1. The royal palace and Wat Phra Keo, the temple of the Emerald Buddha
2. Wat Arun, the temple of the Dawn
3. Wat Saket, temple of the Golden Mountain
4. Wat Pho, temple of the Reclining Buddha
5. Wat Benchamabopit, the Marble Temple
6. The Swan Pakkard Palace
7. Sao Ching-Cha, temple of the Giant Swing
8. Jim Thompson's house
9. National Museum (formerly the palace of Prince Wang Na)
10. Lumpini Park
11. The old Oriental Hotel
12. National Assembly
13. Sanam Luang, the Royal Field
14. Chitralada Palace
15. Vimnanvek Palace
16. Erawan Shrine

**On the gold standard**  Bangkok's jewellery stores, mostly owned by ethnic Chinese, are a haven at times when people lose faith in paper money.

**Calling for the rain**  The different postures of the Buddha each carry their own meaning. This one, standing with arms reaching straight down, is a call for rain to fall on the rice fields.

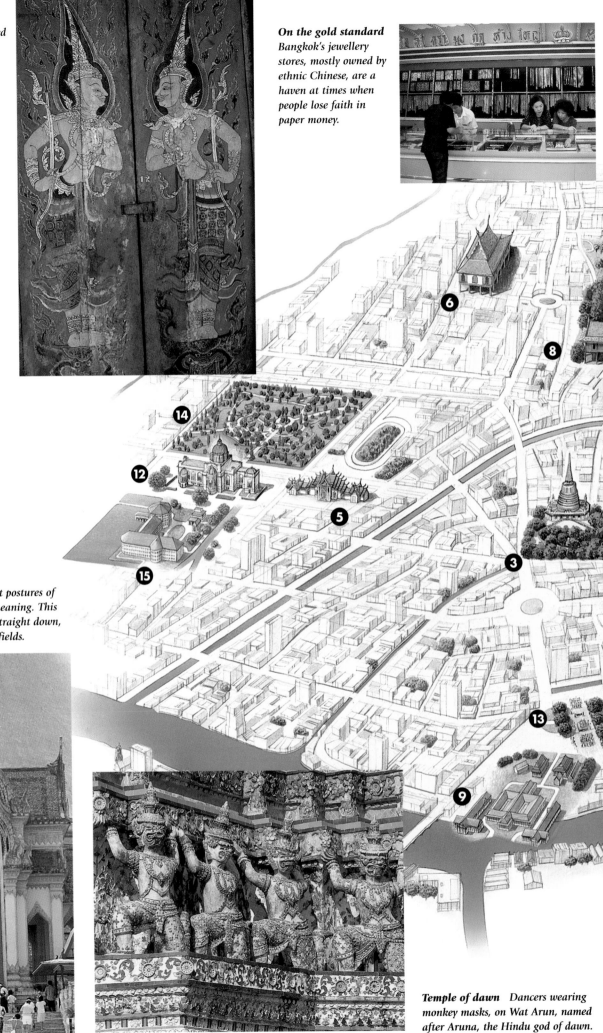

**Temple of dawn**  Dancers wearing monkey masks, on Wat Arun, named after Aruna, the Hindu god of dawn.

# Bangkok, the supercharged city

Bangkok can be steamy in more than one sense of the word. With a mean annual temperature of 32°C (89.6°F) and lying in the path of the monsoons, it is one of the hottest, muggiest cities in the world. And since the era of the Vietnam War, when American dollars poured into the city, it has become notorious for its massage parlours, nightclubs and go-go bars. But there is another Bangkok, too – a place of temples, museums, libraries, art galleries, gilded Buddhas, quiet canals, a royal palace and a gently gliding river. Until the 1930s, Bangkok, the capital of Thailand since 1782, was a quiet city shaded by palm trees and criss-crossed by canals. The 1950s saw an economic boom as Thailand, staying out of the war itself, was enriched by the long conflict in Indochina. The postwar years saw a frenzy of speculation and of building, halted by an economic downturn in the late 1990s.

**Floating market**   Peasant women sell mangoes, durians and vegetables from their canoes on one of Bangkok's canals.

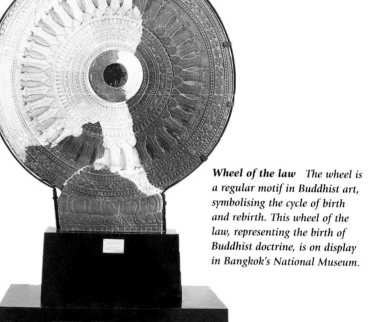

**Wheel of the law**   The wheel is a regular motif in Buddhist art, symbolising the cycle of birth and rebirth. This wheel of the law, representing the birth of Buddhist doctrine, is on display in Bangkok's National Museum.

**Golden secret**   The 10 ft (3 m) high Buddha of Wat Traimit hid its secret for centuries beneath a coat of plaster. In 1953 the plaster was chipped away, revealing it was made of 5 tons of solid gold.

**Home of the Emerald Buddha**   The royal palace houses ceremonial halls, government buildings and, in Wat Phra Keo, the Emerald Buddha, the holiest relic in the land.

# Bangkok

1. Wat Saket, a temple in whose grounds stands a man-made hill, the 256 ft (78 m) high Golden Mountain.

2. The city's reputation as a garish 'sin city' is centred on just two streets – Patpong 1 and Patpong 2.

3. The reclining Buddha of Wat Pho, at 151 ft (46 m) in length, is the largest in Thailand. It is entirely covered in gold leaf and the soles of its feet are inlaid with mother-of-pearl.

4. People wanting to avoid traffic jams take a waterbus on one of the city's picturesque canals.

5. A treasure in teak – the pavilion of King Chulalongkorn (reigned 1868-1910), who filled it with precious items collected in Europe.

6. Bangkok's modern 'Underground', which runs overground, on supporting stilts.

7. As if canals were not enough, these office buildings have more than a touch of Venice.

8. Jim Thompson's house. He was an American who traded in Thai silk and filled his home with beautiful examples of Thai arts and culture.

**Where dreams come true** The Erawan Shrine, built to bring good luck during the building of a hotel, is now used to pray for luck on any occasion, from marriage to exams.

**City of angels** For Thais, Bangkok is Krung Thep, the 'City of Angels', watched over by gods like this one in the royal palace.

**Starting young** Children in Thailand are taught from an early age to honour the Buddha. A toddler places an offering at the feet of a gigantic gilded statue.

**A monarch remembered** Every year, on October 23, the anniversary of the death in 1910 of King Chulalongkorn, flowers are laid in front of the National Assembly in his memory.

**East meets West** Marble impor from Carrara, in Italy, was used build Wat Benchamabopit, the Marble Temple, and its design combines the styles of East and West. The temple, which was designed by a half-brother of Kin Chulalongkorn, was built in 190

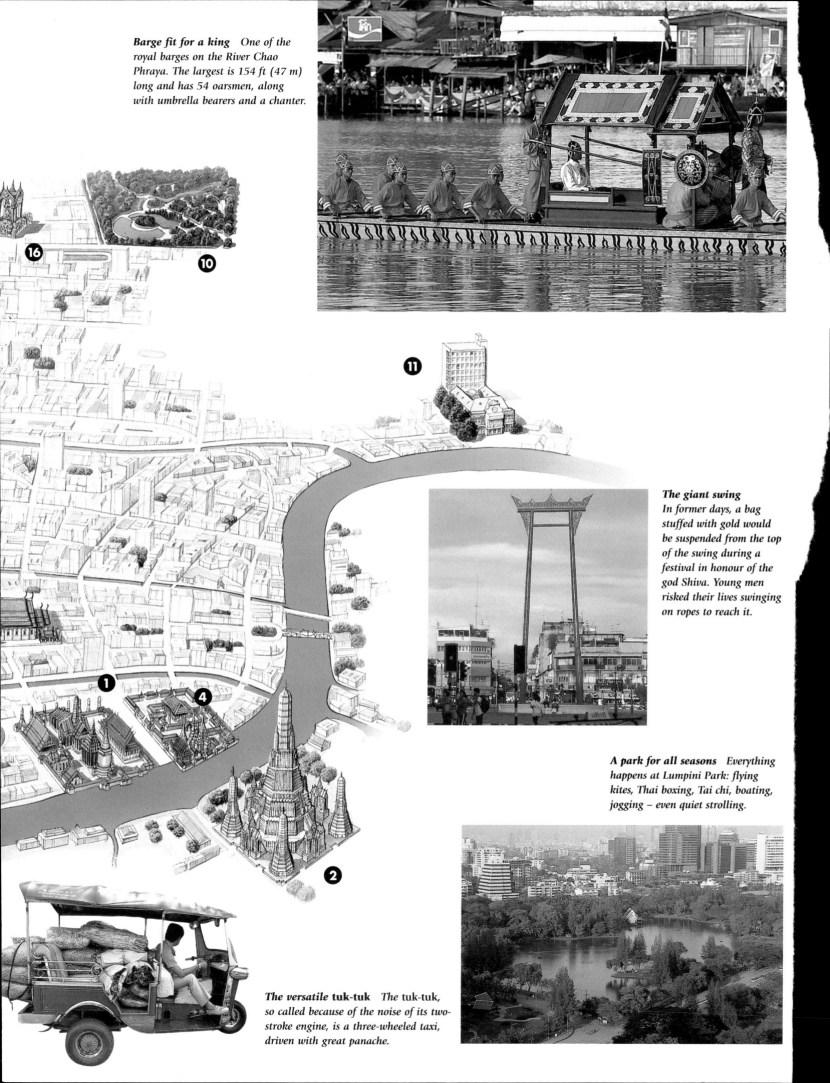

**Barge fit for a king** One of the royal barges on the River Chao Phraya. The largest is 154 ft (47 m) long and has 54 oarsmen, along with umbrella bearers and a chanter.

**The giant swing**
In former days, a bag stuffed with gold would be suspended from the top of the swing during a festival in honour of the god Shiva. Young men risked their lives swinging on ropes to reach it.

**A park for all seasons** Everything happens at Lumpini Park: flying kites, Thai boxing, Tai chi, boating, jogging – even quiet strolling.

**The versatile tuk-tuk** The tuk-tuk, so called because of the noise of its two-stroke engine, is a three-wheeled taxi, driven with great panache.

# Hanoi, a capital city that kept its provincial charm

*Although the Vietnamese made it abundantly clear that the French were not welcome in their country as rulers, much of the charm of their capital comes from the French style that was absorbed during the colonial era. Streets alive with the noise and bustle of the East are lined with buildings that would not look out of place in Paris.*

**Pastel city**   *The colours of houses in Hanoi have been washed out by centuries of humidity.*

Hanoi is a city of legends, and the atmosphere conjured up by its tranquil lakes and tree-shaded boulevards makes it easy to more than half-believe them. It was founded, so one legend says, by a king who saw a golden dragon rising into the sky from the site. Another legend tells how the gods gave Emperor Le Thai To a magic sword to help him to drive the Chinese out of northern Vietnam. With his mission accomplished, he ventured onto a lake in the middle of the city, to give the sword back, but a golden turtle snatched it from his hand and dived to the lake's bottom. Since then, the lake has been known as Hoan Kiem ('The Lake of the Returned Sword'). Today, Hoan Kiem is a gathering place for citizens absorbed in Tai chi exercises, or in jogging.

**Hanoi that might have been**   *A brief property boom in the early 1990s made an impression on the city without spoiling its charm.*

## Reminders of the war

Hanoi was heavily bombed during the Vietnam War, but more than a quarter of a century later, most of the gaps have been filled and reminders of one of the most ferocious wars of the 20th century are to be found mainly in museums and monuments. The most revered site in the city, indeed in all of Vietnam, is the mausoleum that holds the body of Ho Chi Minh, leader in the long struggle for independence. The Army Museum contains scale models of major battles, including that of Dien Bien Phu, in which the French army was finally defeated. What is left of the grim Hoa Lo prison, known during the war as the 'Hanoi

**Early risers**   *It is only 5 am, but people are already performing Tai chi on the banks of Hoan Kiem.*

Hilton' because captured US air-crew were imprisoned there, is now a museum. Among its exhibits is a less charming reminder of French rule – a guillotine.

The best way to tour Hanoi is by bicycle or cyclo, a pedal-powered rickshaw, carried along on the tide of other cyclists, who have made the streets their own, despite strong competition from motorbikes. Around the Dong Xuan market and near the banks of the Red River, people work, eat and enjoy themselves in the open air. Greengrocers prepare papaws, grandmothers keep bowls of noodle soup simmering on stoves placed on the pavement, smiling florists make wreaths or sell posies, while young girls serving behind the counters of family shops look out on old men in berets, playing cards beneath the shade of tamarind trees. Aromatic wreaths of smoke waft into the streets from Confucian and Buddhist temples.

**Bridge over the Red River** *Built between 1899 and 1902 the Long Bien Bridge is just over a mile (1.6 km) long.*

with the old-style communist bureaucracy. Driven back on their own resources, the people of Hanoi rediscovered what, for political and historical reasons, they had long disdained: the city's unique wealth of colonial buildings. The French occupied Hanoi in 1882 and promptly announced their colonial presence and intentions by demolishing the city's walls and gates, as well as a number of prominent buildings. The Ba Tieng Pagoda, for instance, was pulled down to make way for the Roman Catholic cathedral of St Joseph's. The Municipal Theatre, built in 1901 and better known as the Opera House, was modelled, in opulent beaux-arts style, on the Paris Opera House. The centre of Hanoi began to take on the look it has today – that of a late 19th century French city.

## Rediscovering the colonial past

Although it has more than 2 million citizens, and is the capital of a nation of nearly 80 million, there is nothing grandiose or overwhelming about Hanoi: everything is on a human scale. A building boom got under way in the 1990s, but it petered out with the economic crisis at the end of the 1990s and with a flagging enthusiasm on the part of overseas investors for dealing

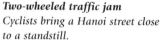

**Two-wheeled traffic jam**
*Cyclists bring a Hanoi street close to a standstill.*

### Ho Chi Minh City, formerly Saigon

When communist tanks rolled into Saigon in April 1975, the US-backed South Vietnamese regime was in its death throes, and the long agony of the Vietnam War was about to end. To mark their triumph, the winners gave Saigon a new name: Ho Chi Minh Ville, after their revolutionary leader. But the official name is no more than that – a name used by officials: most of the 3.2 million inhabitants call their city Saigon. It was founded at the end of the 17th century by sailors and traders of the Khmer Empire, and within a few decades was important enough to be described by the Portuguese as 'the best port in the kingdom of Cochin China'. The French, arriving in 1859, built avenues and villas, drained marshes and even gave the city a tram

service. In the 1950s and 1960s the population soared as people flocked in from a surrounding countryside that was ravaged by a guerrilla war. Whatever its name, Ho Chi Minh City is well on the way to becoming Vietnam's powerhouse. It has an American-style business centre, and its skyline is punctuated by skyscrapers.

Sixty per cent of the country's industrial production and 45 per cent of its foreign trade are concentrated in the city, and its people earn three times as much per head as their compatriots in the rest of the country. As well as being the richest city, it is also the most Westernised. It has high-rise housing, modern restaurants, karaoke bars and even those twin banes of big-city living – traffic pollution and a drugs problem.

**School's out** *Students head for home, on bicycles and mopeds.*

# The faded splendour of Hué

*The emperors of Vietnam gave Hué all that befitted an imperial capital, but when it came to 19th-century power politics, they were no match for the French, who became the real rulers of the country. Today, crumbling colonial villas add their charm to the pomp of Hué's imperial past.*

Hué has a sleepy air, with its palaces and pagodas, terraces and temples, stretching along the banks of the Perfume River, so called because of the medicinal and aromatic shrubs that grow along its banks. Sampans and other small boats ply their trade through the morning mists of the river, as they have done for centuries. The pace of the ancient capital, now a city of 350 000 inhabitants, is unhurried. It has escaped rapid industrialisation and the unchecked construction boom that normally comes with it, but it did not escape devastation during the Vietnam War. In the 1968 Tet (New Year) offensive, the communist Vietcong stormed the imperial citadel and held out for 24 days against furious counterattacks by American troops. Many of the buildings destroyed in the fighting have since been rebuilt by the Vietnamese government, with the help of UNESCO and of private donors.

**On the Perfume River**  *Sampans – highly manoeuvrable flat-bottomed boats – on the Song Huong, the Perfume River, in a scene that has hardly changed since the days of French colonial rule.*

## A Chinese citadel with French defences

Hué, which means harmony, became the seat of the powerful Nguyen family at the end of the 16th century. In 1802, after Nguyen Anh defeated his rivals to become the first ruler of north and south Vietnam, it became the nation's capital. The new emperor, taking the title Gia Long, owed a debt to the French, for he had called in the aid of French mercenaries to win the throne. It was not Gia Long, but his heirs who were to pay that debt. Later emperors persecuted French missionaries and their Vietnamese converts, and Napoleon III seized upon the outrages to send a punitive expedition to Vietnam in 1858. So began a conquest that was to bring all of Indochina – Vietnam, Laos and Cambodia – under French colonial rule, and to leave the emperors as figureheads rather than rulers.

### Protection from on high

Hué was laid out according to the precise dictates of the Chinese art of geomancy, or feng shui, the selection of sites so that benign influences will be brought into play, and bad influences deflected. Practitioners of feng shui believe that high places, whether man-made or natural features, attract well-meaning spirits, so hills and pagodas are sources of protection. The heights of Thien Mu (Celestial Lady), crowned by a seven-tiered pagoda built in 1601, are especially auspicious. So, too, is the Hill of the Royal Screen, which acts as a barrier against negative winds.

**Two different worlds**  *The tomb of Emperor Khai Dinh, finished in 1931, combines European and Asian styles.*

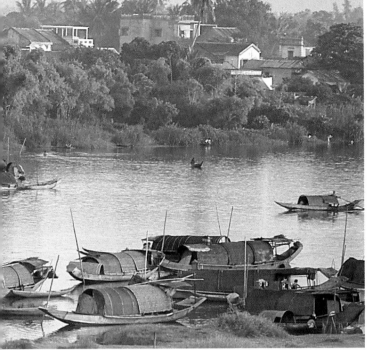

Everything about the Nguyen court was designed to inspire awe. In the Palace of Supreme Peace, the emperors sat on a golden throne to conduct ceremonies and receive the homage of high officials and foreign delegations.

## Tombs of the emperors

Near Hué, in the valley of the Perfume River, lie the tombs of the Nguyen emperors. Stone elephants, mandarins and soldiers stand on eternal watch over courtyards, terraces, pavilions, sepulchres and steles – upright slabs on which the achievements and virtues of the emperors are chiselled. The actual burial sites are reverently hidden behind high walls and heavy brass doors. As in life, so in death: the Nguyen emperors set out to impress. It took the work of nearly 3000 men to build the tomb of the fourth emperor, Tu Duc. The tomb of the 12th emperor, Khai Dinh, mixed Ming architecture with a heavy-handed attempt at the European rococo style.

The last emperor of Vietnam, Bao Dai, who was educated in France, turned out to be a playboy. He abdicated in 1945, and died in France in 1997. His admiration for French culture did not prevent him from having a tomb made for himself at Hué.

To make his capital impregnable against the weaponry of the day, Gia Long employed a French officer to build fortifications modelled on those of Sebastien de Vauban, the military engineer who became a legend in Europe because of the fortresses he built for Louis XIV. Escarpments, bastions and parapets added defensive strength to a massive wall 7 miles (11 km) long and 26 ft (8 m) high, surrounded by a moat and enclosing the royal citadel. Inside, set among gardens and lotus pools, were sumptuous temples, libraries and shrines, inspired by the architectural style of Imperial China's Ming dynasty (1633-1707). The Imperial City, enclosed within the citadel, housed mandarins, scholars, eunuchs and concubines, but the Purple Forbidden City, modelled on that in Beijing, and protected by yet another wall, was reserved for the emperor, his wives and children.

*Many hands make a masterwork* Tomb of the 19th-century emperor Tu Duc, which took the labour of nearly 3000 men.

*The guardian* Statue at the tomb of Khai Dinh.

*Instant art* Visitors take brass rubbings from one of nine massive urns that stand in front of the Pavilion of Splendour in the imperial city, Hué.

*Gateway to the Imperial City* One of four ornate and imposing entrances.

# Kuala Lumpur, California in Asia

*Kuala Lumpur was not even a name 150 years ago – it was a waterlogged stretch of tropical Malayan jungle, in a place where two rivers meet. Today, it is a capital city of 1.5 million people, with its feet set firmly in the present and its sights fixed on the future. In many ways it seems more Californian than Asian: just as Los Angeles is 'LA' to Angelinos, so to those who live there, or even to businessmen who pay a visit, Kuala Lumpur has become 'KL'.*

Toyota cars and Yamaha motorbikes choke every crossroads. Market stalls crammed with hi-fi equipment, or with bogus Rolex watches, spill across the pavements. Gaudy neon signs advertise the delights of cool drinks or of hot nightclubs. Kuala Lumpur today is a multi-highwayed city of skyscrapers, mosques and office blocks; a major centre of government, finance, trade and entertainment. But it has not always been like this.

### A city founded on tin

Around the middle of the 19th century, the Sultan of Selangor sent his brother and his nephew to find new deposits of tin, a mineral long exploited in the Malay Peninsula. Out of nearly 100 miners who set out on the journey from the royal city of Kelang, only 18 survived. The others were carried off by malaria or taken by crocodiles. But at Ampang, where the Kelang and Gombak rivers meet, they discovered a fabulous vein of tin. Two Chinese among the prospectors made small fortunes by setting up a trading post, naming the site Kuala Lumpur, 'Muddy Junction'. With an ever-growing world demand for tin, the settlement became a boom

***The blue pearl*** *The rich colours of Pinang, 'Pearl of the Orient'.*

town, with no law except that of the knife, the machete, the fist and the gun. Chinese and Malay miners fought over mining claims, gambling debts and water rights. In one such battle, in 1878, much of the settlement was burned to the ground. A strong arm leader named Yap Ah Loy, alias 'Captain China', imposed his own order. A British representative arrived in 1880, imported Chinese and Indian labour and, alongside Yap Ah Loy, laid the foundations of a modern city. In 1896, when the Federation of Malaya was formed, Kuala Lumpur was made its capital, a status that was retained when Malaya won its independence from British rule in 1957.

### Western Malaysia

## Pinang, the perfumed island

The idyllic island of Pinang, off the west coast of Malaysia, swamps the senses with its sights, sounds and scents. Bathed in the heat of the tropics, it is a land of herbs and spices, where incense smoke drifts from Chinese temples. To wander around the market stalls of George Town, the capital, is to breathe in an unforgettable array of aromas and perfumes. The island was home to a handful of fishermen and a refuge for pirates when, in 1786, Captain Francis Light claimed it for the British East India Company. He beat off an attempt by the Sultan of Kedah to win it back and founded the capital George Town in honour of King George III. The English used it as a staging post for the illicit opium trade with China and as a base for smuggling pepper and tin out of Dutch territories on the mainland. Pinang became a place of commercial and strategic importance, a rival to the Dutch settlement of Malacca farther south. Workers were attracted from all over the region – Indonesians, Malays, Indians, Arabs and Chinese. This explains Pinang's many little temples, dedicated to Vishnu, Shiva, Buddha or Confucius.

***Where Buddhas gather*** Kek Lok Si temple, Pinang, contains the images of 10 000 Buddhas.

***Palace of justice*** *The palace of Sultan Abdul Samad, with its copper domes and pink-shaded brickwork, is the seat of Malaysia's Supreme Court.*

At the dawn of the 21st century, despite South-east Asia's economic crisis, Kuala Lumpur has continued its expansion. Industrial suburbs have proliferated around new factories, built for the production of textiles, machinery and electronic goods. Big banks and international hotel groups have established their presence in new commercial centres such as Weld, the Putra World Center, and the Ampang Complex. The United Malays National Organisation (UMNO) has built an ultramodern party headquarters in the capital. But another consequence of progress has been the growth of slums and shantytowns.

***A night to remember*** *Broad smiles as citizens celebrate Merdeka ('Freedom') Day, August 31, the anniversary of Malaysia's independence.*

## History in stone

Much of Kuala Lumpur's brief history is written in its architecture. Before the business-driven expansion that began in the 1970s, the prevailing styles were English colonial and Indian 'mogul'. The colonial villas of smart suburbs such as Damansara and Bangsar Heights are straight out of a Somerset Maugham short story. The Royal Selangor Club in Merdeka ('Freedom') Square is a rich slice of Edwardian England, transported to the Far East in all its half-timbered mock Tudor splendour so that planters, army officers and colonial civil servants could relax in familiar surroundings after a game of polo, rugby or cricket. The former residence of the British governor, which is now a luxury hotel, is dwarfed by the vertiginous architecture around it. The Twin Towers of Petronas – which at 1483 ft (452 m) are among the tallest buildings in the world – are the headquarters of a giant oil-exporting company. The most spectacular example of the 'mogul' style is the railway station, a mosque-like fantasy with white minarets and towers, built by a British architect in 1911.

But the heart of Kuala Lumpur lies in its Chinatown, which has a bustling night market, the Pasar Malam, and in its Little India. Bearded and turbanned Sikhs, Indian women in saris and elegant Chinese in silk cheongsams mingle with Malays wearing Islamic caps, and medicine men selling traditional remedies. Pastry shops with fronts of coloured stucco nestle close to the painted gods that adorn the Hindu temple of Sri Maha Mariamann. Not far away from the Great Mosque is the Chinese temple of See Yeoh, with huge incense burners in its courtyard. It was built with money provided by Captain China, in the days when KL was still a rumbustious mining town.

***Built to last*** *The Petronas twin towers are built to withstand earthquakes and typhoons: the foundations go down 390 ft (120 m).*

CHAPTER 5

# CITIES OF THE ANCIENT GODS

In 1860, French naturalist Henri Mouhout sighted the pinnacles of the lost city of Angkor Thom rising above the rain-forest canopy. He had stumbled upon the capital of the ancient Khmer Empire, left to its fate 500 years earlier after repeated invasions by Mongols from the north and Thais from the west. Its towers, sculptures and terraces were to yield their secrets to scholars in the decades that followed. On a bend of the River Irrawaddy, in Myanmar, stand the remains of 5000 Buddhist temples, built during the golden age of ancient Burma. Borobudur, in central Java, is the site of one of the world's greatest Buddhist relics. It is rivalled in beauty and in its aesthetic impact by Ayuthaya, the royal capital of Siam until it was laid waste by the Burmese in 1767.

*One of 172 gigantic stone heads adorning the temple of Bayon, Angkor Thom.*

# Marvels and mysteries of Angkor

*When the French naturalist Henri Mouhout stumbled across the 'lost' temples of Angkor Wat, deep in the Cambodian rain forest, the forest people told him that they had been built by giants. And so, in a way, they had.*

The temples of Angkor, a gigantic achievement of the human imagination, have been described as the eighth wonder of the world. These towering monuments to the glory of the Hindu gods, to the Buddha and to the god-kings of ancient Cambodia, were abandoned by their kings and priests in the 15th century and left to the encroaching tendrils of the rain forest.

The power of Cambodia's Khmer Empire, founded at the end of the 9th century by Jayavarman II, was based on the labour of thousands of peasants and on the fertility of rice fields, watered by an elaborate irrigation system that took advantage of the annual flooding of the Tonlé Sap, the Great Lake. The empire lasted for more than six centuries, stretching at its height from Burma deep into Vietnam, and was ruled by a dynasty of god-kings. It left two colossal monuments: Angkor Wat and Angkor Thom.

## A masterpiece in sandstone

King Suryavarman II (ruled 1131-50) used the immense reserves of wealth, manpower and craftsmanship at his command to build the temple complex of Angkor Wat, a stepped pyramid with five ornate towers, surrounded by a rectangular

*City centre   The temple of Bayon, in the exact centre of Angkor Thom, was built to honour the Buddha.*

moat. This masterpiece of construction in pink-tinged sandstone is dedicated to the Hindu god Shiva, with whom Suryavarman identified himself. It contains half a mile (800 m) of bas-relief sculptures, illustrating tales from the Indian epics the *Mahabharata* and the *Ramayana*. They depict battles between gods and demons, the punishment of the damned, and the churning of the sea of milk in search of the elixir of eternal life. Voluptuously curved *apsaras*, the sacred dancers, are frozen for ever in stone. There are also scenes of everyday life, of hunting, feasting, fortune-telling and peasants working in the fields.

The other master builder at Angkor was Jayavarman VII (ruled 1181-*c*.1200), a devout

### The novelist who fell into temptation

As a young man, the novelist André Malraux (1901-76) was so spellbound by stories of the splendours of Angkor that he wanted to see them for himself. He had heard of some exceptionally well-preserved statues in the tower shrines of Banteay Srei, just outside Angkor, and with the confidence of a 22-year-old, he assumed they were his for the taking. He had a number of bas-reliefs cut away, but when he tried to get them out of the country, he was arrested for theft and spent a brief time in prison. He was never allowed back into Cambodia, despite his later eminence as a writer and, from 1959 to 1969, as Minister of Culture in De Gaulle's Fifth Republic.

**'Temple of Women'** Bas-relief at Banteay Srei (left).

**A work of giants** Locals believed that Angkor Wat (below) was built by giants, and that the architect was inspired by the byres where the gods kept their cattle.

Buddhist. He built a new capital at Angkor Thom, placing the 'temple mountain' of Bayon at its centre. The city walls enclosed some 75 sq miles (190 km²), but it was not a city for the people, and its temples were not thronged with worshippers: it was built exclusively for the god-kings, their servants and their priestly retinues.

### The last days of Angkor

A succession of wars with Chams, Thais and Mongols sapped the power of Angkor, and three times it fell to Thai invasions. The last collapse, in 1431, was the final blow. The complex irrigation works, on which everything depended, were destroyed and rapidly became silted up. The Khmer sovereigns abandoned Angkor as their capital and within a few decades the rain forest had claimed back its own. But its existence was never totally forgotten, and the 'lost' temples were rediscovered by French naturalist Henri Mouhout in 1860, almost by chance, as he marched along a path in the rain forest. The publication of his notes and sketches caused a sensation in Europe and many

archaeologists, particularly from France, devoted their lives to deciphering the records in the ruins and unveiling the splendours of the Khmer civilisation.

**Nature strikes back** A banyan tree, sacred to both Hindus and Buddhists, wraps a temple doorway at Angkor in the smothering embrace of its roots.

### The battle to save Angkor

Many of the *apsaras*, the sacred dancers carved on the temples of Angkor Wat, are headless. Plundering, both by professionals and tourists, has been added in modern times to the destruction and dilapidation brought about by war and centuries of neglect. Heads, limbs and even entire statues from Angkor have appeared in antiques shops, museums and auction houses worldwide. A special police force now keeps watch on the site, and the International Council of Museums issues regular lists of items stolen from Angkor. Preservation work has been carried out since 1991, when UNESCO launched an international campaign to save Angkor, on the basis of a plan drawn up by a Japanese art historian.

**Sacred relic** *The Shezigon pagoda houses a replica of the Buddha's tooth.*

# Pagan, cradle of the Burmese nation

*On a bend in the middle reaches of the River Irrawaddy lies the ancient Burmese capital of Pagan. Entrancingly beautiful Buddhist temples and shrines stretch along the valley as far as the eye can see.*

In the 9th century the Burmese, a Himalayan people migrating in search of fertile land, shouldered aside the Pyus and Mons of the Irrawaddy valley and founded a fortress-capital at Pagan. It grew in wealth and strength, but its days of glory were not to begin until the reign of King Anoratha (1044-77). He proclaimed Theravada Buddhism to be the state religion and started a programme of temple-building. In this he was aided by his capture, in 1057, of the Mon capital, Thaton. Among the spoils of victory were craftsmen, artists and 30 elephant loads of sacred writings – all put to use at Pagan. Anoratha was killed by a wild buffalo in 1077, and none of his successors had his drive and energy. But they carried on temple-building, each attempting to leave a legacy that would outshine those of their ancestors.

Burmese architecture, strongly influenced by the styles of Ceylon and Indonesia, passed through a period of dazzling achievement. At Pagan there are more than 5000 Buddhist temples and stupas (dome-shaped shrines), each a jewel in its own right, serenely watched over by huge statues of the Buddha. Many were left in ruins when Kublai Khan's Mongols sacked Pagan in 1287. Nearly seven centuries later, in 1975, the city faced an ordeal almost as terrifying – a major earthquake. But dedicated local craftsmen, with the help of UNESCO and of the French School of the Far East, have done much to repair and restore these unique monuments.

**Life on the walls** *Frescoes in the Ananda Ok Kyaung monastery depict myths and scenes of daily life.*

**Living history** *Despite the ravages of man and nature – it was sacked by the Mongols and badly damaged in modern times by an earthquake – Pagan has been restored so that it has the same air of serenity today as it had 1000 years ago.*

# Borobudur: a Buddhist sermon in stone

*In the heart of Java rises Borobudur, one of the world's greatest religious monuments. This jewel of Indo-Javanese architecture, lying among rice fields and surrounded by volcanoes, is a three-dimensional representation of the Buddhist faith.*

***On the Pilgrim's Way*** *One of nearly 1500 bas-reliefs lining the Pilgrim's Way at Borobudur.*

The stupa-crowned pyramid of Borobudur, in the plain of Kedu in central Java, is an allegory of the Buddhist religion. It was built under the Sailendra and Mataram kings between the 8th century and the middle of the 9th century, on the plan of a mandala, the sacred wheel that symbolises the universe and the cycle of birth, death and reincarnation. At the same time, it represents the journey of the human soul, seeking release from the selfish cares, passions and sorrows of life in its search for the state of enlightenment known as nirvana. By the end of the 10th century, power had shifted from inland Java to the trading empires of the east coast, and Borobudur was abandoned. Buddhism itself was to be deposed in Java by the tide of Islam that submerged most of the islands of Indonesia. For centuries, the massive and venerable stones of Borobudur lay more than half-forgotten, shrouded beneath a layer of volcanic ash.

## Three levels of existence

Their glory was uncovered in 1814 by the Englishman Sir Stamford Raffles. The pyramid-temple of Borobudur is a description in stone of the teachings and cosmology of Buddhism. Three levels of existence are depicted in nearly 1500 bas-reliefs along the 3 mile (5 km) Pilgrim's Way that spirals round its terraces. The carvings at the base represent the human world of passions and desires. The middle level tells of episodes in the life of the Buddha during his various incarnations. The third level depicts the world of total abstraction, and the domed stupa, crowning the whole, contains a statue of the Buddha experiencing nirvana. The monument has suffered subsidence, because the hill on which it was built has become waterlogged, but a massive aid programme was undertaken in the 1970s and 1980s.

### Sir Stamford Raffles, the rescuer of Borobudur

During the centuries after it was abandoned as the royal capital, Borobudur lay neglected beneath a layer of volcanic ash – a Buddhist relic in a Muslim country. It was not until 1814 that it was rediscovered by Sir Stamford Raffles, then governor of Java, who had the site cleared, revealing its full majesty.

***Age of reason*** *The Buddha in front of the central stupa, in the pose of reason.*

# Ayuthaya: Venice of the East

*The ancient capital of Siam, surrounded by rivers and crossed by canals, was for five centuries the centre of an empire that extended into Burma, Laos and Cambodia. In 1767 Ayuthaya was destroyed by the Burmese, but it still has reminders of an opulent past.*

*City of temples  Monks at Ayuthaya, a city that once had 400 Buddhist temples.*

The story of Ayuthaya begins and ends in war. It began as a Khmer stronghold, built on an artificial island at the meeting point of three rivers some 50 miles (80 km) north of present-day Bangkok; but although well fortified, it was captured by the Thais. Rama Tibodi, the prince of U Thong, made it the capital of Siam in 1350 and became the first of a dynasty of 33 kings. Incessant wars pushed the frontiers of their empire well into present-day Laos, Cambodia and Myanmar, but the enemies of Siam had their successes, too. Ayuthaya's days of glory came to an end in 1767 when it was captured and sacked by a Burmese army.

*Sleeping survivor  A Buddha that escaped the sacking of Ayuthaya.*

### The guardian Buddhas
Before it was pillaged, Ayuthaya contained more than 2000 statues of the Buddha. Today, the greatest Buddha statue in Thailand, cast by bronze-workers in the 15th century, sits on its throne among the ruins of the city. One of the best-preserved buildings is the 14th-century royal Wat of Phra Sri Samphet, whose 52 ft (16 m) Buddha was melted down for its gold by the Burmese invaders. Surviving mosaics on the walls of Wat Ratburana present Buddhas seated on royal thrones, in a kaleidoscope of colours with highlights picked out in gold.

Portuguese missionaries and traders arrived in Ayuthaya early in the 16th century, and were followed by Dutch, British, French, Chinese and Japanese merchants. Trade brought prosperity, and people from other parts of Siam thronged to the capital. By the 17th century it had a population of 1 million, including an important European community.

### An ambassador to the Sun King

In 1685, Louis XIV, the 'Sun King' of France, and the most powerful monarch in Europe, sent a delegation to Siam to establish trade relations and to attempt to convert the subjects of King Phra Narai to Christianity. A member of the delegation, the Abbé François Timoleon de Choisy, was noted not only for a habit of dressing himself up as a woman, but also for his lively curiosity about the world around him. He was a keen observer of life  at the court and in the countryside. His *Journal of a Journey through Siam* describes everything in the most minute detail. It was an immediate success on publication, and became the most celebrated French travel book of the 17th century.

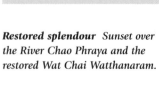

*Restored splendour  Sunset over the River Chao Phraya and the restored Wat Chai Watthanaram.*

# The temples of Vietnam: the heart and soul of the nation

*Vietnam paid a heavy price, both in human lives and in the destruction of ancient buildings, in its 20th-century wars for independence and reunification. But throughout the land, in villages, small towns and big cities, there are still hundreds of temples, restored or ancient, dedicated to saints and sages, to gods, guardian spirits, and heroes and heroines who have become gods. These sacred places are the heart and soul of the nation.*

Everywhere in Vietnam there are gods, ancestors and guardian spirits watching over the welfare of the people. The villages of the rice-growing areas are under the protection of spirits that inhabit the *dinh* – communal houses raised on stilts. Villagers gather at the *dinh* to celebrate their moments of joy and to seek solace in times of grief. The *dinh* also fills the role of council offices and administrative centre for village business. In the *dinh* of the 16th and 17th centuries, wooden carvings portray festivals and show people working in the fields, as well as gods and saints.

### Homage to heroines, and to scholars

Chinese culture put down deep roots during the Middle Kingdom's 1000 year occupation of northern Vietnam, leaving scores of Confucian and Taoist temples – the *den* and the *quan*. The Temple of Literature in Hanoi, dedicated to Confucius and the home of Vietnam's earliest university, contains 82 steles borne by stone tortoises, to commemorate scholars who were successful in the state examinations for the higher civil service in the years 1442-1779. Apart from being used for ceremonies, the temple is a centre for exhibitions of calligraphy, poetry readings, music and dance. The Den Hai Ba Trung, also in Hanoi, commemorates the Trung sisters, who led a rebellion against the Chinese occupiers in around AD 40 and, when defeated, drowned themselves in the Red River.

Another kind of temple, the Buddhist *chua*, is what in the West would be called a pagoda. In origin it is a reliquary, a shrine that holds religious relics: the word pagoda comes from the Chinese *baigu ta*, which means 'tower of whitened bones'. Hanoi's much-

**The sage in the temple**  *Confucius sits serenely in the Temple of Literature.*

restored One Pillar Pagoda was, according to legend, raised on its single column by the 11th-century King Ly Tai Tong in gratitude to the goddess Quan Am for the birth of a male heir. Buddhists revere all forms of life, and this shows in their pagodas. The Chua Co, the 'Stork Pagoda', near Tra Vinh in the Mekong delta, shelters hundreds of storks, while the gardens of the Chua Doi, the 'Bat Pagoda' at Soc Trang in the southern tip of the country, are home to thousands of fruit bats.

**Faiths for all seasons**  *The Vietnamese will pray to Buddha over matters concerning the afterlife, but take their everyday worries to other temples.*

**The Perfume Pagoda**  *Festival time at Chua Hong, the Perfume Pagoda, set among hills in the Red River delta.*

CHAPTER 6

# CULTURE: THE PAST, PRESENT AND FUTURE

The arts, crafts, customs and festivals of South-east Asia owe much to China and India. Individual countries have added their own flavours: in the field of music, for example, these range from the gamelan orchestras of Java and Bali, with their gongs, drums and bamboo xylophones, to the one-stringed lute of Vietnam, the *dan bao*, which produces a plaintive sound curiously like the human voice. The contributions of Islam and of the West were grafted on to societies whose cultural identities had been established for centuries. Craftsmanship began in the days when rulers could call on the entire resources of their nations: they saw it as their duty to bring glory to their dynasties by creating luxurious courts and beautifying palaces and temples.

The delicacy of a contemporary screen, inlaid with mother-of-pearl, or the deep lustre of today's lacquerwork, are proof that the old skills have not vanished.

*A sumptuously decorated royal barge carries a statue of the Buddha onto Lake Inle, Myanmar.*

# Something to celebrate, all year round

*South-east Asia contains an extraordinary diversity of religions, ethnic groups, nationalities and traditions. It is hardly surprising that not a month – indeed, hardly a week – goes by without a colourful festival being held somewhere in the region.*

**Free at last!** *A young Thai liberates a bird from its cage during the festival of Makha Bucha.*

Peasant societies have always looked to the gods for protection against the forces of Nature and the unforeseeable catastrophes of life – a failed harvest, a serious illness, barrenness, floods or storms. And in South-east Asia, even city dwellers are only a few generations at the most removed from the land. This explains why so many festivals are designed to placate the gods and to frighten off evil spirits. Apart from nationwide festivals, every village has its folk festivals, and every temple and pagoda its anniversaries to celebrate. Then there are the national days and royal anniversaries. In socialist countries, such as Laos and Vietnam, May 1 is International Workers' Day, when high-ranking party officials and bemedalled army officers review parades of marching soldiers and military hardware.

## Celebrating the New Year

Wherever there is a sizable Chinese community, or where the Chinese cultural influence has been strong, the liveliest festival of the year is the one to welcome the New Year. It falls between January 21 and February 19, for like most of the ancient festivals it is based on the lunar calendar, in which a month starts with the new moon and lasts for approximately 29$\frac{1}{2}$ days. In Vietnam, where the festival is known as Tet, the entire country seems to be on the move, with hordes of people travelling to visit their families and friends. Hotel rooms and seats on trains, planes and buses have to be booked well in advance.

The spirit world is on the move, too: Tao Quan, the god of the

hearth, goes up to heaven to present to the Jade Emperor his report on how the household has behaved in the past year. If they have settled all their debts and paid the proper homage to the ashes of their ancestors, a good report will follow. Great precautions are taken to fend off evil spirits. The Vietnamese decorate their homes with branches of peach or apricot blossom and erect bamboo poles outside, with clay tablets and yellow cloth on top. Make-believe dragons dance through the streets, scaring away demons. Until a few years ago, fireworks were let off, with the same objective, but following a series of tragic accidents, real fireworks were banned, so most Vietnamese make do nowadays with tape recordings of their noise.

**Procession on water** *A golden water bird, aboard a raft at a Buddhist festival on Lake Inle, Myanmar.*

*Messages of love  Thai girls launch boat-borne wishes during the Festival of Lights.*

## Honouring royalty in Thailand

In Thailand, everything that touches on the royal family has a sacred character. Chakri Day, April 6, is a public holiday in honour of King Rama I, who founded the ruling Chakri dynasty in 1782. The building housing the royal tombs is opened so that homage can be paid to dead kings. The present king, Bhumibol Adulyadej, was crowned on May 5, 1946, another national holiday. At the start of the rice-planting season (mid May to mid June) thousands gather in Bangkok to watch the king turn the first furrow in the Royal Ploughing Ceremony. The queen's birthday on August 5 and the king's birthday on December 5 are both public holidays.

On the first day of the New Year, families welcome back the spirits of their ancestors, burning incense and sandalwood on household altars and offering the spirits rice cakes stuffed with pork and other fillings. This is also the day for visiting relations, for feasting and exchanging presents. In a custom that is remarkably similar to the first-footing tradition of Scotland and northern England, on the other side of the world, the first visitor to cross the threshold in the New Year will bring a year's good luck – provided that he is of good character. The second day of Tet is for young lovers. Youths and girls stand on the shores of a lake and make a wish that the person of their dreams will appear.

In South-east Asia today, as in the West, many families see in the New Year by watching television. Following the Chinese custom, each year is placed under the patronage of one of a dozen animals – rat, ox, tiger, hare, dragon, snake, horse, goat, monkey, rooster, dog or pig – and takes on some of their characteristics. So 2001 was the year of the dragon, 2002 the year of the snake, 2003 the year of the horse, and so on.

In Burma, Laos, Cambodia and Thailand, all of them Buddhist countries, the New Year starts in mid April, in the middle of the hot season. The celebrations are based on water and everybody gets soaked. Images of the Buddha in the temples are reverently sprinkled with perfumed water, but outside the rejoicing is more boisterous. Laughing children throw buckets of water over parents, friends, neighbours and passers-by. On the second day of the three-day festival, the grown-ups join in the gigantic water fight, using hoses, water trucks, and anything they can commandeer. Dancing, banqueting and processions of elephants add to the general fun. Working life, apart from what is necessary to keep planes, buses, trains, hospitals and so on running, comes to a complete standstill. During the years when the Khmer Rouge were trying to create a new social order, such festivals were banned in Cambodia because they were regarded as frivolous, and were associated with religion and the monarchy.

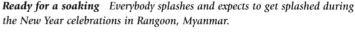

*Ready for a soaking  Everybody splashes and expects to get splashed during the New Year celebrations in Rangoon, Myanmar.*

## Songbirds and candles

In Laos and Thailand the festival of Makha Bucha, in February, commemorates a sermon preached by the Buddha. Dense throngs pack into the temples to offer gifts of fresh fruit and lotus flowers, and to rub gold or silver leaf onto the statues. One charming tradition of Makha Bucha is the freeing of songbirds from their cages. Bystanders will pay a few baht to have a bird released, and even if it is captured again by young boys, it has a good chance of being freed yet again by some soul seeking merit.

In Myanmar and the neighbouring Buddhist countries, November sees the Festival of Lights, a celebration that dates back to before the arrival of Buddhism. The Thais make little boats of wood or bamboo and launch them with lighted candles aboard, with a prayer that the fragile craft will carry away bad deeds and thoughts, and convey their feelings to the one they love.

## Fasting and penance

Malaysia and Singapore, because of their rich ethnic mix, have an unusually high number of festivals. At the end of the ninth month of the Muslim year, the Muslims celebrate the end of Ramadan, the month-long fast during which neither food nor water is allowed between sunrise and sunset. The three days of Hari Raya Puasa are given over to feasting and to visiting friends, with gifts of new clothes.

**Proud day** A Laotian girl takes part in a Buddhist procession in Luang Prabang.

**Ship of fortune** Jubilant Cambodians launch a toy boat, laden with gifts of food, incense and money, in the hope that the spirits in return will grant them good luck, happiness and wealth.

***The sacred way*** *Devout Hindus in procession to Pura Besakih, the most holy temple in Bali, on the slopes of Mount Agung, the sacred volcano.*

The following month brings Lailatul Qadar, the 'Night of Greatness', commemorating the revelation of the Koran to Muhammad. Devout Muslims spend all night praying in the mosque, and village houses are decorated with rows of illuminated lamps.

In late January or early February, Malaysians of Indian origin celebrate Thaipusam in honour of Subramaniam, the son of Shiva, the destroyer. Penitents file into the streets with a *kavadi*, a framework holding flowers and fruit, attached to their bodies by hooks. Having prepared for the ordeal by observing a strictly vegetarian regime, they pierce their throats, cheeks and breasts with spears, swords and hooks. Some go so far as to nail the heavy *kavadi* to their tongues. In October or November, during the festival of Diwali, some devout Hindus celebrate the triumph of light over darkness by walking over glowing coals.

## Volunteers for crucifixion

Christian festivals, too, can involve the willing acceptance of what looks to outsiders very much like pain. Flagellants walk through the streets of Manila during Holy Week, scourging themselves with whips until the blood flows. In some parts of the Philippines, men volunteer to be crucified for a few minutes. Their wounds, treated with a preparation that contains holy water and oils, soon heal. Vietnam and Laos have added the celebration of more recent political and military events to their festivals. Both countries mark May 1, International Workers' Day, and on May 7 the Vietnamese commemorate their 1954 victory over the French at Dien Bien Phu.

***Peach trees for protection*** *Army officers select peach blossom in Hanoi flower market. During the New Year celebrations it will deflect evil spirits from their barracks.*

***'Romans' in the Philippines***
*Children dressed as centurions and Roman soldiers march around the towns and villages of Luzon, in the Philippines, during the Moriones festival of Holy Week.*

123

# Classical drama, shadow plays and a touch of slapstick

*Despite the popularity of movies, television and videos, the traditional theatre still exerts a powerful fascination on audiences in South-east Asia. What began as an offshoot of religion, and as a form of entertainment and instruction for kings and their courts, developed into a robust theatre of the people. Adaptability and variety are the secrets behind the lasting success of traditional theatre: it ranges from the most rigid classical drama to slapstick and social satire.*

Every gesture, every expression, every eye movement in the classical theatre of South-east Asia conveys a precise message to the audience. It might be an emotion, such as anger, fear or sexual attraction; it might be an insight into the character on stage – that he or she is honest, cowardly, heroic or cruel. Costumes and make-up signify a character's social status or profession – king, princess, general, high official, magistrate or clown. The region's drama is ruled by conventions that date back for centuries, and the skill of the actors lies in breathing life into those conventions.

Classical theatre began with performances outside temples, as a way of honouring and diverting the gods. Adapting sacred texts, such as the Hindu *Mahabharata* and *Ramayana*, it still presents gods and humans on stage through such epics as the Indonesian *wayang orang*. Other forms of theatre deal with less exalted themes. The Javanese *ketoprak* and *ludruk*, the Malayan *gadoi* and the Vietnamese *hat cheo* are anchored in everyday life and sometimes incorporate proverbs and popular sayings. In the *hat cheo*, musicians sit on the stage, and like pianists in the days of silent movies in the Western world, play music that fits the action or heightens a mood.

**Shadow theatre**  Wayang kulit puppets at Alor Setar, Malaysia.

**A master at work**  A wayang kulit *puppet-master in Malaysia projects his characters onto a blank screen, illuminated by an oil lamp.*

Songs, comedy, social satire and discreet political criticism accompany the drama. Clowns interrupt the action to harangue the players, and the audience can demand an 'action replay' of any scene they have especially enjoyed. The acting is stately and stylised – so much so that Westerners in the audience can find themselves nodding off. But they are soon woken up by the noise and bustle of the duels and the uncontrollable laughter that greets the clowns.

A theatrical performance can be staged in front of a pagoda as part of a religious festival, or it can add glamour to a wedding, a fair,

## Myths that fill the stage with spectacle

Two ancient Hindu epics provide the theatre of South-east Asia with a feast of plots, characters and spectacle. The *Mahabharata* tells of a great civil war between five Pandava princes and their usurping cousins, the Kauravas. On the eve of the final battle, the Pandava prince Arjuna is smitten with anguish at the sight of so many kinsmen in the ranks of his enemies, but is persuaded by the god Krishna to take up arms and defeat the Kauravas. The *Ramayana* tells of the wanderings of Prince Rama, who is cheated out of the throne and whose wife, Sita, is kidnapped by the demon king Rawana. With the help of the monkey god, Sugriwa, and the monkey general, Hanuman, Rama wins a great battle, rescues Sita and regains his throne.

or any other local event. The Burmese *zat pwe*, with an emphasis on slapstick comedy, can last all night. Another tradition in Myanmar is the *anyeint*, a kind of open-air entertainment that is performed in the streets, free of charge. The performers are hired by influential families who wish to mark a special occasion by putting on a public treat.

Palace intrigues, the limitations of human power, amorous conquests and the daring deeds of warriors follow one another on stage in the Vietnamese *hat tuong*. A modern style of theatre, influenced by the West, emerged in the 20th century: the Vietnamese *cai luong* and *kich noi*, and controversial productions by young Indonesian theatre groups, who lay themselves open to censorship.

### The magic of marionettes

Most of the countries of South-east Asia have a long tradition of puppet theatre, but it is under pressure in places because of the expense and because skilled puppeteers are increasingly hard to find: in Myanmar, the 4 ft (1 m) high marionettes used in *yok-thei pwe* can have as many as 60 strings, including one for each eyebrow. In Vietnam, the annual flooding of the Red River plain gave rise to a tradition of water puppets. It can take four people, standing in water up to their waists and using long bamboo poles, to control a single puppet. Puppet sizes and designs vary considerably. *Wayang klitik*, in east Java, uses flat wooden puppets, whereas the puppets of *wayang golek* in other parts of Indonesia are three-dimensional. The *hun krabok* of Thailand uses hand puppets, which are viewed from the waist up, as in a Punch and Judy show.

***Make-up with a meaning*** A wayang orang *actress concentrates on her make-up, to ensure it conveys exactly the message intended.*

The worlds of myth and of reality are represented by nothing more substantial than shadows in *wayang kulit*, a form of theatrical entertainment that began in Java and has been raised to the level of art. The puppets are made from buffalo hide, their outlines cut with a knife and details carved with a chisel. The puppet-master, the *dalang*, sits behind a blank screen, with a light source behind him and his puppets at hand – as many as 200 of them, with the good characters to the right and the evil ones to the left. The *dalang* is a man of at least 200 voices, for he has to bring to life a vast gallery of characters from fairy tales and Hindu epics. He also has to direct the gamelan orchestra as it interprets the action. Performances stretch from sunset until dawn the following morning. Simply introducing the characters takes until midnight. Then comes a phase when the bad characters seem to be winning. Then the *dalang* sends in the clowns. Eventually, the forces of evil are overthrown, and with dawn comes the victory of the hero. Children stretch and yawn on their mothers' laps, and rub their eyes into wakefulness. The show is over.

***An epic on stage*** *A scene from the* Ramayana, *performed in Java. It tells how Prince Rama regains his throne and frees his wife, who has been kidnapped by a demon.*

# Dancing for the gods

*Dancing began as a way of honouring the gods and enlisting their help to fight the forces of evil. It is still a sacred art, ruled by conventions in which every gesture carries a fixed meaning. But it has also become a way of expressing human dreams, desires, frustrations and triumphs.*

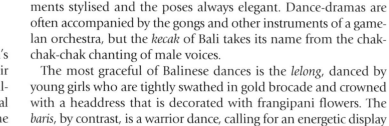

The traditional dance of South-east Asia is a language with a vocabulary, a grammar and a punctuation of its own. Every movement has a precise meaning, and no gesture is superfluous. In Burmese dancing there are 28 different eye movements alone, and 24 ways of moving one hand. An authority on classical Khmer dancing has listed 1165 principal stances, allotting a name to each, like words in a dictionary. But there are no training manuals and nothing is written down for learners. The teachers themselves are living dictionaries and the pupils copy their every move.

**Wicked witch** *Mask of the witch Rangda, who attacks a village in the* barong, *a Balinese dance.*

## Passion, revenge and heroism

To Western eyes, one of the most striking features of the region's traditional ballet is the astonishing flexibility of the dancers. Their gestures are the essence of grace and fluidity. The neck, the shoulders, the torso, the wrists, the very fingers of a Balinese or traditional Khmer dancer seem able to move independently of the rest of the body. This suppleness comes from starting in childhood – some of Bali's most renowned dancers are girls as young as eight.

The tales of passion, kidnapping, revenge, cruelty and heroism recounted in the dances are drawn from Hindu epics such as the *Mahabharata* and the *Ramayana*, and from folk stories or fairy tales. The choreography is often influenced by the ceremonial style of kings and courts. In central Java,

**Royal dance** *The* khon, *a Thai dance originally reserved for the royal court.*

**Moment of peril** *In the grip of a trance,* barong *dancers in Bali turn their swords on themselves.*

for instance, great stress is placed on stateliness and on keeping the emotions under control. The dancer's face is impassive, the movements stylised and the poses always elegant. Dance-dramas are often accompanied by the gongs and other instruments of a gamelan orchestra, but the *kecak* of Bali takes its name from the chak-chak-chak chanting of male voices.

The most graceful of Balinese dances is the *lelong*, danced by young girls who are tightly swathed in gold brocade and crowned with a headdress that is decorated with frangipani flowers. The *baris*, by contrast, is a warrior dance, calling for an energetic display of anger, pride and martial prowess.

Most of Bali's traditional dances evolved centuries ago, but a number were created as late as the 19th century, and the *kebyar duduk*, during which the dancer remains seated cross-legged on the stage, was developed as recently as the 1920s.

## Dance and trance

So-called 'trance dances', which began as rituals for driving evil spirits out of a village, are found throughout the region. In Bali, two girls, inducing themselves into a trance by swaying over incense

fumes, dance the *sanghyang dedari* with their eyes tight shut. In the *sanghhyang jaran*, a barefoot boy, also in a trance, rides a hobby-horse around and through a fire of coconut husks, sometimes stepping, without visible harm, on the live embers. In both dances, the trance is broken by a priest, who applies holy water. The *barong* and *rangda* is a kris (wavy-edged sword) dance. The *barong keket*, half dog, half lion, defends a village against the *rangda*, a witch whose staring eyes, fangs, viciously long nails and necklace of human entrails make her character and intentions plain. She puts the *barong*'s supporters into a trance in which they turn their weapons on themselves. The trance is real enough, for however fiercely the dancers try to stab themselves, only rarely is the skin broken. Good triumphs over evil in the end, and the dancers are brought out of their trances by being sprinkled with holy water in which the beard of the *barong* has been dipped.

During Cambodia's years of ordeal under the Khmer Rouge, the royal corps de ballet was persecuted. It had no place in the brutal new revolutionary society that was being created. But following the overthrow of the regime in 1978, traditional Khmer dancing has been revived. Westerners may find it difficult sometimes to follow the plot, but all agree that to experience a Khmer ballet is an enchantment – and especially compelling if it is staged against the grandeur of the temples of Angkor. The costumes are sumptuous, the battles between monkeys and demons exhilarating, and the music of xylophones, woodwind and gongs hypnotic.

### When spirits get loose

In some Burmese dances, a spirit called a *nat* is invited to take over the mind and body of a shaman. *Nats* are full of mischief, and they can sometimes cause consternation by entering a member of the audience instead. In remote villages of Vietnam, too, spirits can enter the performers. A dancer seized by the warlike spirit *hang quan* will take up a sword. Inhabited by a female spirit, he dances with a fan. If the spirit is that of a prince, he holds a bow or a whip.

**Back from the brink**   *The classical Khmer ballet suffered severely under the Khmer Rouge, but is now firmly re-established.*

**Sheer grace, with a meaning**   *A student at Phnom Penh's National School of Khmer Dancing takes up the pose 'Putting a Flower on the Pillow'.*

# Music with a message

*A Western ear, listening for the first time to the music of South-east Asia, has to accustom itself to unfamiliar instruments, melodies, rhythms and harmonic scales. An appreciation of music's role in the life of the region makes it easier to understand it.*

**Summoned by gongs**
*A legend says gongs were created to call the gods.*

With the exception of the Philippines, the countries of South-east Asia have drawn their musical traditions from the two cultural colossi of the Orient – China and India. The earliest music in the region would have been made with the materials at hand – bamboo and reeds. Formal music began in association with religious rituals and royal courts, and it always had a meaning. In 15th-century Vietnam, for instance, there were several different kinds of music, including music to commemorate dead emperors, another kind to honour the Chinese sage Confucius, and yet another to help the sun and moon to survive an eclipse. Away from the courts and the temples, the music of ordinary people developed a vigorous life of its own, through lullabies, work songs, folk songs and love songs; and today, especially in the cities, there is an eager market for Western pop music.

## Drums, gongs and stone xylophones

Many of the instruments used in South-east Asia have counterparts in the Western orchestra, though there are some striking differences. The xylophone, for instance, has keys of either bamboo or stone. There is an enormous variety of percussion instruments, for drums and gongs play a central role in setting the tempo and creating a musical mood. Some drums have double skins; others have the skin coated with rice paste and ash, allowing the drummer to muffle the sound. Male drums produce a deep, booming sound, while female drums are both larger and shriller. Many percussion instruments originated in India. They range in size from tiny kettledrums to the gigantic *rebarna besar* of Malaysia. There are flutes made of reed or bamboo, oboe-like woodwind instruments, 16-stringed zithers, 3-stringed violins and, especially among the hill tribes, instruments similar to the mouth organ.

Other instruments do not exist in the West. The *gangsa*, or metallophone, used in the gamelan orchestras of Java and Bali, consists of bronze bars mounted over resonating pipes of bamboo, and they are struck with a wooden mallet. The *dan bau* of Vietnam, with a single string stretched over a wooden resonating chamber, is uniquely suited to the music of that country. In the Vietnamese language, the same word can have six different meanings according to the tone in which it is pronounced, and the haunting notes of the *dan bau* can produce a sound that is astonishingly like the modulated tones of the female singing voice. For this reason it is a popular accompaniment to romantic songs and is used in films and in the theatre. Dance and drama have been inseparable

**Repeat performance** *Repetition is a key element in Burmese music (above).*

**The graceful harp** *The 13-stringed* saung, *or Burmese harp (right) is shaped like a boat.*

128

*Music to honour the dead* *Musicians at a funeral in Vietnam.*

clarinet, and the *gengong,* a kind of jew's harp. This ensemble creates a gently murmuring stream of music that sounds like the waters of a fountain splashing into a pool. Its music interprets the action and enhances the mood of classical dance-dramas and of shadow plays, in which puppets are projected onto a screen. Most villages in Java and Bali have their own gamelan orchestra, and complex though the music is, nothing is written down. Musicians absorb the sounds of the gamelan from birth and play by heart and instinct. This approach is said to be useful for mastering the emotions and inculcating habits of self-control. Two scales are used: the lively pentatonic (5-tone) scale and the more stately heptatonic (7-tone) scale. The Western chromatic scale, with semitones between the full tones, is unknown in South-east Asian music, which is one reason why it can sound strange to Western ears.

### The impact of the West

Malaya and Indonesia adopted some of the musical traditions of the Middle East, but the most dominant outside musical influence has been that of the West. Films, radio and television, stereos and compact discs and, more recently, the Internet, have all helped to spread Western fashions to the cities. Disco music is played in the nightclubs of Bangkok, and rock 'n' roll has lost none of its popularity since it was introduced by GIs to the bars, clubs and dance halls of Vietnam.

Indigenous music has an enduring vitality, too. Fishermen in Vietnam have their own songs, the *hat ba trao,* to placate the spirits of the sea. Wherever there are Buddhist temples there is musical chanting, sometimes accompanied by the beating of a drum.

from music since the earliest times, and in Myanmar, Malaysia, Indonesia and other countries powerfully influenced by Indian culture, the two great religious epics, the *Mahabharata* and the *Ramayana,* have inspired all three.

### Vibrations to the sound of the gamelan

According to an old Javanese legend, the god Sang Hyang Guru made the first gong to summon the other gods to his mountain home. He soon found that he needed a second gong, and then a third, and so on. In this way he created the first gamelan orchestra. Today, a gamelan has around 30 instruments: metallophones, bamboo xylophones, a series of drums, gongs and cymbals, stringed instruments such as the zither, bamboo flutes held like a

### King of the sax

King Bhumibol Adulyadej of Thailand, who came to the throne in 1946, is an outstanding musician – a saxophonist who played alongside such all-time jazz greats as Louis Armstrong, Benny Goodman and Lionel Hampton, sharing the adulation of jazz fans with them in the New York of the 1960s. In Thailand he was wildly popular as a player, and his music sold 350 000 CDs.

The classical music of the West has won a following in South-east Asia. Vietnamese pianist Dang Thai-Son has a worldwide reputation as an interpreter of Chopin, and has played with some of the world's greatest orchestras.

*Playing without a score*
*A gamelan orchestra in Bali.*
*Nothing is written down:*
*the musicians play by ear.*

129

# Craftsmen of genius

*South-east Asia's living tradition of superlative craftsmanship is one of the happiest legacies of the centuries when kings and courts ruled in splendour, and neither effort nor expense were spared to beautify palaces and temples.*

The industrial revolution came late to South-east Asia, and when it arrived it dovetailed neatly into a tradition of craftsmanship and a history of making the most of the materials at hand. In such areas as the back country of Cambodia, or the villages of Java, the houses are still made of wood and their roofs of interwoven leaves. The great construction plants of Singapore or Jakarta are full of surprises: in a forest of cranes, with bulldozers and heavy-duty trucks grinding about their business, the safety helmets of the workers are likely to be made of tightly woven reeds and the scaffolding is not steel, but bamboo. In fact, bamboo is much stronger than it looks, and it has the advantages of flexibility and ready availability. The drainage systems are made of bamboo, as are many household objects: partitions, screens, mats, bags, baskets and furniture. Straw hats keep both the sun and the rain at bay.

**The mat-makers**
*Traditional skills are still alive among the region's ethnic minorities.*
*Right: An Iban woman in Sarawak, Malaysia, plaits straw into a mat.*
*Below: Mat-making in Java, with dyed straw and reeds.*

## A life-or-death secret

Producing such articles calls for nothing more than a few tools and a little skill; other artefacts require long training and a perfect mastery of the materials, for example silk. The Romans esteemed this shimmering fabric, brought to them by caravans of merchants along the Silk Road from China. The Chinese guarded the method of its manufacture jealously and prohibited the export of silkworms on pain of death. But around 140 BC, according to legend, a Chinese princess risked her life to smuggle out the secret. In villages in Laos and Thailand, silk is still produced in the old way, without the help of machinery, and it is especially admired for the delicacy of its colours.

## The lustre of lacquer

Another craft that calls for skill and dedication is lacquering, used to decorate furniture, vases, screens, trays, dishes and a host of other objects in common use. Lacquer is a resinous gum, the sap of a sumach tree, which turns from grey to black or a beautiful reddish brown on contact with the air. It can be applied to almost any natural surface, from wood and metal to bamboo and porcelain, but the application is a lengthy process. It involves smoothing the surface, sealing it with raw lacquer, applying a base of ash mixed with lacquer, and then painting on up to 35 coats of lacquer, each taking at least a day to dry before it can be burnished with pumice, pine soot or the ash of deer antlers. Powdered gold or silver and various natural pigments are added to the final layers of lacquer to

give it lustre and colour. The decoration may be raised in relief, and it can either be ornamental, or show animals or scenes from the life of Buddha. The finished product is resistant to damp and heat.

## Incense and mother-of-pearl

The unmistakable, calming and sweetly smouldering smell of incense, burned to honour the gods and drive away demons, is all-pervading in homes and temples throughout South-east Asia.

**Sun-blockers** *The village of Bor Sang, in Thailand, is famous for its gaily coloured paper umbrellas.*

**Tribal history in cloth** *The brightly coloured cloth known as ikat, woven by women in the Indonesian islands of Sumba and Flores, depicts heroes and battles from a tribal past. Traditionally, it was used for sarongs and shawls.*

**In a lacquer workshop** *Two girls in Chiang Mai, northern Thailand, engaged in the painstaking work of mixing colours and applying lacquer.*

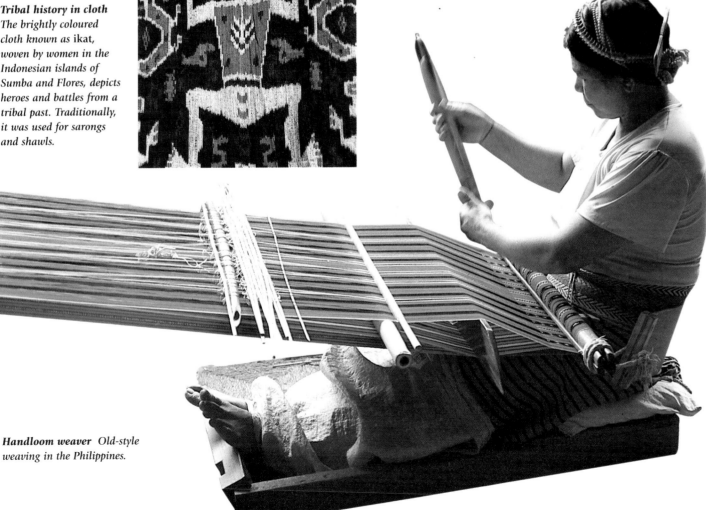

**Handloom weaver** *Old-style weaving in the Philippines.*

Incense sticks are made by craftsmen, many of whom are also candle-makers. The underlying aroma is created by resins, especially that of the spice bush known as the benjamin bush. Black incense is based on a paste of powdered charcoal and grains of resin, rolled onto thin sticks. Some incense sticks are covered with a fine, pleasant-smelling powder, held in place by a light spiral of paper.

The whole is perfumed with candied cinnamon and sugar cane, which adds a restful sweetness to the smouldering incense.

Encrusting objects with mother-of-pearl is another regional speciality, known for at least 2000 years. The craftsmen use several kinds of seashell, among them the freshwater mussel, which is cut into tiny pieces. They are cleaned, then pasted onto a paper pattern which carries the design that will be reproduced on wood. Then comes the delicate work of chiselling out from the wood a tiny

*Two arts in one*  Mother-of-pearl on a lacquer background (Vietnam).

piece that has the same shape and bulk as the fragment of mother-of-pearl that will replace it. The base material used is a hard rosewood called *trac* in Vietnam. Houses in Vietnam often contain furniture, plates, screens, boxes and other objects adorned in this way.

### Life is one long meal for a silkworm

The silkworm begins life as an egg, which hatches out as a caterpillar so tiny that it takes some 35 000 to weigh just 1 oz (28.3 g). At this larval stage it feeds voraciously on mulberry leaves, increasing in size 10 000 times in 25 days. This diet helps it to produce a filament of silk from glands on the underside of its body, and when the larva is mature it wraps this filament around itself, creating a cocoon in which, if left to nature, it would develop into a moth, *Bombyx mori*. The silk farmer sets aside a few cocoons for the next generation of moths and plunges the others into hot water. The filaments are unwound and spun into a silk thread, which is dried, dyed and woven into fabric. The silk in a single cocoon can be more than 1000 yd (1 km) long. Domesticated for so long, the silkmoth is no longer found in the wild.

**Spinner**  *Making Thai silk.*

**The incense-maker**  *Gathering bundles of incense sticks after they have dried in the sun.*

# Literature: freedom and full-scale censorship

*The first stories in South-east Asia were handed down by word of mouth: poems, fairy stories, legends and versions of Hindu epics that offered both drama and moral instruction. Today, some countries in the region are making major contributions to world literature, while free expression in others is stifled by censorship.*

**Writer and fighter**   *The Vietnamese novelist Duong Thu-Huong, who joined her country's struggle against America, but whose work was later banned because it criticised the regime.*

A literary archaeologist, looking for the foundations of the literature of South-east Asia, will find most of them in ancient India. In Thailand, for instance, the 48 000-line *Ramakien* tells how King Ram renounces his throne, goes on a long journey, wins a battle against demons with the help of the monkey general Hanuman and rescues his beautiful wife Seeda from the evil King Ravana. All of these elements are taken from the Indian epic the *Ramayana*, but the subplots draw heavily on Thai history and folklore. In Cambodia, the *Ram Ker* ('In Praise of Rama') recounts the same story, using the Indian names Rama and Sita.

## A long wait for the alphabet

Vietnam is an exception to the general rule. The north of the country was occupied by China for roughly 1000 years, and this left an indelible mark on the national culture. A Vietnamese version of Chinese picture-writing was developed in the 13th century, and a French Jesuit missionary introduced a Romanised alphabet in the 17th, but it was not adopted as the national script until 1920.

Another important strand in the literary tradition throughout much of the region was the *Jataka*, tales and sayings of the Buddha, especially popular in Cambodia and Thailand. The Thai text *Tray Phum* ('The Three Worlds'), dating from 1345, has been likened to a Buddhist version of Dante's *The Divine Comedy*.

The written word came late to many parts of the region, and the printed word later still. Printed books were introduced to Burma (Myanmar) by American missionaries in the 19th century. In Malaysia, stories and records were handwritten or committed to memory and passed on orally until the printing press was introduced by the British in the 19th century.

A tradition of dissent in Vietnamese writing dates back to Ho Xuan Huong, an 18th-century poetess who criticised the corruption of high officials. The dissent was continued

by Nguyen Du, himself an official at the court of the emperor Gia Long (reigned 1802-19). His *Kim Van Kieu*, a novel written in verse, throws into sharp relief the vices of Vietnamese society, as it tells the story of a woman who has to turn prostitute to free her father from prison.

## Jailed for a novel

Poetry has always been held in high regard in Vietnam: even political slogans are written in verse, in order to give them wide appeal. Prose writing was introduced by the French during the colonial period. During Vietnam's 20th-century struggle for independence and unity, publishing was strictly censored. Censorship still exists, but it is now possible for books critical of the government to be printed. In 1991, the war veteran Bao Ninh published *The Sorrow of War*, a horrifying account of the damage war inflicts on men's minds, as well as on their bodies. In the same year, the novelist Duong Thu-Huong, a former resistance fighter against the Americans, spent seven months in prison for crimes against the socialist state. Her novel *Without a Name* reflects badly on the conduct of the government and communist party officials during the war. The official policy in today's Vietnam favours greater openness, but writers are still encouraged to take an optimistic stance.

Criticism is more readily accepted in Thailand. Bhotan, in *Letters from Thailand*, denounces the miseries inflicted on Chinese immigrants and Pira Sudham, in *Land of the Monsoon*, focuses on the poverty of the peasants of Issan, a neglected region in the east of the country. Myanmar, under its unyielding military government, is one of the last refuges of full-scale censorship in South-east Asia. Bookshops are full of works on the arts, but the only writings allowed to touch on politics are those approved by the regime. The Malaysian government frowns on any authors who write in the English language.

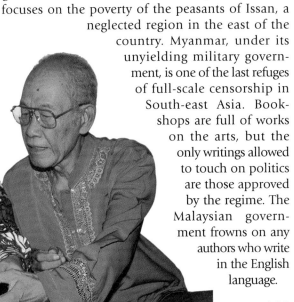

**Return of the exile**   *The dissident Indonesian writer Pramoedya Ananta Toer, who was deported in 1966, discusses his work, 14 years later, with President Wahid – a leader he also criticised.*

133

# Painting comes out of the shadows

*For centuries, painting in much of South-east Asia was confined to religious themes and ranked as the poor relation of architecture, sculpture and pottery. But in the modern era nobody challenges its claim to be one of the major arts.*

**On the temple walls** *The murals of Wat Yai Suwannaram in Petchaburi, Thailand, painted in the 17th century, are particularly well preserved.*

In the ancient civilisations of South-east Asia, artists were anonymous figures. Like the monks of medieval Europe, who patiently illuminated manuscripts without thought for personal glory, they put their skills at the service of religion. Paintings of the Buddha, or of scenes from Hindu epics, were decorative rather than works of art in their own right. In Vietnam, where Chinese cultural dominance was established during a 1000-year occupation, scholar-artists practised the elegant arts of calligraphy and painting on silk. Because of the humidity of the climate and the fragility of the material, little of their output has survived, but the work of the 15th-century artist Nguyen Trai hints at a world in which figures and objects float in space, unconfined by the rules of perspective.

### Talent-spotting colonial rulers

Spanish missionaries taught talented Filipino artists to paint in the European style and employed them at first on religious works. In the 19th century, the canvases of Juan Luna (1857-99), a Filipino who studied in Madrid, were much admired in Spain. He favoured epic subjects such as *The Death of Cleopatra* and *The Battle of Lepanto*. Luna's compatriot Resureccion Hidalgo (1853-1913) went to Paris and painted landscapes and seascapes in the impressionist style.

During the centuries when all forms of art in Vietnam were heavily influenced by Chinese culture, Vietnamese artists were famed for their landscapes and for the delicacy of their paintings on silk. In modern times, the talent of local artists was discovered and fostered by the colonial power. In the 1920s a School of Fine Arts, staffed by French teachers, was founded in Hanoi. Among the graduates, Bui Xhan-Phai built an international reputation for his street scenes of old Hanoi, and Nguyen Tu Nghiem combined ancient and modern traditions in his work. During the Vietnam War, painters in the north turned out giant canvases of triumphant workers, peasants and national leaders. But after victory such grandiose efforts fell into disrepute. Painting today has absorbed Western traditions such as impressionism, abstract art and surrealism without losing sight of its origins.

### Ubud, the village that lives for art

In the 1930s, a Balinese prince, trying to boost the tourist trade, invited the German musician and artist Walter Spies to set up as a painter in the village of Ubud. In those days painting meant applying natural pigments to shadow puppets or hand-woven cotton. Spies introduced the vibrant colours of oils and the pastel shades of watercolours. With Belgian artist Rudolf Bonet he founded an artists' colony and Ubud is now world famous.

**Chariots of war** *Battle scene from the Hindu epic* Ramayana, *on the walls of a pagoda in Phnom Penh.*

# New nations in search of a new architecture

*After winning independence from Western rule, most countries in South-east Asia boldly announced their new identities in bricks, glass and mortar. The old colonial style of building, no matter how gracious, belonged to the past.*

**Modern living, Asian-style**  *Singapore built a dozen new towns to rehouse some 3 million people in high-rise apartments.*

The triumph of nationalism in South-east Asia led to an urgent demand for flagship buildings – modern parliaments and imposing new offices to house important new ministries. In the early years of nationhood, these were designed by Western architects, in the 'international' style. The emergence of a modern Asian style of architecture had to wait until the 1970s. By this time, some cities were growing so rapidly that the housing shortage was acute and slum clearance had become an urgent priority. Deciding what to build in place of the slums gave Asian architects the chance to show their ingenuity. Singapore, which began its slum clearance in 1960, is a striking example of the evolution of an Asian style. Faced with the necessity of housing nearly 3 million people, the state set out to build good public housing at affordable prices, which inevitably meant high-rise flats that were more or less similar in appearance. Carefully landscaped parks were laid out as the 'lungs' of the new estates, and in 1973 the architects William Lim and Tay Khen Soon constructed the Golden Mile Shopping Centre and the People's Park, the first great business centres in South-east Asia, in a style that was resolutely original.

## Exuberant 'mini-Manhattans'

President Sukarno, who guided Indonesia through its first two decades of independence, tried to make Jakarta a capital whose buildings would win the admiration of the world. He left behind a massive sports stadium, one of the world's biggest mosques and a number of grandiose statues and monuments. Other cities in the region added their own exuberant touches to the modern international style, and began to look like mini-Manhattans with a dash of the East. Kuala Lumpur in Malaysia began 150 years ago as a mud-spattered mining town. Today, with its Petronas Twin Towers soaring to 1483 ft (452 m) against a skyscraper skyline, it has jumped into the modern age feet first. The experimental techniques of such architects as Kean Yeang and Robert Hamzah have created a futuristic city of elegant terraces, swooping spirals and courtyards in the air. In a playful mixing of different styles, buildings are often given an Islamic look, their swelling domes contrasting with the straight-sided glass and steel skyscrapers around them.

**Babel in Bangkok**  *A dragon winds around the medieval-style Tower of Babel Hotel in Bangkok.*

**Money machine**  *This giant glass robot is Bangkok's Bank of Asia.*

135

# Batik, the ritual art of writing with wax

*In Java, Bali and other parts of Indonesia, children wear batik for their first haircut. Grown-ups wear it when they marry, exorcise evil spirits or attend a funeral. It raises any occasion to the level of a ceremony.*

**Original colours** Batik from north Java.

Since its beginnings in 6th century Java, batik has become more than a colourful decoration on clothing. Wearing batik is a tradition with a spiritual significance: it gives an aura of solemnity to festivals and to the ceremonies that mark the rites of passage.

Batik is a Javanese word that means 'writing with wax' and describes a process that calls for a combination of artistic gifts and great technical skill. Patterns and motifs are applied with liquefied wax to a piece of fabric and allowed to solidify. The fabric, usually cotton or silk, is then dropped into a vat of dye. When the wax is removed, by scraping or boiling, the areas it covered retain the natural colour of the cloth and those that were uncovered take on the colour of the dye. New areas are then waxed, and the fabric is soaked in a different dye: this is repeated as many times as there are new colours to be added. The wax may be applied with a canting, a copper crucible with a handle and tiny spouts, which allow fine lines to be drawn. This method is reserved for women. Another technique, developed in the 19th century, is to print the wax onto the fabric with an iron or wooden stamp, called a cap. In Sulawesi (formerly the Celebes) the wax used to be applied with strips of bamboo.

**Artist at work** A woman applies wax, using a canting.

## The once-sacred art of dyeing

An entire rainbow of colours is used in batik today, but the original colours were vibrant blues and reds – the blues from the leaves of the indigo plant; the reds from the pounded bark of mangrove trees. Before the 1930s, when chemical dyes were introduced, the dyeing of the cloth was a sacred process, carried out by elderly women because they were held to be ritually pure. In the days when only natural dyes were used, it was possible to pinpoint where an item of batik originated from the colours used.

The batik tradition is so ancient that the designs have acquired their own names. Among the geometric designs are the *ceplok*, consisting of stylised squares and circles, the *ganggong*, a swirling arrangement of crosses and stars, and the *nitig*, which has the shape of a beehive. Other traditional designs have the shape of shells, or of plaited or woven cloth. Non-geometric designs can include the shapes of human beings, animals, insects and plants.

### Sarongs, sashes and turbans

Batik is not a single garment but three separate pieces of dyed cloth, all of them wrapped around the body. The *iket kepala*, used mainly by men, is a square of cloth that is worn on the head, like a turban. A sash 6-9 ft (2-3 m) long, called the *slendang* by men and the *kemben* by women, is wrapped around the waist. And finally comes the *kain panjang*, or sarong, which is worn by both sexes like a skirt.

*Special occasion* Batik adds a touch of brightness and an aura of dignity to a procession in Bali.

# The magic and power of the kris

*What the kukri is to a Gurkha, the assegai to a Zulu, or the samurai sword to a Japanese, the kris is to a Malay or an Indonesian – the mark of a warrior. In the old days, it was an indication of social rank and in the modern age, though no longer used as a weapon, it is a family heirloom that links generation to generation, for the powers of the ancestors are stored in its blade.*

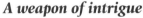

In Java, Bali, Sumatra, Kalimantan, Sulawesi and the southern parts of the Philippines, the double-edged, wavy-bladed kris is believed to have supernatural powers. Its point, it is said, will deflect malevolent forces. Its blade will warn the wearer of an enemy's presence by vibrating in its scabbard. It can deflect the flames of fire or the waters of a flood, and even kill an enemy just by being pointed at his footprint.

The kris is such a fearsome-looking weapon that its reputation hardly needs to be bolstered by such stories. Traditionally, the blade was made of steel, using iron and nickel obtained from meteorites. Several layers of metal were laminated together and damascened – decorated with wavy patterns of inlay, often in gold or silver. Making a kris was a ritual in its own right. The armourers would fast before beginning work, to make themselves worthy. Then, chanting to summon supernatural powers, they would temper the steel in clear, pure water and rub it with the juice of unripe lemons, mixed with a little arsenic. They might also dip the blade in the intestines of a snake or a scorpion, so that it

***Embracing fear*** *Tense moment in a Balinese kris dance.*

would take on their venomous power. Naga, a mythical serpent, inspired the sinuous form of the kris blade, which always has an odd number of bends, known as *lok*. These bends are symbolic: a five-lok blade, for example, is a reference to the five Pandava brothers of the Hindu epic *Mahabharata*.

## A weapon of intrigue

The finely sculpted handle of a kris may be in wood, ivory or silver – or, for a person of royal blood, gold. It often depicts a mythological figure and may be inlaid with precious stones. The scabbard is made of precious wood, such as sandalwood or teak, and is sometimes covered with a chasing of gold or silver leaf. The top can be given a shape such as the outline of a ship. Historically, the kris has been more often used in palace intrigues and assassinations than on the field of battle, but it still has a powerful aura of fascination and fear.

### When the kris goes looking for a bride

It was once the custom in Malay society for a young man in need of a wife to formally kidnap his bride. If wooing were not enough, he would force his way into her parents' home, kris in hand. But in a society where losing face is one of the worst punishments that can be inflicted, the eager young lover was taking a terrible risk. He might be refused by the girl or her parents, or he might be chased out of the house by her brothers; worse still, the entire community would know about it. This was probably the origin of the later custom of simply sending a kris to the family. If the young man was not wanted, the kris was quietly returned, with no danger of his losing face in public.

***Dagger that confers status*** *Tucked into a sash, carried against the small of the back and pointing left to ward off evil, the kris is a powerful status symbol in Malaysia, Indonesia and the Philippines.*

# MAPS, FACTS AND FIGURES

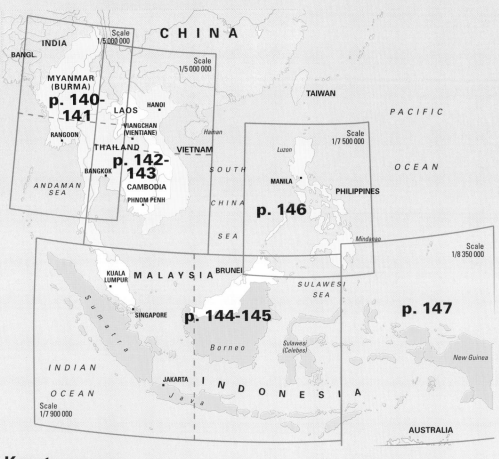

India · BANGL. · CHINA · Scale 1/5 000 000 · Scale 1/5 000 000 · MYANMAR (BURMA) · **p. 140-141** · HANOI · LAOS · VIANGCHAN (VIENTIANE) · TAIWAN · PACIFIC · RANGOON · THAILAND · VIETNAM · Hainan · Scale 1/7 500 000 · OCEAN · Luzon · BANGKOK · **p. 142-143** · SOUTH · MANILA · PHILIPPINES · ANDAMAN SEA · CAMBODIA · PHNOM PENH · CHINA · **p. 146** · SEA · Mindanao · Scale 1/8 350 000 · KUALA LUMPUR · MALAYSIA · BRUNEI · SULAWESI SEA · **p. 147** · Sumatra · SINGAPORE · **p. 144-145** · Borneo · Sulawesi (Celebes) · New Guinea · INDIAN · JAKARTA · INDONESIA · OCEAN · Java · Scale 1/7 900 000 · AUSTRALIA

## Key to maps

### Place names

■ CAPITAL     ● City

● Major city     • Town

### Borders

—— International land frontier

- - - - International maritime frontier

### Topography

▲ Mt Hkakabok Razi 5881 m    Summit

**MAOKE MTS**    Mountain range

### Elevation tints

Metres

5000
4000
3000
2000
1000
500
200
0

### Depth tints

Metres

- 200
- 500
- 1000
- 2000
- 3000
- 4000
- 5000
- 6000

# Myanmar (Burma)

CHINA

Guangxi Zhuang Autonomous Region

MIAO LING

DUPANG LING

YUNKAI DASHAN

Guilin
Liuzhou
Nanning
Guiping
Wuzhou
Hexian
Liuzhou
Hechi
Duyun
Anshun
Kunming
Gejiu
Mengzi

VIETNAM

HANOI
Haiphong
Nam Dinh
Thanh Hoa
Vinh
Ha Tinh
Dong Hoi
Cao Bang
Ha Giang
Lao Cai
Dien Bien Phu

LAOS

VIANGCHAN (VIENTIANE)
Louangphrabang
Xiangkhoang
Plain of Jars
Plateau de Xiangkhoang
Louang Namtha

Phou Bia 2 819 m
Phou Loi 2 257 m
Phan Si Pan 3 143 m

LUANG PRABANG RANGE

AILAO SHAN

WULIANG SHAN

NU SHAN

BAICAO LING

QINGSHUILANG SHAN

HAINAN
Haikou
Danxian (Nada)
Baoting

Wuzhi Shan 1 867 m

DONGHAI DAO
NAOZHOU DAO
WEIZHOU DAO
DAO CAT BA

Gulf of Tonking

Zhanjiang
Maoming
Qinzhou
Beihai

Chiang Mai
Lampang
Uttaradit
Nong Khai
Udon Thani
Nakhon Phanom
Sakon Nakhon

Sirikit Reservoir

RAKHWHAENG

Nam Ngum Reservoir

Tropic of Cancer

Mekong (Mènam Khong)

Red River (Yuan)

Black River (Song Da)

142

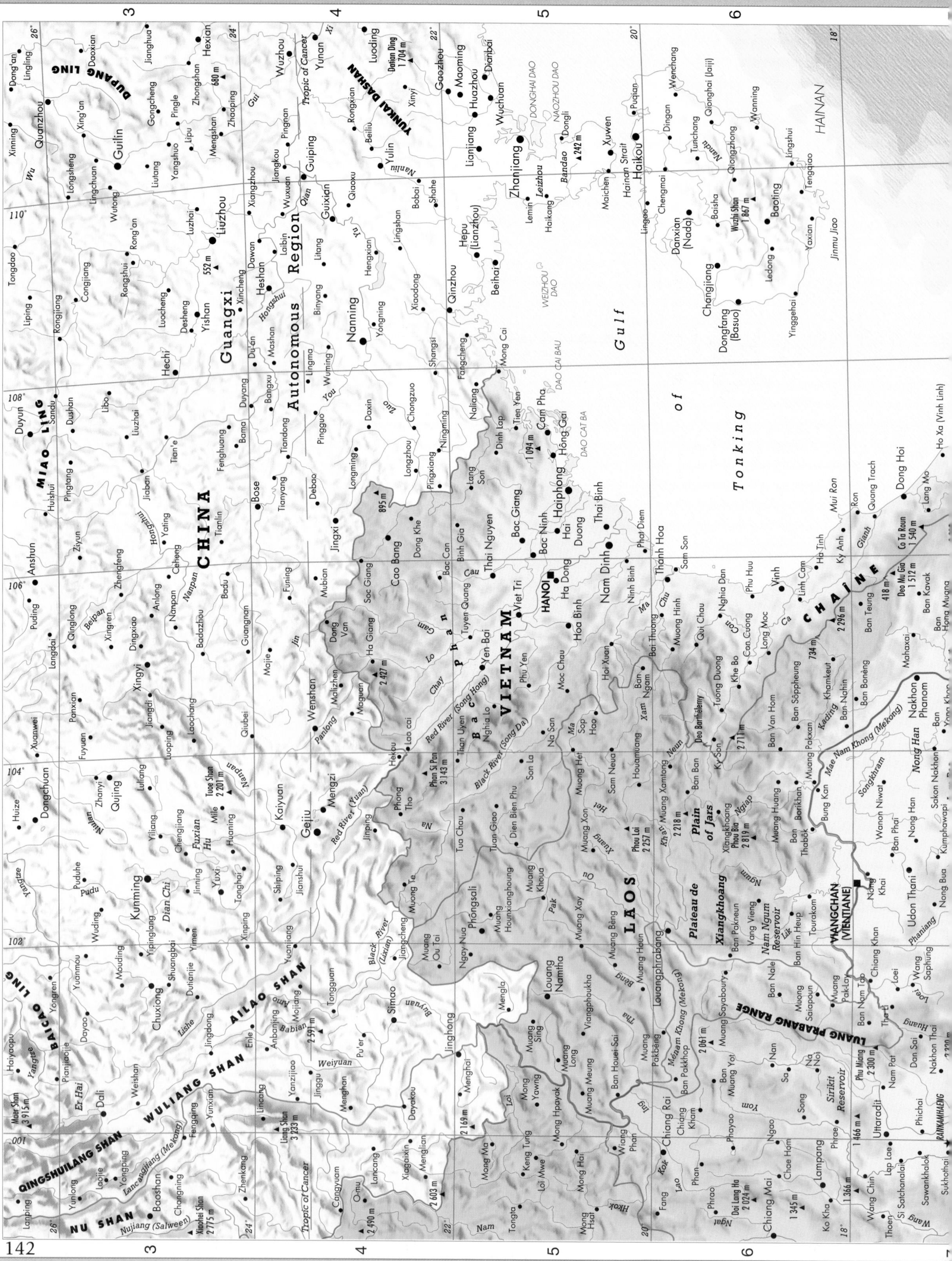

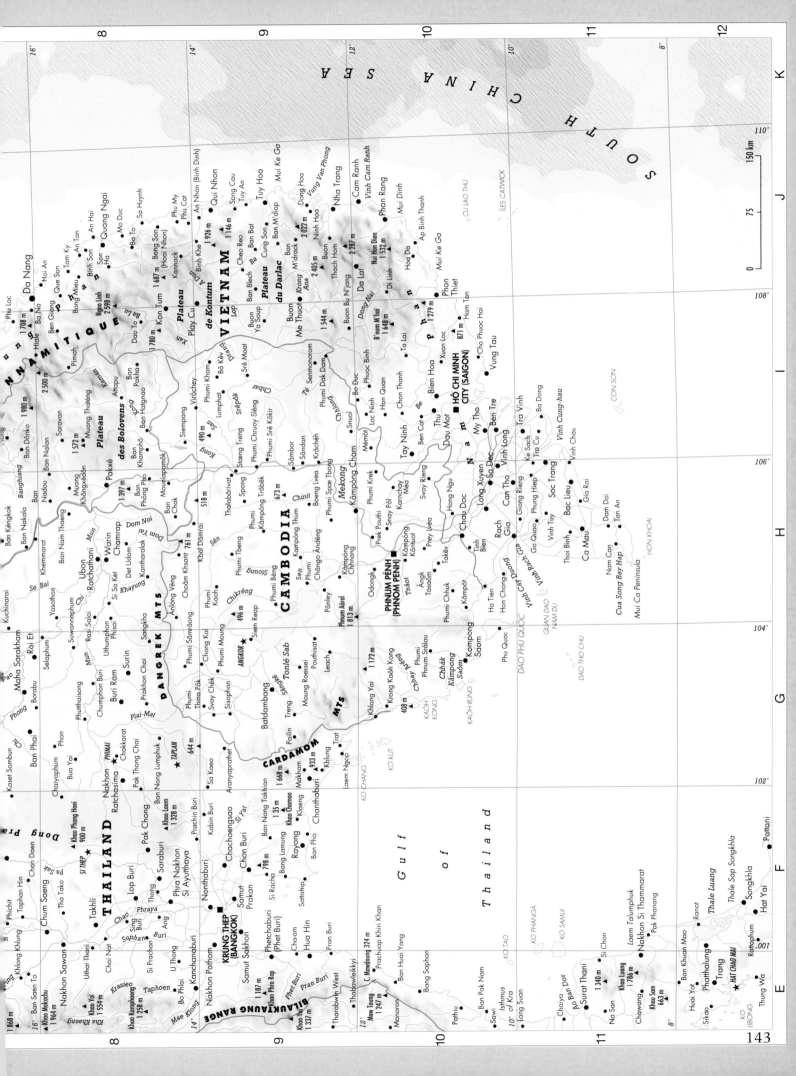

# Malaysia • Sumatra

**A** **B** **C** **D**

SOUTH CHIN

SEA

MALAYSIA

Trang
Kantang
Songkhla
Thale Sap Songkla
KO LIBONG
Hat Yai
Pattani
BUTANG GROUP
Sai Buri
LANGKAWI
Yala
Narathiwat
Alor Setar
Kota Bharu
REDANG
MALAY PENINSULA
George Town (Penang)
Butterworth
Gunong Lawit 1 517 m
Kuala Terengganu
Bertam
TENGGUL
PINANG
Taiping
Gunong Chamah 2 170 m
Bertam
Gunong Tahan 2 187 m
Kuala Dungun
Ipoh
Gunong Batu Puteh 2 130 m
Tapis 1 511 m
C. Penunjok
Cukai
PULAU LAUT
NATUNA BESAR
Telok Anson
Kuantan
2 985 m
Bireun
Lhokseumawe
Bentong
Pahang
Pekan
Takengon
Langsa
Gunung Abongabang 2 983 m
Gunong Lembu 2 983 m
Pangkalansusu
Binjai
Medan
KUALA LUMPUR
ANAMBAS ISLANDS
Binjai
GunongLeuser 3 381 m
Belawan
Kelang
Seremban
TIOMAN
JEMAJA
AIRABU
Meulaboh
Labuhanhaji
Binjai
Tebingtinggi
Port Dickson
Segamat
AUR
Bakungan
Pematangsiantar
Tanjungbalai
Melaka (Malacca)
K. Rompin
SIMEULUE
Danau Toba
SAMOSIR
Labuhanbilik
Muar
Batu Pahat
RUPAT
Sinabang
Singkil
2 078 m
Rantaupratpat
Bagansiapiapi
BENGKANS
Johor Bahru
Tanjur Api
KEPULAUAN BANYAK
Tarutung
Sibolga B.
Sibolga
Barumun
Rokan
SINGAPORE
BINTAN
KEPULAUAN TAMBELAN
Singkawang
MUSALA
Padangsidempuan
Sebanga
PADANG
Tanjungpinang
LEMUKUTAN
Gunungsitoli
Kotatengah
TEBINGTINGGI
KEPULAUAN RIAU
KEPULAUAN BADAS
Mempawah
NIAS
Telukdalam
Gunong Surikmerapi 2 145 m
Pekanbaru
Kampar
Natal
PINI
Gunong Talakmau 2 912 m
Sungaiguntung
KEPULAUAN LINGGA
Ponti
SIMUK
SUMATRA
Equator
TANAHMASA
Bukittinggi
Payakumbuh
Indragiri
Rengat
LINGGA
SINGKEP
TANAHBALA
BATU GROUP
Padangpanjang
SIBERUT
Padang
PEGUNUNGAN BARISAN
Hari
TIGAPULUH HILLS
Hari
Selat Berhala
Tanjung Jabung
PULAU-PULA KARIMATA
Muarasiberut
Gunung Kerinci 3 800 m
Jambi
BANGKA
SIPURA
Selat Bungalaut
Sungaipenuh
Tembesi
Mangsang
Selat Karimata
Selat Sipura
Gunung Masurai 2 933 m
Muntok
Pangkalpinang
PUGAI UTARA
Surulangun
Selat
1 554 m
Selat Gaspar
Tanjungpandan
Musi
Palembang
PAGAI SELATAN
Lubuklinggau
Kayuagung
BELITUNG
Lais
Prabumulih
Tanjung Lumut
Lahat
Gunung Dempo 3 159 m
Komering
GREATER
Bengkulu
Baturaja
MEGA
Manna
Tulangbawang
Menggala
Kotabumi
2 232 m
Gunung Resag
Krui
Tanjungkarang-Telukbetung
JAVA SEA
Kotaagung
INDIAN
ENGGANO
Teluk Semangka
Selat Sunda
JAKARTA
Tanjung Idramay
Cireb
Tanjung Cina
Bogor
3 078 m
Tanjung Cangkuang
Teluk Pelahuanratu
Bandung
GunungCiremay
3 42
Sindangbarang
Tasikmalaya
Purv

OCEAN

CHRISTMAS ISLAND (Australia)

0    100    200 km

144

# Philippines

0 75 150 km

1

2

3

4

5

TAIWAN

PACIFIC

OCEAN

20°

ITBAYAT
BATAN
ISLANDS
BATAN

BABUYAN
ISLANDS
CALAYAN

CAMIGUIN

Babuyan Channel

Cape Bojeador
Bangui
Laoag
Aparri
Cape Escarpada
San Nicolas
Gonzaga
Mount Sicapo
2 234 m
Tuguegarao
Vigan
Lubuagan
Candon
Bontoc
Ilagan
Mount Palanag
1 212 m
San Fernando
Mount Pulog
2 929 m
Solano
Lingayen
Baguio
Bani
Dagupan
Lingayen
San José
LUZON
Tarlac
Cabanatuan
Angeles
POLILLO
ISLANDS
Olongapo
Matolos
POLILLO
MANILA
Quezon City
Cavite
Pasig
Lamon Bay
LUBANG
ISLANDS
Santa Cruz
Daet
Calauag
Batangas
Lucena
Naga
Caramoan Peninsula
Cape Calavite
CATANDUANES
Mount Halcon
2 585 m
Calapan
Boac
Bondoc Peninsula
Mount Mayon
2 424 m
MINDORO
MARINDUQUE
BURIAS
Legaspi
Mount Baco
2 487 m
SIBUYAN
Bulusan Volcano
PHILIPPINES
Roxas
SIBUYAN
San José
Aroroy
Catarman
TABLAS
Masbate
Oras
MASBATE

SOUTH

CHINA

SEA

PHILIPPINE

SEA

12°

16°

CORDILLERA CENTRAL
SIERRA MADRE
ZAMBALES MTS

CALAMIAN
GROUP
BUSUANGA
SEA
VISAYAN
BILIRAN
SAMAR
CULION
Kalibo
Roxas
SEA
Tacloban
El Nido
PANAY
Bogo
Ormoc
Taytay
CUYO
ISLANDS
LEYTE
DUMARAN
Iloilo
Bacolod
Sogod
Loreto
Roxas
1 593 m
Canlaon
San Carlos
DINAGAT
PALAWAN
CEBU
SIARGAO
Puerto
Princesa
Honda Bay
Panay
Gulf
Binalbagan
BOHOL
Dapa
Aborlan
Tagbilaran
Surigao
Quezon
SULU
NEGROS
Dumaguete
SIQUIJOR
Butuan
Tandag
Mt Mantaliagajan
2 054 m
SEA
BOHOL SEA
CAMIGUIN
San Juan
PANDONAN
BUGSUK
Mount Dapiak
2 560 m
Iligan Bay
Cagayan
BALABAC
Sindangan
Illigan
Cateel
Balabac Strait
Lake
Lanao
BALAMBANGAN
BANGGI
Pagadian
Mount Ragang
2 815 m
Hijo
Kudat
CAGAYAN SULU
Sibuco
OLUTANGO
Midsayap
Mount Apo
2 954 m
Caraga
Kota Belud
JAMBONGAN
Zamboanga
Moro
Gulf
MINDANAO
Kota Kinabalu
(Jesselton)
Gunong Kinabalu
4 094 m
Sandakan
Basilan Strait
BASILAN I.
Datu
Piang
Lake Buluan
Malita
Surup
Ranau
Tanjong
Hog
PANGUTARAN
GROUP
SAMALES
GROUP
JOLO I.
Glan
Tinaco Point
LABUAN
Beaufort
Segama
TAWITAWI
SARANGANI ISLANDS
BANDAR SERI
BEGAWAN
Sabah
Tenom
Lahad Datu
SUBUTU
Kuala
Belait
Lawas
BRUNEI
BRASSEY MTS
Seria
Semporna
Miri

DIUATA MTS
Agusan
Davao Gulf

SULU ARCHIPELAGO

8°

146

116°

120°

124°

128°

MINDANAO

Hijo
Caraga

Davao Gulf
Surup

inaca Point

ARANGANI ISLANDS

KARAKELONG
KEPULAUAN TALAUD

SALEBABU

SANGIR

SIAU
TAHULANDANG

IARO

Klabat

ator

KASIRUTA
Labuha
MANDIOLI
BISA
OBILATU
MANGOLE
SANANA

OBI

KEPULAUAN OBI

BURU
Namlea

AMBELAU

Piru
Amahai
Ambon

CERAM SEA

SERAM

Selat Manipa

KEP. PENYU
KEP. LUCIPARA

BANDA SEA

KEP. BARAT DAYA

VETAR
Ilwaki
KISAR

ATAURO

DILI
2 315 m
Vikeke

TIMOR SEA

AST TIMOR

BACAN

MOROTAI
Wayabula

Galela
Tobelo
Tatam

Jailolo

Ternate
Tidore
1 508 m

Weda

Teluk Weda

Tanjung Gamcak

HALMAHERA

Teluk Buli

GEBE

Selat Bougainville

HALMAHERA SEA

Tanjung Libobo

BATANTA

KEP. BOO

SALAWATI

MISOOL

Wahai

Bula

Selat Dampier

Sorong

WAIGEO

Teminabuan

Inanwatan

Tanjung Sabra

Onin Pen.
Fakfak

KARAS

KEP. GORONG

Karufa

Tanjung Papisoi

ADI

KEP. WATUBELA

KEP. BANDA

SERUA
NILA
DAMAR
TEUN
ROMANG
BABAR
MOA
SERMATA
KEP. LETI
KEP. BABAR

WULIARU
SELU
SELARU

MOLU

LARAT
YAMDENA

KEP. TANIMBAR

KEP. TAYANDU

KAI KECIL

KEPULAUAN KAI

KAI BESAR

DOBO

MAIKOOR

TRANGAN

WOKAM

KOBROÖR

KEP. ARU

PULAU DOLAK

Tanjung Vals

SONSOROL ISLANDS

PULO ANNA

MERIR

TOBI

HELEN ISLAND

KEPULAUAN ASIA

KEPULAUAN AYU

Tanjung Jamursba

TAMRA MTS
3 000 m
Kwaka

Mts Arfak
2 939 m
Ransiki

Wasian
Steenkool

Teluk Berau
Babo
Wasior

Wasado
1 069 m

Kaimana

Teluk Kamrau

Modowi

Umari

PACIFIC

OCEAN

NEW GUINEA

Manokwari

SUPIORI

KEP. PANDAIDORI

BIAK

Bosnik

NUMFOOR

Selat Sorenarwa

Teluk Cenderawasih

Napan

Nabire

3 550 m

YARAMANIAPUKU MTS

SUDIRMAN MTS

Kokonau

Irian Jaya

Teluk Flamingo

Oscanep

Tanjung Cook

Tanjung Deyong

YAPEN

Serui

Waren

Dom
1 340 m

Tariku

Napan

Pk Jaya
5 030 m

Bagusi

VAN REES MTS

Mamberamo

Angemuk
3 741 m

MAOKE MTS

Pk Trikora
4 750 m

JAYAWIJAYA MTS

Tanjung d'Urville

Sarmi

Ansudu

Demta

Jayapura
(Sukarnapura)

Vanimo

Taritatu

Sobger

Pk Mandala
4 760 m

DIGUL MTS

Agats

Kepi

Tanahmerah

Mapi

Muting

Digul

Moli Channel

Okaba

Wan

KOMORAN

Merauke

ARAFURA SEA

AUSTRALIA

Cape Van Diemen

CROKER I.

C. Cockburn

Cape Wessel

Apsley Strait

Cobourg Pen.

GOULBURN ISLANDS

WESSEL IS.

BATHURST ISLAND

MELVILLE ISLAND

Van Diemen Gulf

Boucaut Bay

ELCHO I.

C. Fourcroy

Clarence Strait

Dundas Strait

0    100    200 km

# South-east Asia: the statistics

*Of the ten countries that make up South-east Asia, some are part of the continent (Cambodia, Laos, western Malaysia, Myanmar, Singapore, Thailand, Vietnam); others are islands (Brunei, Indonesia, eastern Malaysia, the Philippines).*

**MYANMAR**

**LAOS**

**THAILAND**

**CAMBODIA**

**VIETNAM**

M A L A Y

**SINGAPORE**

**I N D**

## CAMBODIA

**Official name:** Kingdom of Cambodia
**Capital:** Phnom Penh
**Area:** 69 898 sq miles (181 035 km²)
**Population:** 11 757 000
**Density:** 168 per sq mile (65 per km²)
**Ehnic groups:** Khmer 89%, Vietnamese 5.5%, Cham 2.3%, Chinese 1%, others 1.7%
**Religions:** Buddhist 89%, Christian 4%, Islam 4%, others
**Currency:** Riel
**Languages:** Khmer, French, English, Vietnamese, Chinese
**Type of government:** Constitutional monarchy with elected National Assembly and appointed Senate

## LAOS

**Official name:** Lao People's Democratic Republic
**Capital:** Vientiane
**Area:** 91 429 sq miles (236 800 km²)
**Population:** 5 690 000
**Density:** 62 per sq mile (24 per km²)
**Ehnic groups:** Lao Loum (Laos) 67%, Lao Theung (Mon-Khmers) 16.5%, Lao Thai (Thais) 7.8%, Lao Soung (Miaos and Yaos) 5.2%, others 3.5%
**Religions:** Buddhist 60%, tribal religions 34%, Christian 2%, others 0.4%
**Currency:** Kip
**Languages:** Lao, French, English
**Type of government:** Single-party People's Republic with a National Assembly which elects the president. The ruling party is the Lao People's Revolutionary Party

## MALAYSIA

**Official name:** Federation of Malaysia
**Capital:** Kuala Lumpur
**Area:** 127 310 sq miles (329 733 km²)
**Population:** 22 710 000
**Density:** 178 per sq mile (69 per km²)
**Ehnic groups:** Malay 59%, Chinese 25.8%, Indian 14.8%, others 0.4%
**Religions:** Muslim 53%, Buddhist 17.6%, Chinese faiths 11%, Hindu 7%, Christian 6.4%, others 5%
**Currency:** ringgit
**Languages:** Bahasa ('Market') Malay, English, Chinese dialects, Malay
**Type of government:** Federal, under a constitutional monarchy (sultanate) with two legislative chambers – the Senate and the House of Representatives. The constitution contains special safeguards for Sabah and Sarawak

## INDONESIA

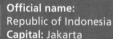

**Official name:** Republic of Indonesia
**Capital:** Jakarta
**Area:** 735 358 sq miles (1 904 569 km²)
**Population:** 212 560 000
**Density:** 289 per sq mile (112 per km²)
**Ehnic groups:** Javanese 61.7%, Chinese 2.7%, Acehnese, Batak, Dyak, Madurese, Sundanese and others 35.6%
**Religions:** Muslim 88%, Christian 9%, Hindu 2%, Buddhist 1%
**Currency:** rupiah
**Languages:** Bahasa ('Market') Indonesian, Dutch
**Type of government:** Federal republic with two legislative chambers, the House of People's Representatives and the People's Consultative Assembly

## THE PHILIPPINES

**Official name:**
Republic of the Philippines
**Capital:** Manila
**Area:** 115 736 sq miles (299 756 km²)
**Population:** 75 300 000
**Density:** 651 per sq mile (251 per km²)
**Ehnic groups:** Tagalog 29.7%, Cebuano 24.2%, Ilocano 10.3%, Biolano 5.6%, Samar Layte 4%, Pampangano 2.8%, Hiligaynon 1.8%, Pangasinan 1.8%, others 19.8%
**Religions:** Roman Catholic 84%, Church of the Philippines 6%, Muslim 4.3%, Protestant 3.9%, others 1.8%
**Currency:** Philippines peso
**Languages:** Tagalog (Filipino), English, Spanish
**Type of government:** Republic with a president and two-chamber Congress, the Senate and the House of Representatives

## THAILAND

**Official name:** Kingdom of Thailand
**Capital:** Bangkok (Krung Thep)
**Area:** 198 447 sq miles (513 975 km²)
**Population:** 61 800 000
**Density:** 311 per sq mile (120 per km²)
**Ethnic groups:** Thai 80%, Chinese 10%, Malay 4%, Khmer 2.7%, others 3.3%

**Religions:** Buddhist 93%, Muslim 4%, others 3%
**Currency:** Baht
**Languages:** Thai, Chinese, Malay, English
**Type of government:** Constitutional monarchy with a parliament consisting of two chambers, the Senate and the elected House of Representatives

## VIETNAM

**Official name:** Socialist Republic of Vietnam
**Capital:** Hanoi
**Area:** 128 065 sq miles (331 689 km²)
**Population:** 79 500 000
**Density:** 621 per sq mile (240 per km²)
**Ethnic groups:** Vietnamese

85%, Chinese 2%, Thai 1.5%, Khmer 1.4%, Cham, Hmong and other Montagnards, 10.1%
**Religions:** Buddhist 68%, Roman Catholic 8%, others 24%
**Currency:** Dong
**Languages:** Vietnamese, French, English, Khmer
**Type of government:** Single-party Socialist Republic with a National Assembly

P H I L I P P I N E S

B R U N E I

## BRUNEI

**Official name:** Brunei
**Capital:** Bandar Seri Begawan
**Area:** 2226 sq miles (5765 km²)
**Population:** 322 000
**Density:** 145 per sq mile (56 per km²)
**Ethnic groups:** Malay 68%, Chinese 16%, indigenous 6%, Indian and others 10%
**Religion:** Muslim
**Currency:** Brunei dollar
**Languages:** Malay, English, Chinese dialects
**Type of government:** Monarchy. The sultan rules by decree and is advised by a privy council. There are no elections, no legislature and no political parties

## SINGAPORE

**Official name:**
Republic of Singapore
**Capital:** Singapore
**Area:** 239 sq miles (619 km²)
**Population:** 4 017 000
**Density:** 16 810 per sq mile (6490 per km²)
**Ethnic groups:** Chinese 77%, Malay 14%, Indian (including Sri Lankan) 8%, others 1%
**Religions:** Buddhist 54%, Muslim 15%, Christian 14%, Hindu 3.5%, no professed religion 13.4%
**Currency:** Singapore dollar
**Languages:** Malay, Chinese (mainly Mandarin), English, Tamil
**Type of government:** Republic, with an elected parliament and a directly elected president, who appoints the prime minister and cabinet

## MYANMAR (BURMA)

**Official name:** Union of Myanmar
**Capital:** Yangon (Rangoon)
**Area:** 261 228 sq miles (676 578 km²)
**Population:** 49 340 000
**Density:** 189 per sq mile (73 per km²)
**Ethnic groups:** Burman 68%, Shan 9%, Karen 7%, Arakanese 4.5%, Barmar,

Chin, Kachin, Mon and others 11.5%.
**Religions:** Buddhist 89%, Christian 4%, Muslim 4%, others 3%
**Currency:** kyat
**Languages:** Burmese, Mon Khmer, Thai, English
**Type of government:** Military dictatorship, ruling through the State Peace and Development Council

N E S I A

# Climate, relief and vegetation

*South-east Asia stretches from the peaks of northern Myanmar to the islands of Indonesia, and covers more than 1 730 000 sq miles (4 490 000 km²) of rugged mountains, fertile plains and dense tropical forests. The prevailing climate is hot and humid – ideal for plant and animal life.*

Extending for almost 2200 miles (3500 km) from north to south, and with altitudes ranging from sea level to well above 13 000 ft (4000 m), the region provides a prodigious variety of niches for living things.

## A hot, sticky climate

In the northern part of the region the pattern of the climate is set by the monsoon winds, which give two distinct seasons. From November to March, winds that are dry and cool blow from the interior of Asia towards the coasts. From April or May to October, winds laden with moisture blow in from the sea. Before the monsoons burst, the humidity can be oppressive, with temperatures soaring well above 32°C (90°F). The rains are the signal for the start of rice-planting. They can also bring devastating floods, and winds at sea can build up into typhoons, which ravage the coasts. In 1916, at Bogor, in Java, a storm lasted for a record 322 days. In the region's more southerly part, where the climate is equatorial, warmth and humidity are present all year and the farming season is almost uninterrupted. Even in the driest month of the year, Pontianak, in Indonesia, which lies on the Equator, is drenched by 6.6 in (167 mm) of rain.

### WHERE THE SUN SHINES
*(hours per year)*

| | Total |
|---|---|
| Vientiane | 3200 |
| Bandar Seri Begawan | 2700 |
| Manila | 2510 |
| Phnom Penh | 2466 |
| Bangkok | 2450 |
| Rangoon | 2 448 |
| Jakarta | 2331 |
| Kuala Lumpur | 2238 |
| Singapore | 2056 |
| Hanoi | 1097 |

**Paddling to safety** *A woman in Hoi An, Vietnam, and her bedraggled-looking dog make for dry land after torrential rains flooded the town in 1999.*

CLIMATE ▼

**Climate**
- equatorial
- tropical
- subtropical
- warm and humid
- high altitude

### The calamitous floods of the year 2000

Floods are an ever-present menace for those who live along the banks of the Mekong. In 1999, following torrential rains, more than 100 people were drowned in central Vietnam. That toll was exceeded in September 2000, when the worst floods along the Mekong for 40 years claimed more than 400 lives in Cambodia and Vietnam. Communications in entire provinces were thrown into disarray, with main roads impassable, and 350 000 people were forced to flee their homes. Almost all of the 34 000 homes in the Vietnamese district of An Phu, some 125 miles (200 km) south of Ho Chi Minh City, were under water. These floods, the result of exceptionally heavy monsoon rains, were made worse, said United Nations experts, by the massive deforestation of previous years.

### RAINFALL *(in inches/mm)*

| | Total | Wettest month | Driest month |
|---|---|---|---|
| Bandar Seri Begawan | 111.5/2830 | 13.6/345 (Dec) | 5.1/130 (Feb) |
| Rangoon | 103.4/2625 | 22.9/580 (July) | 0.08/2 (Jan) |
| Singapore | 95.5/2425 | 10.4/265 (Dec) | 6.5/165 (July) |
| Kuala Lumpur | 93.2/2365 | 11/280 (Nov) | 5/125 (June) |
| Hanoi | 70.7/1795 | 13.2/335 (July) | 1/25 (Dec) |
| Jakarta | 70.7/1795 | 11.8/300 (Jan) | 1.8/45 (Aug) |
| Manila | 68.9/1748 | 18.9/480 (Aug) | 0.08/2 (April) |
| Vientiane | 66.4/1686 | 15.2/385 (Sept) | 0.04/1 (Dec) |
| Bangkok | 58.7/1491 | 12/305 (Sept) | 0.28/7 (Jan) |
| Phnom Penh | 55.2/1402 | 10/255 (Oct) | 0.28/7 (Jan) |

### MEAN TEMPERATURES *(°C/°F)*

| | January | July |
|---|---|---|
| Bandar Seri Begawan | 28/82.4 | 32/89.6 |
| Kuala Lumpur | 27/80.6 | 29/84.2 |
| Singapore | 26/78.8 | 29/84.2 |
| Bangkok | 24/75.2 | 29/84.2 |
| Hanoi | 16/60.8 | 29/84.2 |
| Manila | 26/78.8 | 28/82.4 |
| Phnom Penh | 25/77 | 28/82.4 |
| Jakarta | 26/78.8 | 27/80.6 |
| Rangoon | 25/77 | 27/80.6 |
| Vientiane | 21/69.8 | 27/80.6 |

| Relief |
| --- |
| height in metres |
| 3000 |
| 1000 |
| 200 |
| 0 |

## ▲ RELIEF OF SOUTH-EAST ASIA

### Mountains, plains and rivers

More than half the land area of South-east Asia is made up of islands. The Indonesian archipelago alone, a garland of more than 13 000 islands, accounts for more than three-quarters of a million square miles (nearly 2 million km²). During the last Ice Age, with vast amounts of water locked up in the polar ice caps, and sea levels much lower than they are today, land bridges connected the archipelago and Borneo with the Asian landmass. On the mainland, the mountains that curve in an extended U-shape around the central plain of Myanmar, and that rise in the north and west of Thailand, are extensions of the Tibeto-Himalayan range. Those that dominate Laos and sweep down the central regions of Vietnam are extensions of the hills of southern China. Both Indonesia and the Philippines are part of the 'Ring of Fire', the arc of volcanoes and earthquake-prone regions encircling the Pacific Ocean. Indonesia has some 300 volcanoes, 50 of them active.

Five great rivers descend from the mountains, irrigating and sometimes flooding the lands through which they run: the Irrawaddy and the Salouen in Myanmar; the Chao Phraya in Thailand; the Mekong in Cambodia and Vietnam; and the Red River in Vietnam. Their well-watered valleys, flood plains and many-branched mouths are very fertile: the Irrawaddy and Mekong deltas and the central plain of Thailand are among Asia's most productive rice bowls.

*Under the volcano*
*Buffaloes and a Filipino farmer on Luzon, beneath the Mayon volcano.*

### Where life flourishes

The region's all-pervading heat and moisture have created the most favourable environment for plant life on Earth. Before human beings cleared these vast spaces to plant crops, almost the entire region was covered with rain forests. Today, despite deforestation, forests still cover nearly half the land surface. The trees include teak and other hardwoods and a record number of species of bamboos and palms. Some 2500 different genera of flowering plants, comprising 25 000 species, have been recorded in the islands. Insects and cold-blooded animals, which have little or no internal control over their body temperatures, can operate at peak efficiency in the heat of the sun, so butterflies, moths, spiders, snakes, frogs and lizards can grow to giant sizes. And with a profusion of plants and insects for food, the bird life flourishes.

*Daybreak  Early morning mist on the Mekong at Luang Prabang, Laos.*

| RIVERS (in miles/km) | |
| --- | --- |
| Mekong | 2610/4200 |
| Salouen | 1740/2800 |
| Irrawaddy | 1300/2100 |
| Chao Phraya | 750/1200 |
| Red River (Song Hong) | 750/1200 |

| THE HIGHEST MOUNTAINS (altitude in ft (m)) | | |
| --- | --- | --- |
| Mount Hkakabo Razi (Myanmar) | 19 294 | (5881) |
| Puncak Jaya (Indonesia) | 16 535 | (5040) |
| Mount Kinabalu (Indonesia) | 13 697 | (4175) |
| Mount Kerinci (Indonesia) | 12 467 | (3800) |
| Mount Semeru (Indonesia) | 12 060 | (3676) |
| Pic Fan Si Pan (Vietnam) | 10 312 | (3143) |
| Mount Apo (Philippines) | 9695 | (2955) |
| Mount Bia (Laos) | 9350 | (2850) |

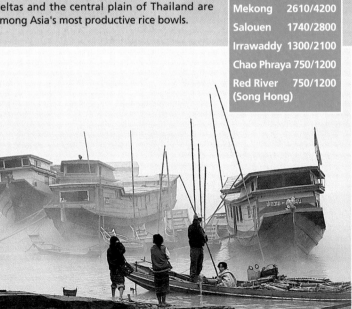

| ISLANDS (area in sq miles/km²) | |
| --- | --- |
| New Guinea | 303 000/785 000 |
| Borneo | 284 000/736 000 |
| Sumatra | 162 000/420 000 |
| Sulawesi (Celebes) | 66 400/172 000 |
| Java | 47 900/124 000 |
| Luzon | 40 150/104 000 |
| Mindanao | 36 536/94 630 |

| FORESTS (as a percentage of total area) | |
| --- | --- |
| Brunei | 82.4 |
| Indonesia | 60.6 |
| Cambodia | 55.7 |
| Laos | 53.9 |
| Malaysia | 47.1 |
| Myanmar | 41.3 |
| Vietnam | 28.0 |
| Thailand | 23.0 |
| Philippines | 22.7 |

# Population, economy and society

*From Myanmar to Vietnam, between the Indian Ocean and the Pacific, half a billion people make up the population of South-east Asia. Some spend hectic lives, buying, selling and bargaining amid the pulsating rush of city life. Others live at the pace of the bullock cart, and are still waiting for prosperity to take them by the hand.*

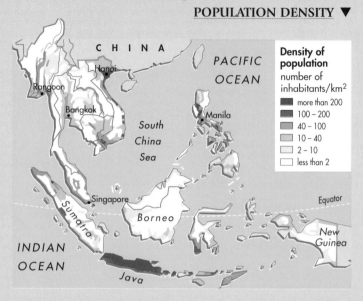

**Density of population**
number of inhabitants/km²

- more than 200
- 100 – 200
- 40 – 100
- 10 – 40
- 2 – 10
- less than 2

The slogan of the Indonesian government, 'Unity in Diversity' could be applied to South-east Asia as a whole. The nations have much in common, notably a profound reverence for the past, for ancestors and for the family. Many of their cultural and religious traditions can be traced back either to India or to China. With the exception of Thailand, every country in the region has shared the experience of being colonised by a Western power. Until the economic blizzard at the end of the 1990s, they also shared the dream of being led into an era of ever-expanding prosperity by the 'mini-tigers' of Singapore, Malaysia, Thailand and Brunei.

But there are also forces within South-east Asia that pull in the direction of diversity rather than of unity. There is little in common between the half-million Papuans of the Indonesian province of Irian Jaya and the 1 million Kachins of northern Myanmar. The Kachins arrived as refugees, centuries ago, from the mountains of southern China. The Papuans, living at a Stone Age level for thousands of years in the rain forests of New Guinea, may have been more than faintly puzzled when, in 1962, they passed from under Dutch colonial rule and were absorbed by Indonesia.

Within the frontiers of new nations, forged since the collapse of colonialism, linger traces of ancient kingdoms and empires. Malaysia was created from 14 hereditary sultanates and four other states, and a little over half of its people are ethnic Malays, the *bumiputra*, or 'sons of the earth'. There are also sizable Chinese and Indian minorities. Tensions between Malays and Chinese led to bloody riots in 1969. Indonesia contains an astonishing diversity of peoples – some 300 ethnic groups, speaking nearly 650 different languages and dialects. The government has tackled this problem by declaring Bahasa (Market) Indonesian

to be the official language. Its drive for unity met with bitter resistance from separatist movements in Aceh, Sumatra, and in East Timor, which was annexed in 1976 and finally allowed independence in 2002. Myanmar, too, faces the challenge of welding a bewildering variety of races into a single nation. Among its 49 million inhabitants are 67 ethnic groups who between them speak 242 different languages and dialects. Some of the main groups (apart from the Burmese, who

amount to 68 per cent of the total) are the Karens of the south, the Kachins and the Chinese of the north and the Shan in the centre of the country. In Thailand, by contrast, some 80 per cent of the population are ethnic Thais. Chinese make up the largest minority, at 10 per cent, and the remainder.

**Man of the forest** *A Papuan in the rain forests of Irian Jaya, the Indonesian part of the island of New Guinea.*

## LIFE EXPECTANCY

|  | Men | Women |
|---|---|---|
| Singapore | 76 | 80 |
| Brunei | 74 | 78 |
| Malaysia | 70 | 75 |
| Thailand | 66 | 73 |
| Vietnam | 66 | 72 |
| Philippines | 66 | 72 |
| Indonesia | 64 | 67 |
| Myanmar | 57 | 62 |
| Laos | 52 | 55 |
| Cambodia | 51 | 55 |

## TOTAL POPULATION
*(in millions)*

| | |
|---|---|
| Indonesia | 212.6 |
| Vietnam | 79.5 |
| Philippines | 75.3 |
| Thailand | 61.8 |
| Myanmar | 49.3 |
| Malaysia | 22.7 |
| Cambodia | 11.8 |
| Laos | 5.7 |
| Singapore | 3.9 |
| Brunei | 0.32 |

## AGE PYRAMID ▼

**Cambodia**

50%
40%
30%
20%
10%

under 15 / 15 to 29 / 30 to 44 / 45 to 59 / 60 to 74 / over 75

**Singapore**

50%
40%
30%
20%
10%

under 15 / 15 to 29 / 30 to 44 / 45 to 59 / 60 to 74 / over 75

are mainly hill tribes – among them Mons, Khmers and Hmongs. Vietnam is racially the most homogenous nation in the region, with 85 per cent of its people Vietnamese. It also has Hmongs, Tays, Nungs and other hill tribes, who tend to be pushed into areas where nobody else wants to live.

## Thailand's black economy

Thailand is notorious for producing pirate editions of films, videos and computer software and unauthorised versions of luxury goods, carrying bogus designer labels. But these activities make up only part of the country's 'black' economy. Profits from drugs, prostitution, undercover trading in arms and oil, illegal betting, illegal employment practices and the sale of stolen antiques have a considerable impact on Thailand's economy. Between 1993 and 1995, such activities brought in an estimated 286 to 457 billion bahts a year. The total profits of the black economy probably amount to more than 20 per cent of Thailand's gross national product.

IMPORTS AND EXPORTS: SINGAPORE, CAMBODIA AND VIETNAM
*(in billions of US dollars)*

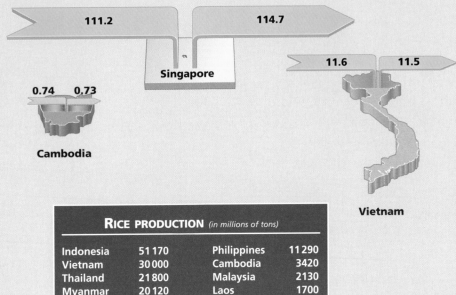

| RICE PRODUCTION *(in millions of tons)* | | | |
|---|---|---|---|
| Indonesia | 51 170 | Philippines | 11 290 |
| Vietnam | 30 000 | Cambodia | 3420 |
| Thailand | 21 800 | Malaysia | 2130 |
| Myanmar | 20 120 | Laos | 1700 |

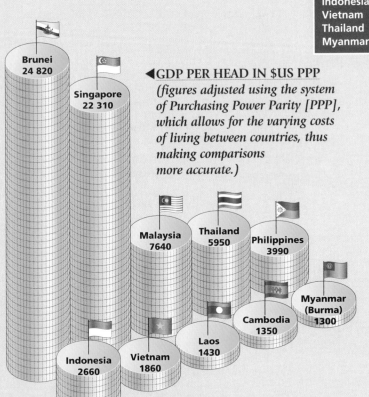

◄ GDP PER HEAD IN $US PPP
*(figures adjusted using the system of Purchasing Power Parity [PPP], which allows for the varying costs of living between countries, thus making comparisons more accurate.)*

| | |
|---|---|
| Brunei | 24 820 |
| Singapore | 22 310 |
| Malaysia | 7640 |
| Thailand | 5950 |
| Philippines | 3990 |
| Indonesia | 2660 |
| Vietnam | 1860 |
| Laos | 1430 |
| Cambodia | 1350 |
| Myanmar (Burma) | 1300 |

## Working together for progress and prosperity

In 1967, Thailand, Malaysia, Singapore, Indonesia and the Philippines agreed that, in a highly competitive world, there was much to be said for cooperation. They founded ASEAN, the Association of Southeast Asian Nations, with the objectives of stimulating economic growth and social progress, fostering cultural development and promoting regional peace and stability. The founder members were joined by Brunei in 1984, by Vietnam in 1985, by Laos and Myanmar in 1997 and by Cambodia in 1999. The individual member nations, prosperous though some of them are, might easily be overshadowed by the economic powerhouse of Japan and the vast economic potential of China. But through ASEAN they can talk to their giant neighbours on more equal terms. Together, they occupy a strategic position between the Indian and Pacific Oceans, they hold valuable reserves of oil and other raw materials, and they have an internal market of half a billion people. At the 1992 summit meeting, faced with the economic challenge of Japan and Taiwan, ASEAN set up a common market – AFTA, the Asian Free Trade Area.

| THE WAGES OF SIN: THE PROFITS FROM ILLEGAL ACTIVITIES IN THAILAND *(in billions of bahts)* | |
|---|---|
| Illegal gambling | 138 to 277 |
| Prostitution | 100 |
| Drug trafficking | 28 to 33 |
| Arms trafficking | 6 to 31 |
| Illegal trading in oil | 9 |
| Illicit employment | 5 to 7 |

▼ WORLD RANKINGS FOR KEY PRODUCTS

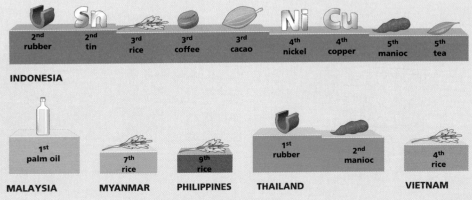

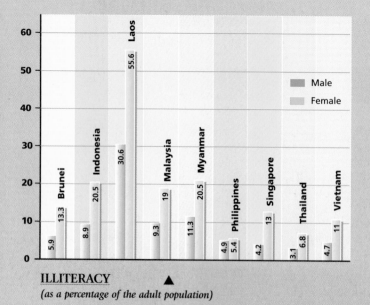

**ILLITERACY**
*(as a percentage of the adult population)*

Male
Female

Brunei — 5.9 / 13.3
Indonesia — 8.9 / 20.5
Laos — 30.6 / 55.6
Malaysia — 9.3 / 19
Myanmar — 11.3 / 20.5
Philippines — 4.9 / 5.4
Singapore — 4.2 / 13
Thailand — 3.1 / 6.8
Vietnam — 4.7 / 11

## THE TOURIST TRADE
*(Millions of visitors)*

| | |
|---|---|
| Thailand (1998) | 7.8 |
| Singapore (2000) | 7.7 |
| Malaysia (1996) | 7.1 |
| Indonesia (1996) | 5.1 |
| Philippines (1999) | 2.2 |
| Vietnam (1998) | 1.7 |

## THE BIG CITIES
*(number of inhabitants)*

| | |
|---|---|
| Jakarta | 9 113 000 |
| Manila | 8 594 000 |
| Bangkok | 7 358 000 |
| Singapore | 4 017 000 |
| Ho Chi Minh City | 3 200 000 |
| Nakhon Ratchasima | 2 700 000 |
| Rangoon | 2 513 000 |
| Bandung | 2 400 000 |
| Hanoi | 2 200 000 |
| Medan | 1 942 000 |

## PUBLIC HEALTH SERVICES ▼

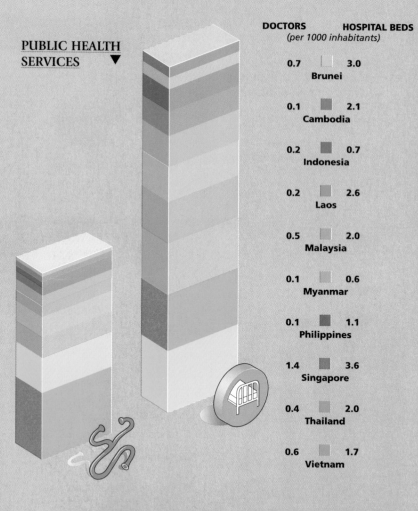

|  | DOCTORS | HOSPITAL BEDS |
|---|---|---|
| | *(per 1000 inhabitants)* | |
| Brunei | 0.7 | 3.0 |
| Cambodia | 0.1 | 2.1 |
| Indonesia | 0.2 | 0.7 |
| Laos | 0.2 | 2.6 |
| Malaysia | 0.5 | 2.0 |
| Myanmar | 0.1 | 0.6 |
| Philippines | 0.1 | 1.1 |
| Singapore | 1.4 | 3.6 |
| Thailand | 0.4 | 2.0 |
| Vietnam | 0.6 | 1.7 |

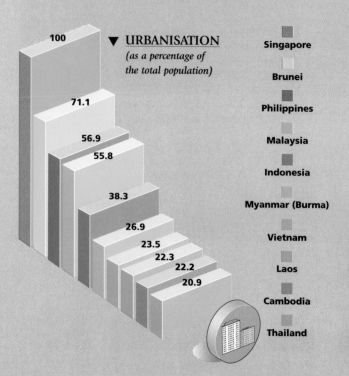

▼ **URBANISATION**
*(as a percentage of the total population)*

| | |
|---|---|
| Singapore | 100 |
| Brunei | 71.1 |
| Philippines | 56.9 |
| Malaysia | 55.8 |
| Indonesia | 38.3 |
| Myanmar (Burma) | 26.9 |
| Vietnam | 23.5 |
| Laos | 22.3 |
| Cambodia | 22.2 |
| Thailand | 20.9 |

## Population pressures in the island of Java

Java takes up only ¹/₁₄th of the land area of Indonesia, yet more than half the country's total population lives there. In Indonesia as a whole, the population density averages 289 inhabitants per sq mile (112 per km²); in Java, the figure is 2256 per sq mile (871 per km²). The problem is even worse in the cities because they act as magnets to people from the countryside. Jakarta, Surabaya and Bandung at least hold out to poor peasants the promise of a better life. Java's population has been growing rapidly since the 16th century, when the powerful Islamic kingdom of Mataram was based there, drawing its wealth from the spice trade. Today, Jakarta has more than 9 million inhabitants. For several years the state, adopting a policy first applied by Dutch colonisers in 1905, has been encouraging the Javanese to emigrate to other islands. There are vast spaces in Kalimantan, Borneo, that are populated sparsely, if at all. But incomers are not always welcome there: at the turn of the millennium, thousands of settlers from Madura, an island off the coast of Java, fled from Kalimantan after a series of massacres by the indigenous Dyaks.

# Index

Page numbers in italics denote illustrations. The letter and number references in brackets are the co-ordinates for places in the map section, pp. 140-7.

# Acknowledgments

Abbreviations: t = top, m = middle, b = bottom, l = left, r = right.

FRONT COVER: *Along Bay, Vietnam*, SDP/J. Rey
BACK COVER: *Buddhist monks, Thailand*, HOA QUI/
J.-L. Dugast

Pages 4/5: DIAF/Ch. Pratt; 6/7: COSMOS/T. Van Sant; 8t: HOA QUI/Ch. Vaisse; 8/9: HOA QUI/Ph. Body; 9mr: DIAF/Ch. Frégier; 10tl: COSMOS/R. Gordon; 10bl: RAPHO/M. Friedel; 10/11: DIAF/B. Merle; 12tl: COSMOS/R. Gordon; 12/13: RAPHO/G. Sioen; 13t: BIOS/C. Ruoso; 13b: DIAF/Ch. Frégier; 14t: GAMMA/L.-H. Fage; 14m: G. DAGLI ORTI/Museum of Anthropology, Turin; 14b: RMN/Th. Ollivier/bronze pot, Dong Son culture, Vietnam/musée Guimet, Paris; 15t: HOA QUI/M. Troncy; 15m: HOA QUI/Ph. Body; 15b: COSMOS/R. Smolan; 16b: RMN/J. Goldings/musée Guimet, Paris; 16/17: HOA QUI/V. Durruty; 17l: HOA QUI/D. Noirot; 17r: RMN/J. Goldings/musée Guimet, Paris; 18t: HOA QUI/Ch. Boisvieux; 18/19: DIAF/Pratt-Pries; 19ml: HOA QUI/*le Monde*; 19mm: HOA QUI/E. Lobo; 19mr: G. DAGLI ORTI/musée Guimet, Paris; 19b: HOA QUI/J.-L. Dugast; 20m: G. DAGLI ORTI/Naval Museum, Lisbon; 20b: G. DAGLI ORTI/Museo Correr, Venice; 20/21: G. DAGLI ORTI/Archives Torre do Tombo Lendas da India de Gaspar correia, Lisbon; 21t: HOA QUI/Ch. Boisvieux; 21b: HOA QUI/J. Paoli; 22t: G. DAGLI ORTI/Marciana Library, Venice; 22br: RMN/Manufacture nationale, Sèvres; 22bl: G. DAGLI ORTI/Navy Historical Service, Vincennes; 23t: Jean-Loup CHARMET/BNF, Paris; 23b: G. DAGLI ORTI/National Museum of Ethnology, Leyde; 24mm: Jean-Loup CHARMET/private collection; 24mr, b, 24/25, 25r: KEYSTONE; 26b: GAMMA/Leroy; 26/27: GAMMA/S. Vichith; 27tr: GAMMA/D. Osborn; 27tm: COSMOS/Impact/D. Faulder; 27m: CORBIS-SYGMA/N. Quidu; 27b: GAMMA; 28/29: AFP/R. Elliott; 30/31: RAPHO/F. Le Diascorn; 32bl: BIOS/C. Ruoso; 32br: ANA/M. Freeman; 32/33t: BIOS/D. Barthélemy; 33m: BIOS/R. Valarcher; 33b: BIOS/D. Heuclin; 34tr: BIOS/A. Compost; 34m: BIOS/R. Cavignaux; 34bl: BIOS/D. Heuclin; 34/35: BIOS/Seitre; 35ml: BIOS/A. Compost; 35r: BIOS/C. Ruoso; 35b: BIOS/OSF/D. Fleetham; 36t: EXPLORER/E. Sampers; 36m: SCOPE/M. Gotin; 36b: ASK IMAGES/Aven; 37t: BIOS/O. Morvan; 37m: RAPHO/D. Riffet; 37b: AFP/Van Song; 38t: HOA QUI/Ph. Bourseiller/Du; 38/39: HOA QUI/Ph. Bourseiller; 39t: HOA QUI/Krafft/I&V; 39b: DIAF/Ch. Travert; 40t: HOA QUI/P. De Wilde; 40m: HOA QUI/Ch. Boisvieux; 40b: HOA QUI/J.-L. Dugast; 41m: HOA QUI/P. De Wilde; 41bl: DIAF/Eurasia Press; 41br: BIOS/Seitre; 42m: HOA QUI/D. Noirot; 42b: HOA QUI/Ch. and J. Lénars; 43tl: BIOS/Seitre; 43bm: EXPLORER/J. Brun; 43br: BIOS/A. Compost; 44/45: HOA QUI/Liaison internationale; 46bl: HOA QUI/D. Joubert; 46br: HOA QUI/Icône/O. Martel; 46/47: HOA QUI/D. Joubert; 47ml: HOA QUI/P. De Wilde; 47mr: BIOS/J. Frébet; 47b: HOA QUI/J.-L. Dugast; 48t: HOA QUI/X. Zimbardo; 48m: HOA QUI/Ch. Sappa; 48bl: CORBIS-SYGMA/A. Tannenbaum; 48br: DIAF/N. Wheeler; 49m: RAPHO/M. Yamashita; 49b: EXPLORER/G. Boutin; 50t: CORBIS-SYGMA/J. Fields; 50m: CORBIS-SYGMA/S. Raymer; 50b: HOA QUI/ALTITUDE/Y. Arthus-Bertrand; 51t: DIAF/Valdin; 51m: HOA QUI/R. Manin; 51b: DIAF/E. Quéméré; 52t: RAPHO/A. Diaz; 52m: AFP/Hoang Dinh Nam; 52b: AFP/STR; 53t: AFP/M. Vidon; 53b: AFP/Branata; 54t: CORBIS-SYGMA/coll. Sean Sexton; 54bl: EXPLORER/P. Montbazet; 54bm: EXPLORER/P. Le Floch; 54/55: EXPLORER/P. Montbazet; 55t: ASK IMAGES/Aven; 56m: CORBIS-SYGMA/Maher Attar; 55b: EXPLORER/P. Montbazet; 56/57: CORBIS-SYGMA/Maher Attar; 57ml: CORBIS-SYGMA/S. Dorantes; 57mr: HOA QUI/M. Renaudeau; 58t: HOA QUI/Serena; 58m: HOA QUI/Icône/O. Martel; 58b: EXPLORER/K. Straiton; 59m: HOA QUI/Icône/O. Martel; 59bl: DIAF/D. Ball; 59br: DIAF/B. Simmons; 60tr, br: AFP/Roslan Rahman; 60m: AFP/Chaiwat Subprasom; 60/61: AFP/Pornchai Kittiwongsakul; 61t:

ANA/G. Deichmann/PHILIPPINES; 62t: OSMOS/Heimo Aga; 62b: DIAF/G. Simeone/El Nido Miniloc Resort at Palawan; 62/63: RAPHO/M. Friedel; 63t: EXPLORER/Ribienas; 63m: COSMOS/Heimo Aga; 63br: EXPLORER/P. Van Riel; 64t: DIAF/Valdin; 64bl: AFP/J. Nito; 64bm, 65t: AFP; 65b: AFP/E. Dunand; 66t: CORBIS-SYGMA/P. de Vallombreuse; 66m: EXPLORER/G. Boutin; 66b: COSMOS/Visum/C. Engel; 67t: RAPHO/M. Yamashita; 67m: BIOS/Fotonatura/Harvey; 67b: COSMOS/Visum/M. Wold; 68/69: SCOPE/A. Jongen; 70t: GAMMA/Saola/E. Pasquier; 70b: DIAF/B. Barbier; 70/71: EXPLORER/S. Grandadam; 71t: EXPLORER/Ph. Roy; 71b: HOA QUI/P. De Wilde; 72t: RMN/Th. Ollivier/musée Guimet, Paris; 72b: ANA/G. Deichman; 72/73: HOA QUI/J.-L. Dugast; 73tl, tr: RAPHO/Ch. Sappa; 74t: COSMOS/T. Raupach/Argus/Focus; 74/75: DIAF/N. Wheeler; 75tl, tr: DIAF/E. Planchard; 75b: RAPHO/B. Wassman; 76t: AFP/Mosista Pambudi; 76m: CORBIS-SYGMA/S. Dorantes; 76b: CORBIS-SYGMA/V. Miladinovic; 77l: AFP/Dimas; 77r: GAMMA/Piat; 78m: DIAF/B. Barbier; 78b: HOA QUI/Duffau; 79m: HOA QUI/X. Zimbardo; 79bl: GAMMA/B. Rieger; 79br: BIOS/J.-E. Molina; 80t: GAMMA/P. Aventurier; 80/81: DIAF/Ch. Frégier; 81t: GAMMA/P. Singh; 81m: RAPHO/M. Yamashita; 81b: DIAF/B. Simmons; 82t: ANA/A. Soldeville; 82b: HOA QUI/P. De Wilde; 83tl, tr: RAPHO/L. Franey; 83b: COSMOS/B. & C. Alexander; 84m: EXPLORER/J. Brun; 84bl: ANA/J.-J. Sommeryns; 84/85: COSMOS/G. Buthaud; 85t: ANA/M. Huteau; 85br: COSMOS/Woodfin Camp/C. Karnow; 86t: HOA QUI/S. Grandadam; 86b: DIAF/D. Thierry; 86/87: DIAF/N. Wheeler; 87: HOA QUI/X. Zimbardo; 88ml: DIAF/J.-D. Sudres; 88mr: HOA QUI/Globe Press/A. Evrard; 88b: HOA QUI/P. Guedj; 89t: HOA QUI/B. Pérousse; 89m: AFP/S. Shaver; 89b: HOA QUI/S. Grandadam; 90t: HOA QUI/E. Valentin; 90b: HOA QUI/R. Manin; 91t: RAPHO/M. Yamashita; 91m: HOA QUI/E. Raz; 91b: HOA QUI/Ph. Body; 92/93: DIAF/Valdin; 94m: HOA QUI/P. Guedj; 94b: HOA QUI/Globe Press/A. Evrard; 94/95: HOA QUI/Globe Press/A. Evrard; 95t: HOA QUI/Ch. Boisvieux; 95b: HOA QUI/A. Wolf; 96t: CORBIS-SYGMA/V. Miladinovic; 96b: EXPLORER/Globe Press/A. Evrard; 97m: HOA QUI/ALTITUDE/G. A. Rossi; 97bl: DIAF/Even; 97br: AFP/Weda; 98/103: RAPHO/G. Gerster; 98tl: HOA QUI/*le Monde*; 98tr, bl: DIAF/B. Simmons; 98br: RAPHO/G. Sioen; 99t: RAPHO/A. Diaz; 99m: HOA QUI/*le Monde*; 99bl: EXPLORER/J.-L. Gobert; 99br: DIAF/D. Ball; 100tl: SCOPE/Ph. Beuzen; 100tr: TOP/G. Sioen; 100bl: TOP/R. Tixador; 100br: DIAF/Valdin; 101t: EXPLORER/W. Rozbroj; 101m: HOA QUI/J.-L. Dugast; 101bl: HOA QUI/P. De Wilde; 101br: DIAF/B. Simmons; 102tl: DIAF/Valdin; 102tr: DIAF/B. Simmons; 102ml: DIAF/N. Wheeler; 102mr: COSMOS/Aspen/J. Aaronson; 102b: HOA QUI/*le Monde*; 103tl: COSMOS/Robert/Bergerot; 103tr: HOA QUI/J.-L. Dugast; 103bl: ASK IMAGES/M. Charuel; 103br: TOP/G. Sioen; 104t: DIAF/D. Thierry; 104m: ANA/S. Amantini; 104bl: ANA/J. Rey; 104/105: DIAF/Ch. Frégier; 105t: CORBIS-SYGMA/Ph. Giraud; 105b: EXPLORER/E. Sampers; 106b: SCOPE/M. Gotin; 106/107: DIAF/N. Wheeler; 107ml: HOA QUI/M. Renaudeau; 107m: SCOPE/M. Gotin; 107mr: SCOPE/P. Desclos; 107b: DIAF/SIME/S. Damm; 108t: HOA QUI/E. Beracassat; 108b: RAPHO/E. Berbar; 109t: COSMOS/Heimo Aga; 109bl: DIAF/J. Miller; 109br: RAPHO/E. Berbar/architect Cesar Pelli; 110/111: DIAF/B. Simmons; 112b, 112/113: HOA QUI/Y. Gellie; 113t, br: DIAF/B. Simmons; 113bm: HOA QUI/Y. Gellie; 114t: DIAF/J.-P. Garcin; 114m: HOA QUI/Ch. Boisvieux; 114b: HOA QUI/Ch. Vaisse; 115t: DIAF/F. Soreau; 115b: HOA QUI/P. De Wilde; 116tr: EXPLORER/H. Matsumoto; 116ml: EXPLORER/K. Straiton; 116b: HOA QUI/Ch. Boisvieux; 117t: DIAF/B. Simmons; 117br: DIAF/Ch. Frégier; 117bl: DIAF/J. Sierpinski; 118/119: GAMMA/Pasquier/Mongi; 120t:

HOA QUI/P. De Wilde; 120/121: HOA QUI/P. Wang; 121t: HOA QUI/*le Monde* 121b: HOA QUI/A. Wright; 122bl: AFP/P. Trouillaud; 122br: AFP/R. Elliott; 122/123: HOA QUI/Ph. Bourseiller; 123bm: AFP/Hoang Dinh-Nam; 123br: HOA QUI/Globe Press; 124m: ANA/M. Durazzo; 124b: ANA/M. Freeman; 125t: COSMOS/Aurora/J.-B. Pinneo; 125b: DIAF/B. Barbier; 126t: EXPLORER/J. Desmarteau; 126bl: RAPHO/B. Wassman; 126br: EXPLORER/S. Fiore; 127m: GAMMA/P. Aventurier; 127b: GAMMA/C. Loviny; 128t: DIAF/Y. Travert; 128bl: HOA QUI/J.-L. Dugast; 128br: HOA QUI/E. Valentin; 128/129: EXPLORER/M. Hosken; 129t: DIAF/Ch. Frégier; 130m: HOA QUI/C. Pavard; 130b: DIAF/F. Huguier; 130/131: DIAF/R. Mazin; 131tr: DIAF/J. Gabanou; 131m: HOA QUI/Ch. & J. Lénars; 131b: RAPHO/F. Huguier; 132t: HOA QUI/Ph. Body; 132bl: DIAF/J. Kerebel; 132br: HOA QUI/J.-L. Dugast; 133t: GAMMA/F. Reglain; 133b: AFP/Agus Lolong; 134t: RAPHO/G. Sioen; 134bl: HOA QUI/H. Ruiz; 134br: HOA QUI/*le Monde*; 135t: HOA QUI/Altitude/G. A. Rossi; 135bl: HOA QUI/Altitude/Y. Arthus-Bertrand; 135br: DIAF/B. Simmons/architect Sumet Jumsai; 136t: AEDTA; 136m: ANA/M. Freeman; 136b: EXPLORER/Ch. Lénars; 137m: EXPLORER/S. Grandadam; 137mr: RMN/R. Lambert/Paris, musée Guimet; 137b: B. DAVID; 138/139: EXPLORER/M. Hiroyuki; 150: AFP/Cong Dien; 151t: COSMOS/Impact Visuals/S. Sprague; 151b: HOA QUI/J.-L. Dugast; 152: HOA QUI/P. De Wilde; 154: CORBIS-SYGMA/S. Dorantes.

Printed and bound in Europe by Arvato Iberia
Colour separations: Station Graphique, Ivry-sur-Seine

617-014-02